Contemporary Saudi Arabia and The Emerging Indo-Saudi Relations

Contemporary Saudi Arabia and The Emerging Indo-Saudi Relations

Edited by
Gulshan Dietl
Girijesh Pant
A.K. Pasha
P.C. Jain

SHIPRA

ISBN: 978-81-7541-373-3

First Published in India in 2007

Contemporary Saudi Arabia and the Emerging Indo-Saudi Relations

Price: Rs. 200, US$ 10

Published by:
SHIPRA PUBLICATIONS
115-A, Vikas Marg, Shakarpur
Delhi-110092, INDIA
Phone: 91-11-65277210, 91-11-22500954
Fax: 91-11-22458662
E-mail: info@shiprapublications.com
www.shiprapublications.com

Contents

Introduction

GULSHAN DIETL

Saudi Arabia is a unique country at least in three specific details. One, it possesses more than a quarter of the global oil reserves and has been the largest oil producer for over half a century and today is the only producer with a spare production capacity. Two, the holiest Islamic shrines are located in Mecca and Medina placing the country in the epicentre of the Muslim sacred space. Three, it is one of the last surviving ruling monarchies and the only one that has named the country after its own family name.

The Saudi political system is so clearly identified with the concept of absolute monarchy that one often tends to ignore various other political institutions that qualify it in an appreciable measure. Some of these institutions have been functioning for a very long time, and others are still in the process of evolution. As the political space is only gradually opening up, people's participation in the system has ranged from polite petitions to mass demonstrations all the way to violent explosions.

The Saudi economy is a one-resource economy, namely the oil. It is a rentier economy, in which the state is the principal recipient of rent from oil. Late last year, it was admitted to the World Trade Organisation. It took twelve years for the country to complete the negotiations, the second-longest accession period after China, which negotiated for fourteen years. The development heralds major changes in Saudi economy. It will boost foreign investment providing funds for diversification of its largely oil-based economy. It will also bring new export opportunities, especially in the petrochemical industry. At the micro-level, the impact will necessarily be uneven.

The population mosaic of the country is rich in details: a very young population, a very discreet presence of women in public space, and a large number of migrants from several countries. A generally religious ambience does not obscure variety in life styles and socio-cultural diversity.

The location of Mecca and Medina on its territory and of one-fourth of global oil reserves under its land makes Saudi Arabia a natural leader in Islamic and oil affairs. The Organisation of Islamic Conference and the

Organisation of Petroleum Exporting Countries reflect Saudi preferences to a great extent. The oil trade as well as the compulsions of regime security have defined the Saudi dependence on the United States. A total lack of relationship with the Soviet Union during the Cold War period have gradually led to the resumption of normal ties with Russia in the post-Cold War period.

A triangular power balance defines the Gulf region: Saudi Arabia, Iran and Iraq. Saudi Arabia has drawn the rest of the five Gulf states within its own orbit through the regional grouping of the Gulf Co-operation Council. Its relations with Iran and Iraq have tended to swing with the changes in domestic circumstances as also with the wider geopolitical developments like the wars, a revolution and a regime change. Its involvement in the Arab world has been mainly driven by its search for a political solution to the Palestine problem.

Over the decades, its relations with India have steadily improved. During the cold war, India chose to remain non-aligned, whereas Saudi Arabia was firmly in the US-led block. The Saudi-led OPEC showed a considerate policy towards India during the oil crisis of 1973. There was no embargo against India. The bilateral relations have been on an upswing since then. The Saudi King Abdullah was the official guest at the Republic Day celebrations on 26 January, 2006. The visit has been significant in many respects. The earlier visit of a Saudi king had been more than fifty years back. The "Delhi Declaration" signed at the end of the visit spoke of a broad strategic vision between the two countries.

Today, the Kingdom is the largest supplier of oil to India. It is the fourteenth largest market for India accounting for seven percent of its total exports. India, in turn, is the fifth largest market for Saudi Arabia accounting for four-an-a-half percent of its exports. Roughly 1.3 million Indians are working in the Kingdom, who are sending back remittances worth $2 billion annually.

Saudi Arabia is worth a scrutiny. The Gulf Studies Programme of the Centre for West Asian and African Studies at Jawaharlal Nehru University held a Seminar towards that end. The political, economic and social situation in the country, its foreign policy and Indo-Saudi relations were the major themes of the seminar. This book is a collection of revised and updated papers presented at the Seminar.

The first four chapters in the book focus on the Saudi political system, economy and society.

Talmiz Ahmad in his paper "The Political Dynamics of Saudi Arabia and the Challenge of Reform" maintains that Saudi Arabia and its people are the product of their terrain, their religious doctrine and their access to the world's largest petroleum reserves, all of which have imparted to their society a sense of disequilibrium. The Kingdom's leaders recognise that in order to sustain their rule they have to pay obeisance to the Wahhabi national ideology even as they attempt to equip their myriad populace to handle the challenge of modernity, while maintaining their own supreme authority. The story of Saudi Arabia is, therefore, the story of an attempt to bring balance to a society unable to shed the burdensome legacy of its past as it seeks to cope with the siren-call of the future.

Ahmad's prognosis for the next few years is that, led by King Abdullah, the Saudi state will continue on its path of modernism and liberalism, with some dollops of political reform and substantial expansion of economic opportunity. While the state will provide some modicum of educational reform, the clergy will continue to receive due respect and it, in turn, will continue to play its role in strengthening the Saudi order and the rule of the royal family. We are not likely to see any movement in the direction of the kind of radical political reform that is being urged by Western and some Arab quarters.

His relatively sanguine future projection is based on a pragmatic consideration: the Al-Saud are confident they can neutralise domestic dissent through co-option; they are convinced that, given their valuable role in terms of US strategic interests in the region linked with oil and the lucrative economic opportunities they provide American and other Western companies, they will be able to moderate US demands on them and persuade the Americans to accept change at the pace set by the royal family. They find no reason why their traditional pragmatism, which has served them so well for so long, will not continue to see them through in the years to come.

Anwar Alam's paper on "State and Opposition in Saudi Arabia: Emerging Trends", provides a stark contrast to Ahmad's analysis. He interprets the nine-eleven as an indication of a general sense of frustration within the Kingdom. He undertakes a historical view of the functioning of the Saudi state and its engagement with different social classes, tribes and regions. He then takes a synoptic view of the sources of legitimacy and support base that has helped in consolidating and institutionalising the al-Saud rule. Inquiring into the causes and context of the opposition, he examines its nature, dimensions and effectiveness.

The issues of equity, representation and evolution of an inclusive society dominate the political discourse in the Kingdom today. The overarching question is "what does it mean to be a Saudi?" That is the question that will shape the relationship between the state and the opposition. Despite vast resources — both material and ideological — the regime lacks legitimacy to contain the appeal of the opposition. That it has granted the right of representation — even if only at the municipal level — is an indication of the success of the opposition.

Girijesh Pant in "Saudi Arabia: From Oil Kingdom to Market" identifies the Saudi accession to the World Trade Organisation in December 2005 as marking a new phase in the country's economic management in which the state will have to retreat and the market will have to step in; the social contract between the state and the society will have to be revised; and the interface between the domestic and the global market will have to be made transparent, accountable and rule-based.

This leap forward is not an unmitigated blessing. The market-led boom has escalated the price of the land; especially as watering the land is costlier and selling it is more lucrative. The food security, in the circumstances, is an obvious casualty. The issues of subsidised services and infrastructure support are acquiring added urgency in view of the growing demand and aspirations. In spite of rent-derived resources, the contradictions between the regional-global interface will be sharp. Revising its social contract of rentier economy without jeopardising its legitimacy will be a delicate task before the Saudi state.

P.C. Jain opens his paper on "Population and Society in Saudi Arabia" with a disclaimer; there are no precise estimates of Saudi Arabia's past or current population for the simple reason that there has never been any comprehensive census: instead estimates are made on the basis of advanced sampling techniques. More than 73 percent of Saudi population is below twenty-nine years of age. This segment of the population is educated, urbanised and modern. The rentier economy and patriarchal polity will not be able to meet their rising expectations.

With wide spread availability of televisions, radios, fax machines, internet and satellite dishes, the Saudis have truly entered the electronic and information age. The inflow of information — in spite of censorship — is now beyond the government and clergy's control. The future consequences of not keeping pace with the global ethos will be decisive.

The next two papers deal with the two of the central issues in Saudi foreign policy; the nuclear programme of Iran and strains in relations with the United States.

In her paper "Iranian Nuclear Programme: Saudi Concerns and Responses", Gulshan Dietl looks at the Saudi policy in response to the proliferation in their neighbourhood. The official Saudi pronouncements on the matter are unexceptionable: we will not join the nuclear race; Iran has assured us that it is not seeking nuclear weapons; there is no possibility of an Iranian attack on Saudi Arabia; the US is partly to blame as it is negotiating with North Korea, signing a nuclear peace agreement with India, and turning a blind eye to Israeli nuclear arsenal. The unofficial statements from the analysts, journalists and others, though, are very different: the Bushehr reactor on the Gulf is closer to the Arab states of the Gulf than to Tehran and an accident there would spell disaster; the old Soviet technology could result in a Chernobyl-type tragedy; Iran is seismically unstable and an earthquake would cause immense problems; the Iran-US confrontation would destabilise the geopolitics of the region even more.

The most interesting Saudi response is a clever make-over of an earlier proposal to make West Asia a nuclear-free zone to the one on the Gulf as a Weapons of Mass Destruction Free Zone (GWMDFZ). That would leave Israel out of its purview and focus exclusively on Iran.

Bansidhar Pradhan in "Saudi Arabia and the US: Contextualising an Unequal Relationship in the Post-11 September Phase" provides an overview of Saudi-US relations going back to decades and examines its current status. Whereas the voices in the US call for lessening dependence on Saudi Arabia by curbing the addiction to its oil; the Saudis are also becoming increasingly critical of their regime's excessive closeness to the US. Apart from the Palestine issue, the perception that the US would like to slice up the country and retain control over the oil-rich Ahsa province has not helped the bilateral ties.

There are far too many considerations binding the two rather than pulling them in different directions. There are, nonetheless, subtle Saudi moves to diversify their foreign policy to gain autonomy in their dealings with and reduce reliance on the US. A fundamental restructuring of Saudi-US relations will depend on the internal dynamics in the Kingdom.

The last two chapters (VII and VIII) assess the historical, political and economic relations between Saudi Arabia and India.

A.K. Pasha in his "Indo-Saudi Relations: Past and Emerging Challenges" traces the bilateral ties from the early maritime contacts. The rise of Islam contributed to an increasing awareness of travels to each other's lands. In modern times, the issues of Kashmir, the Organisation of Islamic Conferences, the destruction of Babri Mosque and Pakistan have greatly influenced the Indo-Saudi relations. In the past five years, the Saudi position on Kashmir has moved to calling for a bilateral process and appealing for peace between India and Pakistan. India's nuclear tests in 1998, growing Indo-Israeli ties, India's emergence in areas of IT, high economic growth rate and rapidly improving Indo-US relations have apparently convinced the Saudis that their pro-Pakistani tilt will be a burden in their quest for better ties with India.

The Saudi King was the chief guest at the Republic Day celebrations in New Delhi on 26 January, 2006. He became the first Saudi king to get that honour. The tradition of inviting a head of state as chief guest at the Republic Day parade every year is now considered a measure of the importance India attaches to that country, apart from serving as an opportunity to showcase the country's military might as well as secular and democratic traditions.

Javed Ahmad Khan in "New Trends in Indo-Saudi Economic Relations" examines two distinctly favourable developments that could take Indo-Saudi relations in a positive direction. One, massive oil revenues have refuelled the development activities in Saudi Arabia, which could accord sound investment opportunities in such varied sectors as oil, gas, petrochemicals, utilities, infrastructure, leisure and tourism, finance and asset management. Two, Saudis have adopted a "Look East" policy in the aftermath of the nine-eleven.

The two can benefit immensely from their complementary strengths. India has a stable polity and democratic framework, a well-developed legal system and independent judiciary to safeguard the 'rule of law', a free press, a rapidly growing economy with a huge market, and a strong tradition of entrepreneurship. Saudi Arabia, on its part, offers opportunities in petroleum and petrochemicals, power, water, railways, roads, telecommunications, information technology (IT), banking, and financial services.

The authors, with different perspectives and on different subjects, have coalesced to put together a volume that is a serious and well-rounded treatment of the theme.

1

The Political Dynamics of Saudi Arabia and the Challenge of Reform

TALMIZ AHMAD

Saudi Arabia and its people are the product of their terrain, their religious doctrine and their access to the world's largest petroleum reserves, all of which have imparted to their society a sense of disequilibrium. The Kingdom's leaders recognise that in order to sustain their rule they have to pay obeisance to the Wahhabi national ideology even as they attempt to equip their myriad populace to handle the challenge of modernity, while maintaining their own supreme authority. The story of Saudi Arabia is, therefore, the story of the attempt to bring balance to a society unable to shed the burdensome legacy of its past as it seeks to cope with the siren-call of the future. The interplay of various factors that contribute to this predicament is examined in this essay.

The Terrain and the People

The heartland of the Kingdom of Saudi Arabia, the original home of its leadership and its unique form of Islam, is the land known as Najd, with the ancient city of Riyadh at its centre. The terrain of this land has had a profound impact on the character of the people residing here and the values and institutions they have developed.

Much of this land is desert and of all the large countries in the world, Saudi Arabia is believed to be the most arid, and no area is more arid than Najd. Najd has a long, hot and almost totally dry summer, with temperatures reaching 48°C and above. There is rain between December and April, but there are extraordinary variations in rainfall from year-to-year and even from day-to-day. It may range from 15 mm in 1966 to 257 mm ten years later; half or even more of a year's rainfall may fall in a single day, causing cataclysmic floods which are known to sweep away entire settlements.

The wadi system and the relatively high water table in certain low-lying areas provide pasture areas, locations for settlements, and halting points on trans-peninsular routes. Riyadh, throughout its history, has been blessed by abundant water resources and good soil for agriculture. Thus, it emerged as an important crossroad on trans-Arabian routes.

The people have adapted to the harshest physical conditions on earth and survived through robust self-sufficiency in isolation from the outside world. The forbidding barriers between Najd and the outside world have produced a society which has been little exposed to outside influences. The almost total absence of resources and the severity of the climate made this region unattractive to invaders. Whenever outsiders periodically claimed suzerainty, such as the Ottomans or the Sharifs of Mecca, they quickly decided to leave the region to tribal control or to local rulers. In such an environment the cooperative virtues of loyalty to family, clan and tribe developed, but without centralised authority.

The Advent of Wahhabism*

The religion followed by the people of the Najd was Islam, but by the middle of the 18th century it had so degenerated in the harsh, isolated environment as to approximate the conditions prevailing before the advent of Prophet Mohammed. Wahhabism, so called after its founder, Mohammed ibn Abdul Wahhab (1703-92), with its emphasis on a return to the simple and pure beliefs of early Islam, austere living and strict application of the *Shariat*, emerged in this inhospitable terrain as an

---

*In my understanding of this frequently controversial and misunderstood concept, I have followed Stephane Lacroix who has said:.

"I define "Wahhabism" as the religious tradition developed over the centuries by the 'ulama' of the official Saudi religious establishment founded by the heirs of Muhammad 'Abd-al-Wahhab', an establishment which in turn considers itself as the legitimate guardian of this tradition. However, the Wahhabis never refer to themselves as such, and always use the terms *Salafi* (with reference to *al-salaf al-salih* or pious ancestors) or *Ahl al-Tawhid* (People professing the absolute unity of God)." ("Between Islamists and Liberals: Saudi Arabia's New 'Islamo-Liberal' Reformists", *Middle East Journal*, Vol. 58, No. 3, Summer 2004, p. 345.)

abiding faith. Indeed, a commentator has described the advent of Wahhabism as "a kind of 'second coming' of Islam in Arabia." Some scholars believe that the Wahhabi reference to the period before their arrival as *jahiliyyah* (period of ignorance) may be the literal truth since inner Arabia might possibly not have been Islamised in any significant way before the 18th century.

Mohammad ibn Abdul Wahhab entered into a religio-political alliance with the then little-known ruler of the township of Dirrayah, near Riyadh, Mohammad ibn Saud, in 1744, an alliance which was to have extraordinary implications for the people of Najd and the history of the Arabian Peninsula. In terms of this alliance, the progenitor of the Al-Saud accepted the doctrine of ibn Abdul Wahhab and in turn promised him the use of his armed force to spread and enforce this doctrine across the Peninsula. The Saudi-Wahhabi movement spread gradually as a result of popular appeal and military force. After bringing all of Najd under their sway, in 1801 the Wahhabis sacked Kerbala, and, in 1806 they expelled the Turks from Mecca and Medina.

Since adherence to Wahhabism plays such a significant role in the establishment and consolidation of the modern Kingdom of Saudi Arabia, it would be useful to note some of its major tenets. The Wahhabis belong to the Hanbali school, which is the most conservative of the four Sunni schools of jurisprudence. Again, they approach Hanbalism through the writings of the Syrian scholar, ibn Taymiah (1262-1328), who provided the most austere and rigid interpretations of the Koran and Hadith: ibn Taymiyah, it is said, 'bowed to no authority higher than the Koran.... and lifted his voice against innovation, saint worship, vows and pilgrimages to shrines.'

Besides asserting the oneness of God, Wahhabism's other emphasis is on the community whose sole purpose is to apply the law of God and establish a society where that law prevails. Since the purpose of the Wahhabi community is to live by God's law, obedience to the ruler or *Imam* is an absolute obligation on the individual. In turn, the ruler's main function is to uphold the law and expand the community until it embraces all men. In pursuit of this goal, the ruler, in counsel with his religious advisers, may force the individual to do those things which he should do anyway: hence, the institution of the *mutawwa* (the "obedience-causer" or loosely called "religious police") who use force to make people pray and who enforce the norms of public decorum, particularly in respect of women.

Wahhabism also advocates *jihad* against the "innovators" (*ahl al-bidah)*, a category includes that all who do not share Wahhabi beliefs. It was interpreted broadly to justify all those policies and regulations of the *Imam* as would bring the community closer to God's will.

The House of Saud in the 20th Century

The military successes of Mohammad ibn Saud were halted by a combination of Ottoman, Egyptian and Sharifian forces and internal family feuds through the rest of the 19th century. Late in the century, the alliance of God and Sword found its new knight in Abdul Aziz ibn Saud (1880-1953), who commenced the restoration of his family's fortunes with the capture of Riyadh in 1902. Then, following in the steps of his great ancestor, he systematically brought all the other tribes in Najd and other parts of the peninsula under his control; he finally captured the Holy Cities of Mecca and Medina in 1926, and proclaimed himself King of the Kingdom of Saudi Arabia, giving to this ancient land the name of his own family.

During his lifetime, King Abdul Aziz sired 43 legitimate sons, the eldest born in 1900 and the youngest in 1948. To avoid internal family feuds, he decreed that succession among his sons would pass from brother to brother, excluding the unfit, and that all family matters would be decided by a council of senior family members. According to present indications, succession among the remaining brothers could continue uninterrupted for another 15 years or so, after which a new arrangement to pass the succession to the next generation would have to be evolved.

Abdul Aziz made certain innovations which imparted to the nascent Saudi state a character that significantly distinguished it from the political arrangements that had gone before. *First*, in a departure from the past, he established a firm centralised authority by ending the autonomy of the tribal chiefs and settling (through a carrot and stick policy) the bedouin population. To drive home his intentions, he chose the palm tree and not the camel as the national symbol of his country!

Secondly, while he had initially used the *Ikhwan* (zealous Wahhabi warriors) in his military campaigns, he, in January 1930, destroyed them, thus asserting his sole authority over the State and declaring emphatically that the religious order, too, would be subordinate to him.

Thirdly, he laid the foundations of the *modern* Saudi state, utilizing the oil revenues generated from 1939 onwards to fund the development of the infrastructure and institutions of this state, while adroit diplomacy (and occasional use of force) set out the rules and norms of engagement of the state with the Kingdom's neighbours and the big powers.

Finally, Abdul Aziz established that his family, the Al-Saud, would effectively dominate every aspect of the Kingdom—political, economic, religious, social and cultural. He laid the foundations of a patronage system that constitutes the central characteristic of the Saudi state, co-opting into the Saudi order all former power-holders, particularly the semi-autonomous tribal chiefs.

The Saudi system is based on patronage, where a prince is the patron who establishes an unequal relationship with a client who is a notable, a tribal Sheikh, or a person of religious or business importance. Thus, through patronage, the royal house has collectively co-opted a large number of interest groups—tribal leaders, religious personages, businesspersons, academics, media persons and youth, who, as beneficiaries of royal patronage, flourish within the system and develop an interest in its continuance and prosperity.[1]

Oil revenues do not mean that adherence to Wahhabism has to be surrendered or even diluted. Acceptance of the Wahhabi doctrine as the national ideology, even as it imposes onerous responsibilities on the leadership, has important positive implications: the Al-Saud could oust the Sharif of Mecca (the descendent of the Holy Prophet) and assert their rule over the peninsula only on the basis that they were fighting for the cause of Islam against corruption and deviation. This conviction gave both legitimacy and a special sanction to their political and territorial claims.

Today, the sinews of the Wahhabi order, including the criminal system based on the Hanbalite interpretation of the *Sharia* and restrictions on women in relation to their dress, movement and employment, not only sustain that legitimacy, they are also an integral part of State authority. They impart to the Kingdom's leadership the moral and legal sanction to demand loyalty and support from their citizens and enforce compliance with their dictates: the *mutawwa*, therefore, are not just agents for the enforcement of public morality; they are also protagonists of the authority of the State, the foot-soldiers of the national ideology that happens to be couched in religious terms.

However, more important than these mutual claims of state authority and political obligation, the Wahhabi ideology is the basis of the *nationhood* of the Saudi state and its people, the one characteristic that is their special endowment, which distinguishes them from other Arabs, and imparts to them an identity that is at once unique and arrogant: the Saudi will bow his head before no one; and the Saudi national flag, with the *Kalimah* supported by an unsheathed sword, will never be lowered.

The flag clarifies that state authority and Islam (in its Wahhabi form) mutually reinforce each other and are indistinguishable aspects of royal power.

The arid desert and the heat of Najd moulded the character of the Saudi, making him insular and self-sufficient; Wahhabism and the triumph at arms re-affirmed to him his special status and sharpened his harsh demeanour. Oil revenues have tamed the terrain and the man, and are every day making inroads into the demanding tenets of Ibn Wahhab.

Islamic Dissent

Islamist dissent against the Saudi state order has made sporadic appearances in Saudi Arabia during the 20th century, most seriously in 1979 when the Haram Sharif in Mecca was occupied by those who opposed the Al-Saud for their corruption and modernity. In recent years, in the last decade of the 20th century, it emerged from within the Wahhabi establishment in the wake of the arrival of a large number of Western, particularly American, troops into Saudi Arabia following the Iraqi occupation of Kuwait in 1990. Sensing a serious threat to the Kingdom from the Iraqi action, King Fahd was able to obtain the support of the *Ulema* to the Kingdom seeking assistance from the West, which the *Ulema* had earlier condemned as infidel and enemy of Islam.

However, in spite of the religious sanction provided by the establishment *Ulema*, a number of young religious preachers under the leadership of Dr. Safar Al Hawali, head of Islamic theology at the Umm al Qura University in Mecca, expressed open dissent. In a public lecture, Dr. Al Hawali condemned the American and Western conspiracy against the Muslim world and declared: "The West is our enemy forever." He also criticised the "guardian" of the Saudi society (a clear reference to the King) for the moral and material corruption and decay of moral values in Saudi society as also for the promotion of a materialist consumer society. Within a few weeks, 1,00,000 copies of the lecture were distributed throughout the Kingdom.

Another religious attack on the Kingdom's leadership came from Sheikh Salman al Audah who condemned the alliance with the USA. The Islamist view of the Gulf crisis and the war was quite clear: the Gulf conflict was masterminded by Washington to strengthen its strategic and economic hold over the oil-rich region. Further, the permanent US presence on Arab soil would *not* give security to the Al-Saud: in fact, "it had invited public outrage in the Muslim world, and started a new and historical movement which would not be stopped." In December 1990, the Islamic reformists published a long list of demands signed by 200 prominent, mostly religious, persons.

Later, after the end of the war against Iraq, 400 prominent personalities submitted a one-page letter of demands calling for 'comprehensive reform' within the framework of the *Shariat* covering every aspect of national life. A year later, the Islamic dissidents published a document consisting of 10 chapters titled "*The Memorandum of Advice*", based on the ten points of this letter.[2] It was submitted to King Fahd in July 1992 and signed by 92 Sheikhs and Islamic personalities. The demands consisted of the following: they proposed a regulatory system for the issue of *fatwas*; an examination of the system of government "in the light of statements and declarations pronounced by leaders at different times"; the establishment of a Shura Council; revival of municipal and district councils (with a suggestion of elections for them, as had already been done in the case of chambers of commerce); a review of the judicial system and the observance of the due process of law; freedom of expression in the media; a comprehensive review of the working of the Committee for the Promotion of the Virtue and the Prevention of Vice (the religious police); opening of areas of public life for women; and radical and comprehensive reform of the educational system.

The Islamic dissident movement culminated, on 3 May, 1993, with the setting up in Riyadh of the Committee for the Defence of Legitimate Rights (CDLR) "to defend the rights of the citizen according to *Shariat*". By September 1994, government tolerance of the dissidents' defiance ran out. In just a few days, the security services rounded up all the prominent leaders of the dissident movement, including the two rebel Sheikhs (al-Hawali and al-Audah), along with many young activists and known Islamists. The government crackdown left the Islamist opposition activists inside prison, under house arrest, in hiding or in exile. This crackdown opened a new chapter in the confrontation as the Islamist dissidents now took their propaganda campaigns abroad.

The current crisis consisting of sporadic terrorist acts in the Kingdom and regular reports of fierce and bloody confrontations between Islamic zealots and Saudi security personnel, which have Osama Bin Laden and his *Al-Qaeda* at their centre, constitutes a new and significantly upgraded Islamist challenge to the Saudi order.

This contemporary challenge has focused unwelcome attention on the contradictions in Saudi policy which consists of a strong political, strategic and defence relationship with the United States while maintaining a rigid Wahhabi order at home and supporting Islamic causes abroad. The problems inherent in this arrangement could be contained in times of prosperity when dissent could be muted by the co-option of clerics and youth into the Saudi order. September 11 exposed the faultlines and compelled the Kingdom's leaders to do some introspection and strategic review to respond to this unprecedented crisis.

At the same time, an important issue frequently addressed in the columns of Western newspapers is the extent to which the Kingdom itself has been responsible for the current crisis. Western observers believe that Wahhabi Islam has been a breeding ground for militant behaviour and an assault on local traditional forms of Islamic practices in different parts of the world. In this regard, there has been considerable attention paid to the Saudi education system which is believed to have inculcated in Saudi youth a fundamentalist mindset and hostility towards the West. Western writers have argued that this education system has woven religious fundamentalism into the history and culture of modern Saudi Arabia while encouraging Islam-based dissent against modernity and secularism.

Saudi Reform

Though Islamic dissent in Saudi Arabia has received considerable attention from scholars and journalists, the demand for reform from the liberal side, which has also characterised Saudi political evolution in recent times, has not been given the same space. The first manifestation of this demand in modern Saudi history was the "Movement of the Liberal Princes", which, between 1958-62, was led by Prince Talal bin Abdul Aziz and had a number of other young princes associated with it. In June 1960, these princes submitted a plan for constitutional reform that would take the Kingdom on the path of becoming a constitutional monarchy. They also proposed a partially elected national assembly and progress in the area of human rights. These proposals were rejected by King Saud and Crown Prince Faisal, after which, in 1962, Talal and his supporter-princes left Saudi Arabia for exile in Cairo.

Besides this rather public demand for liberal reform emanating from within the royal family, Saudi Arabia has had some low-key presence of Baathists and communists whose members came together in the "Union of the People of the Arabian Peninsula," which was set up in 1958 and remained active through the 1960s. This group advocated pan-Arab nationalism and Arab unity, and proposed constitutional reforms and an elected parliament. The movement collapsed, along with other groups of

Arab nationalists, following the Arab defeat in the Arab-Israeli war of 1967. After this, there was no significant liberal reform movement in Saudi Arabia for the next 30 years.

Following the Iraqi invasion of Kuwait and the arrival of US forces, certain liberal elements in the Kingdom attempted to promote reform in the country. This commenced with a '*drive-in*' by 45 women through the streets of Riyadh during which some of them took off their veils and publicly stamped on them. This was followed by a petition submitted to the Government in December 1990 by 43 intellectuals, including former Cabinet Ministers, prominent businessmen, writers and university professors.[3]

The preamble of this petition contained a firm statement of allegiance to the Government and the royal family. Ten specific reforms were proposed: formation of a consultative council; revival of municipal councils; modernising the judicial system; total equality among all citizens; greater freedom to the media; reform of the *muttawwa* (religious police) system; and greater participation of women in public life. In view of the demand for reforms in the *muttawwa* system, the Islamic critics of this petition came to refer to it as a 'secular petition' and its protagonists as 'secularists'.

The "drive-in" and the liberal petition motivated the Islamists to mobilize Saudi public opinion through sermons and lectures, with copies on audiotapes being circulated in the country in their thousands. Though the government cracked down on the Islamists, this fierce onslaught by the Islamists was able to ensure that the Kingdom's liberals were effectively muted through the 1990s and their agenda totally ignored.

In 2002-03, two separate developments pertaining to the region which had a catalytic impact on the reform movement in Saudi Arabia were: first, the publication of the *Arab Human Development Report 2002,* released by the UNDP in July 2002; and, secondly, the increasing political and military involvement of the United States in West Asia, particularly its aggressive military posture *vis-à-vis* Iraq.

The *Arab Human Development Report* painted a devastatingly negative picture of the socio-economic situation in the Arab world in comparison with other regions.[4] The report, *inter alia,* noted:

(i) Over the past twenty years, in the Arab world growth in per capita income was the lowest in the world except in sub-Saharan Africa.

(ii) Labour productivity in the Arab world has been low and is declining.

(iii) The decline in workers' productivity has been accompanied by deterioration in real wages, which has accentuated poverty.

The report made it evident that, in both quantitative and qualitative terms, Arab countries have not developed as quickly or as fully as other comparable regions. From a human development perspective, the state of human development in the Arab world was a cause for concern. Achievement by the Arab region on the Human Development Index (HDI) in the past decade was lower than the world average: although poverty was low compared to other parts of the world, the Arab region was hobbled by a different kind of poverty—poverty of capabilities and poverty of opportunities. These had their roots in three deficits: freedom, women's empowerment, and knowledge. Growth alone neither bridged these gaps nor set the region on the road to sustainable development.

In its conclusion, the report called for comprehensive reforms in the Arab world; it said:

> The way forward involves tackling human capabilities and knowledge. It also involves promoting systems of good governance, those that promote, support and sustain human well-being, based on expanding human capabilities, choices, opportunities and freedoms (economic and social as well as political), especially for the currently poorest and most marginalised members of society. The empowerment of women must be fully addressed throughout.

Even as the shocking findings of the report were being absorbed in the region, West Asia came face to face with an aggressive American posture that included a promise to pursue intrusive policies to 'reform' the region in political, religious and social areas to neutralise the sources of Islam-based terror and to modernise the region's polities by imbuing them with the American virtues of freedom, democracy and free-markets. The region's leaders and people also watched helplessly and with alarm as, throughout 2002, the United States engaged in the harshest possible rhetoric against Iraq (as also, periodically, other countries in the region) and gradually, by the end of the year, put in place diplomatic, political and logistical arrangements for armed assault on Iraq.

Even as the region was mulling over the implications of this US-led initiative for reform (amidst preparations for war on Iraq), a reform programme prepared by the effective Saudi ruler, Crown Prince Abdullah, was published in January 2003. The initiative titled, "Charter to Reform the Arab Condition", included a strongly-worded critique of the Arab situation and incorporated a commitment on the part of Arab leaders to reform the Arab nations.[5]

The Charter noted "the state of weakness and powerlessness" of the Arab nations that had made it an easy target for its enemies. It asserted that the time had come to "reinvigorate the national soul and awaken and rekindle its determination to prove that the Arabs are able to establish themselves as a living nation capable of facing the challenges and threats posed by the ongoing developments and their accelerated ramifications." The most significant aspects of the Charter were the following remarks:

> *Self-reform and the promotion of political participation in Arab countries represent two basic tools for building Arab capabilities.* They provide the conditions needed to realise comprehensive and sustainable development, meet the requirements for positive engagement in international affairs, encourage creative thinking and deal objectively with international changes, notably globalisation and the rise of mega economic blocks, as well as catch up with the rapid developments in such areas as technology, communication and information. (Emphasis added.)

Most of the latter part of the Charter referred to the promotion of economic cooperation among the Arab countries through establishment of a free trade zone, a customs union, an Arab common market, and support and encouragement to the private sector.

Saudi officials had planned for this Charter to be formally approved by Arab leaders at the Arab League Summit in Cairo in March 2003, after which it would constitute the basic document for Arab action in coming years. In the event, given the concerns relating to possible American military action against Iraq, Crown Prince Abdullah announced at Cairo that the time was not propitious to discuss the Charter and that he would place it before the Summit a year later.

Saudi writers expressed fulsome praise for Abdullah's initiative. One commentator said that the initiative "constitutes a complete project for an Arab renaissance."

Soon after the publication of the Crown Prince's "Charter" for reform, news started appearing in the Saudi and foreign media of a Memorandum for reform that had been submitted to Crown Prince Abdullah. It emerged that, on 19 January, 2003, a Memorandum, titled: "A Strategic Vision for the Present and the Future of the Homeland", had been sent to Crown

Prince Abdullah. A few days later, Crown Prince Abdullah actually met 40 of the 104 signatories of the petition.

The *Vision* Memorandum[6] commenced with the praise of the Crown Prince's efforts to listen to popular opinion which was very concerned about the impact on the country of the September 11 events, as also the international and regional environment which included "military threats, indications of interference in international affairs, and suggestions for redesigning the map of the entire region." The petitioners affirmed their commitment to the integrity of the Kingdom of Saudi Arabia and their solidarity with the leadership in confronting the dangers that threaten the present and the future of the country. The petitioners asserted that their Memorandum was in line with the injunction pertaining to *Shura* (consultation) enjoined by the Holy Prophet, and that it was an attempt to promote a comprehensive national dialogue.

The signatories said that their vision for the country envisaged five pivots. Of these, the most basic was that steps had to be taken to set up constitutional establishments based on:

(i) implementation of *Shariat* in regard to religious worship and inter-personal relations; and
(ii) satisfaction of citizens with regard to the efforts made by the country to serve their interest.

To achieve these, the petitioners argued, it was necessary for the leadership to engage in *Shura*, which could only take place on the basis of a Constitution and a system of Rule of Law. The proposed Constitution had to contain provisions for the separation of powers, enshrine the basic rights of citizens, and provide for a representational assembly through popular participation.

Following this basic pivot, the other pivots mentioned in the Memorandum were the following:

(i) to address economic problems;
(ii) strengthening of interaction between society and its leadership;
(iii) launching a political reform programme; and
(iv) setting up of a national forum for dialogue.

In April 2003, Crown Prince Abdullah also received a petition, titled "Partners in One Nation," signed by 450 prominent Saudi Shias, in which the following main points were made:

(i) strengthen the integrity of the *ummah*;

(ii) make a frank declaration of the Kingdom's respect for all Islamic beliefs, including the Shia;

(iii) open the country to different Islamic beliefs and ensure their representation in Islamic organizations such as the Muslim World League, Supreme Council of Mosques, International Islamic Relief Organisation, etc.;

(iv) encourage contacts of religious scholars in the Kingdom with Muslim scholars of other doctrines;

(v) form a national committee of jurists, including qualified Shiites, to look into the question of sectarian discrimination, as also their representation in the Council of Ministers, Government departments, and representation in diplomatic assignments, military and security systems, and in the Shura Council; and

(vi) abrogate all circulars and administrative measures leading to discrimination, criminalisation and condemnation of the Shiite community.

Following the recommendation made in the *Vision* Memorandum of January 2003, in June 2003 the first National Dialogue meeting took place in Riyadh drawing together religious scholars and intellectuals reflecting different points of view. The participants presented the Crown Prince with a summary of the main points of their discussions, which emphasized rational debate, frankness and objectivity, while highlighting the importance of adopting moderate language when discussing Islamic issues. One of its recommendations was the establishment of a national centre for dialogue to serve as a think tank, organizing meetings and conducting research.[7]

Accordingly, the King Abdul Aziz Centre for National Dialogue was set up in Riyadh, in August, 2003. In September 2003, a new petition, signed by 300 intellectuals, including 50 women, was submitted to Crown Prince Abdullah which called for radical reforms in the country's constitutional, political, economic and social institutions.[8]

Between 27-31 December, 2003, the "Second National Dialogue Forum", was held, in Mecca. Attended by 50 clergymen, intellectuals and academics, both men and women, and 10 specialist researchers, its theme was: "Excess and Moderation: A Thorough Review." The Forum made, *inter alia*, the following recommendations:[9]

(i) need to accelerate the political reform process, including elections to the Shura Council, and setting up of trade unions and civil society institutions;

(ii) financial transparency and accountability;

(iii) modernising the religious message;
(iv) promoting dialogue in Saudi society and "responsible free speech";
(v) reforming education to spread the spirit of tolerance and moderation;
(vi) strengthening the role of women in all aspects of life; and
(vii) guaranteeing a fair trial to those accused of violence and terrorism.

In March 2004, the Kingdom set up a National Human Rights Commission, which had been preceded, in November 2003, by the first human rights conference in Riyadh. Again, in mid-June, 2004, the third National Dialogue Forum met in Jeddah, this time focusing on the "Rights and Duties of Women." The Forum reconfirmed that "women could be their own guardian," and recommended expansion of educational and employment opportunities for them.[10]

The 4th and 5th meetings of the National Dialogue Forum took place in December 2004 and December 2005, in Dhahran and Abha respectively. The Dhahran dialogue focused on youth issues and concluded with the consensual recommendation to promote the culture of dialogue, tolerance, respect and acceptance of each others' opinion. The dialogue at Abha took place under the title: "Us and Others", and discussed the contours of a national vision, referring particularly to Sunni-Shia relations and the plight of foreign workers in the Kingdom. This discussion was telecast live throughout the country.

From February 2005, Saudi Arabia witnessed municipal elections commencing with elections for the Riyadh municipal council on 10 February, 2005, and subsequent rounds taking place in different parts of the country upto April 2005. The fact that the franchise was restricted to men evoked considerable criticism from prominent Saudi women (and several men as well).

Referring to the Saudi government's announcement of municipal elections in early 2005, the Saudi scholar, Ghazi Al-Maghlooth, said:

> Be that as it may, at this stage, it is enough that the word "elections" has entered the Saudi vocabulary, and that the concept of elections has been embedded into the conceptual mindset of our Saudi society, and that the stagnant waters of our national life have been stirred. For too long, we have been living in a state of frozen, rock-solid rigidity day in and day out.[11]

The liberal Saudi commentator, Turki al-Hamad, saw in the election announcement "a new way of thinking...tantamount to a systemic revolution in Saudi political thinking and in the philosophy of the Government in the Kingdom." He concluded:

> The mere fact that terms such as 'mass participation,' 'elections,' and 'widened public participation' are being used is extremely significant. It is not important whether or not the Saudi leadership is really persuaded that this is the right way to go. What is important is that the survival of the Saudi state is at risk; this is enough to persuade Saudi leaders to adopt change.
>
> With the measures announced last week, Saudi decision makers.... broke down the psychological barriers between Saudi and the current age; democracy, rational thinking and—most important of all—they tore down the barriers that prevented ordinary Saudis from seeing the interests of their country as being supreme."[12]

The Outlook for Reform in the Kingdom

There is no doubt that, since Gulf War I (1990-91), the Kingdom has seen considerable reform. Soon after the war, *Shariat* laws were codified for the first time and published as the Basic Law of Governance, addressing issues such as administration, local government, royal succession, etc. The Shura Council was set up, and its (nominated) members have steadily increased from the original 60 to 90; from 2001 to 120, and from April 2005 to 150. The Council is a remarkable body in that it includes *Ulema*, Islamic scholars, tribal leaders, former ministers, retired civil servants and senior military officers, academics, economists and media persons, from different parts of the country; it also has two Shia members. More than half its members have doctorates. An analysis of the members' qualifications indicates an overwhelming liberal bias in terms of their background.

Though most of its proceedings are still outside the public domain, the Shura Council seems to be playing an increasingly visible and vibrant role in state affairs, particularly in the area of legislation: in almost every instance, a draft law has been thoroughly revised by the Council before being promulgated as a royal decree. The Council's role as a watchdog is also expanding, and Deputy Ministers from different departments are regularly subjected to intense grilling at the Shura meetings.

Following the events of September 11, Crown Prince Abdullah publicly criticised the extremist approach of religious preachers and held them primarily responsible for leading young people astray. He particularly castigated them for not imbuing Saudi youth with the essential message of Islam, of moderation and tolerance. At the same time, Abdullah accelerated the pace of reform in education, though this has not been given too much publicity so as to avoid embarrassing the clergy on the one hand as also to avoid indications of possible American pressures in this area. School and college syllabi are in the process of being thoroughly revised, with greater emphasis being laid on English and contemporary technical knowledge.

Today, there is a sense that almost all areas of national life are open to debate and review. The media has been radically transformed and publishes detailed criticisms of the state of the economy, government departments, state of municipal services, educational standards, condition of women, etc. Indeed, today, discussions relating to women's role in society in newspaper columns are very frequent: the conclusion is unavoidable that the leadership is carefully preparing public opinion for some important changes in this area in the near future.

The reform of the judicial system, delayed to some extent by the events of 9/11, is now underway: while the lead role of the *Ulema* is likely to remain, there will be a new emphasis on specialisation among judges, particularly in areas such as international commercial law and labour law. Along with this, the legal framework is being quietly reformed, with a number of committees looking at ways to modernise legal codes and procedures to meet international standards and attract foreign business.

Perhaps as a result of sharper international scrutiny, the Kingdom has permitted international human rights groups to pay visits to the country, along with large numbers of Western journalists. Political prisoners, particularly those who had participated in the religious dissent movements of the 1990s, have been released. There is also a new sensitivity to Shia interests which are now being given an unprecedented public airing; these portend a more visible Shia presence in Saudi public life in the near future.

This progress in the sensitive area of religion is accompanied by more rigorous public rhetoric and action against Islamic extremists. The Kingdom is clearly anxious to portray itself not as the patron and harbinger of Islamic extremism but as a co-victim with the USA, and keen to be seen taking harsh action against these elements. Appalled at the carnage wrought by the extremists, the Saudi establishment and political leaders have been articulating the discourse of moderation, tolerance and dialogue, accompanied by the severest criticism of Islamic radicals committing murder in the name of religion. Thus, in his Friday sermon, in April 2004, Sheikh Saleh bin Abdullah bin Humaid, the *Imam* of the Haram Sharif, Mecca, said:

> ...extremism in Allah's religion is a cause for destruction and sedition. They (the extremists) are fanatics regarding the religious scholars they follow and consider some Muslims and their rulers as disbelievers. They isolate themselves from the Muslim society and confuse between ignorance and being unjust to the people. The fate of the extremists is destruction. The methods of extremists through use of violence, carrying out explosions, destruction, robbery and shedding blood, will defeat neither the great values nor will they undermine the great accomplishments. They cannot liberate a people or impose a sect on people.
>
> Terrorism and bloodshed cannot be a respectable system or an acceptable course. Nor can it be a creed or religion. They cannot change any policy and will not win sympathy. They confirm an aggressive nature and a bloody spirit. Therefore, sensible people appreciate this united stance by the *Ummah* against these blatant criminal acts.[13]

The Saudi Islamic writer, Abdul Rahman Al-Rashi, saw extremism as the curse of Islam from its inception; he recommended:

> Islam's enemy has always been, first and foremost, extremism. The people who should fight them are preachers themselves. It is their duty to publicise middle-of-the-road Islam and back moderate preachers.... Since these people (extremists) tried to use Muslim funds under the pretext of a *jihad* that killed more Muslims than members of any other group, it is the duty of charities to turn around and back the awareness campaigns against extremism.... *It is time to rescue Islam from the Islamists and save its reputation.* (Emphasis added.)[14]

Another Saudi scholar, Abdurrahman Al-Shayyal, bemoaned the wave of violence in his country and explained it thus:

> This wave of violence that has swept across Saudi Arabia does not surprise me. The sermons and behaviour that have been a constant feature in our society were bound to lead to this, if not more. How can you expect to convince a 30-year-old fanatic

> that what he is doing is wrong, unethical and pure madness when for the past 20 years of his existence he has been the subject of a long, highly intensive extremism course?
>
> It is painfully ironic, when looking back into the annals of Arab culture, to see how Arabs prided themselves and were known for their honour, generosity and hospitality. Now we are known for a completely different set of qualities, and our honour has been ground into dust. Unless we all stand up and overturn the extremist hold on our country, then we can only expect more bloodshed.[15]

King Fahd of Saudi Arabia, in his speech at the opening session of the Shura Council, described terrorism as "corruption on earth." Noting that Muslims were responsible for some terrorist acts, he said that Islam had nothing to do with such conduct and action. According to him:

> Islam is free of such acts and the Muslim has nothing to do with these actions and has no sympathy for those who carry them out. Islam is the religion of peace, love and tolerance. It calls for doing good and refraining from anything evil and encourages understanding and peaceful coexistence while strongly warning against injustice and aggression.[16]

Prognosis

The most significant feature of the June 2003 Memorandum and the subsequent "national dialogue", that has been taking place in the Kingdom over the last three years, is the fact that it is being supported by a broad band of reformers brought together by its moderate context. This is clearly intended to avoid the fierce opposition of Islamist elements in Saudi society which had emerged in early 1991 in response to the so-called "secular petition" submitted in December 1990. Hence, it avoids some of the more strident demands of Westernised Saudis who reject, *in toto*, the Wahhabi order and the supremacy of the *Shariat* and even question the unassailable position of the Al-Saud family.

Stephane Lacroix in his brilliant essay analyzing Saudi Arabia's contemporary reform scenario, refers to this reform movement as "Islamo-Liberal Reformism" and its protagonists as "Islamo-Liberals." He sees the present scenario in the Kingdom as a call "for democratic change within an Islamic framework, though a revision of the official 'Wahhabi' religious doctrine."[17] He points out that, in the *Vision* Memorandum, Saudi intellectuals have not only managed "to orchestrate a historic rapprochement between two forces long considered mutually opposed, the liberals and the Islamists, but they have, manifesto after manifesto, succeeded in constructing a moderate Islamo-liberal reformist and nationalist discourse, around which they created a wide consensus."[18]

Echoing this analysis, the astute observer of Arab affairs, Abdulwahab El-Effendi, has applauded the fact that reformists had now come together to present a common petition. He sees this as offering Saudi Arabia:

> an historic opportunity to reform itself internally in such a way that the royal family can supervise the tempo of change, taking the people with it. It might yet succeed in responding to change while at the same time maintaining its position.[19]

Wael Mirza, too, criticises the hitherto "compartmentalised approach" of reformers intent on pursuing their own narrow agenda and point of view. He believes that Saudi intellectuals from different schools have been looking for a common ground. In the past, the Arabs had sought their panacea from a single ideology, be it pan-Arabism or "Islam". Just as those "single solutions" had failed in the past, so would "liberalism" fail today if it was not leavened with inputs from other belief systems. Mirza argues that the Arab world is facing such serious political, economic, and social threats that they necessitate a more realistic and comprehensive search for solutions that go beyond the idea of replacing one belief system with another.[20]

What then is the prognosis for "reform" in the country? Two reforms frequently agitated about abroad appear most unlikely, i.e., the uprooting of Wahhabism and ushering in of a democratic order in which the Al-Saud would be a mere constitutional monarchy. However, within these limits, a number of other important changes are likely. Those most visible and urgently undertaken will be in the economic field, covering privatization, legal/judicial changes in the area of commercial law and practice, increasing transparency in budget-making, and curbs on the share of the royal family in oil revenues.

Over the next five years, political reform will primarily pertain to the Shura Council, including the emergence of a partially elected body, expansion of its powers and making its debates more public. There will also be some reduction in disabilities suffered by women in terms of their employment and movement, though public mixing of genders is unlikely to be sanctioned, and the *hijab* and veil will remain in force. Though fully supported by King Abdullah, any significant change with regard to the status of the Shia is unlikely since that would directly conflict with the tenets of the Wahhabi order. A slow evolutionary approach will be followed in this regard, as also in the other sensitive area of educational reform.

The Saudi polity, based on religious and political affiliation between the Al-Saud and Wahhabism, is a remarkably resilient entity. It is made up of well-understood and widely accepted mutual obligations that tie different sections of the social structure, with the royal family at its centre sanctioning privilege and wielding patronage. The Al-Saud directly interact with citizens through the *majlis* and listen to different sections of opinion at their *diwans*. They provide patronage and financial support through tribal leaders, local governors and *Ulema*, and now more often through the Shura Council members. The nature of the Saudi state and its formal institutions ensure that all tribes and broad functional categories of citizens participate to some extent in government.

Most Saudis have now come to equate their state with the royal family; they are convinced that there is no family or system that can replace it, and its departure would mean disintegration of the state into its various regions and tribes. Above all, regardless of what its domestic and foreign critics might say, most Saudis believe that the Al-Saud do defend their state against Western political, economic and cultural encroachment. The Saudi system, thus, is a system that is very difficult for dissidents to penetrate and undermine.[21]

The prognosis for the Saudi polity for the next few years is that, led by King Abdullah, the Saudi state will continue on its path of modernism and liberalism, with some dollops of political reform and substantial expansion of economic opportunity. While the state will provide some modicum of educational reform, the clergy will continue to receive due respect and it, in turn, will continue to play its role in strengthening the Saudi order and the rule of the royal family. We are not likely to see any movement in the direction of the kind of radical political reform that is being urged in Western and some Arab quarters.

The Al-Saud are confident they can neutralise domestic dissent through co-option; they are convinced that, given their valuable role in terms of US strategic interests in the region linked with oil and the lucrative economic opportunities they provide American and other Western companies, they will be able to moderate US demands on them and persuade the Americans to accept change at the pace set by the royal family. They find no reason why their traditional pragmatism, which has served them so well for so long, will not continue to see them through in the years to come.

References

1. Mamoun Fandy, *Saudi Arabia and the Politics of Dissent*, St. Martins Press, New York, 1999, pp. 245-48; hereafter, *Fandy.*
2. *Fandy*, pp. 50-60.
3. *Fandy*, pp. 48-49.
4. *Arab Human Development Report—2002*: Creating Opportunities for Future Generations, UNDP and Arab Fund for Economic and Social Development; downloaded from: www.undp.org/rbas.
5. *Arab News*, Jeddah, 13 January, 2003.
6. Stephane Lacroix: "Between Islamists and Liberals: Saudi Arabia's New 'Islam-Liberal' Reformists", *Middle East Journal*, Vol. 58, No. 3, Summer 2004, Washington DC, pp. 360-61; downloaded from www.mideasti.org; hereafter *Lacroix*.
7. *Arab News*, 4 August, 2003.
8. "A New Saudi Reform Memo", *Al-Quds Al-Arabi*; translation printed in *Mideast Mirror*, Oct. 1, 2003.
9. "Saudi Reform": text of the final communiqué and recommendations of the second National Dialogue Forum, Mecca; translation printed in *Middle East Economic Survey*, 12 January, 2004.
10. "Reports of High Drama at National Dialogue Forum Exaggerated", *Arab News*, Jeddah, 16 June, 2004.
11. Ghazi Al-Maghlooth: "Saudi Elections: Winds of Change", *Al-Watan*; translation printed in *Saudi Gazette*, 20 October, 2003.
12. Turki Al-Hamad: "A Small but Revolutionary Breakthrough", *Al-Sharq Al-Awsat*, London, translation printed in *Mideast Mirror*, 21 October, 2003.
13. Adam Bakr: "Avoid Extremism and Fear Allah", *Okaz*, Jeddah; translation printed in *Saudi Gazette*, 4 April, 2004.
14. Abdul Rahman Al-Rashi: "Time to Rescue Islam from Islamists", *Arab News*, Jeddah, 6 June, 2004.
15. Abdurrahman Al-Shayyal: "Slaughtering Our Honour", *Arab News*, Jeddah, 20 June, 2004.
16. Abdul Wahab Bashir: "Reforms to Suit Saudi Needs", *Arab News*, 21 June, 2004.
17. *Lacroix*, p. 345.
18. *Lacroix*, p. 362.
19. *Al-Quds Al-Arabi*, London, 13 February, 2003.
20. *Al-Watan*, Abha, 6 March, 2003.
21. *Fandy*, p. 243.

2

State and Oppositions in Saudi Arabia
Emerging Trends

ANWAR ALAM

Introduction

The Kingdom of Saudi Arabia has been the focus of world attention ever since it was found that out of 19 hijackers of infamous 9/11, 15 were Saudi citizens. The incident not only rekindled the international debate over the issue of relationship between Islam and the West and the question of democratic reform in the Muslim World but also by targeting the USA, the lone super power and the most important allay of Saudi Arabia, it conveyed a message that all is not well within the Kingdom; that beneath the surface of political stability lies a generalized sense of frustration and anguish against the prevailing state of affairs within the Kingdom. The 1990s and aftermath has witnessed a series of violent and non-violent actions against the Saudi State. Doubts have been raised over the survivability of the Al-Saud regime. What is the nature of oppositions in the Kingdom? What are the prospects of the oppositions? How the Al-Saud regime has responded to these internal challenges? What are the emerging political trends that have aroused out the historical engagements of the Saudi state with the changing character of social classes?

One way of reflecting upon some of the above raised questions is to undertake a historical view of the functioning of the Saudi state system and its engagement with different social classes, tribes and regions. From this perspective this essay, in the first part, takes a synoptic view of the sources of legitimacy and support base that have so far helped in sustaining, consolidating and institutionalizing the Al-Saud's rule. The second part of the essay reflects upon the context and causes of the emerging internal oppositions, its nature, dimensions and effectiveness to the Al-Saud regime. The third part of the essay discusses the political strategies of the regime and its effectiveness to deal with the internal challenges. Finally, while concluding the essay, summarizes the emerging political trends in the kingdom in the light of analysis of this essay.

The Saudi State System: Notable Features

The Saudi state system, having absolutist monarchial form of government, derives its legitimacy and social support to rule from the following sources:

Religious Legitimacy: While Al-Saud's claim to rule is usually conveyed in terms of Islam in general, in practice the Islamic dimension is tied to the Islamic tradition initiated by Muhammad ibn'Abd-al-Wahhab and pejoratively known by others as Wahhabism. The historical narratives of the Saudi state emphasized (only) the 'Islamic' dimension of al-Saud's rule, while tribalism, Arabism, nationalism, localism, regionalism, sectarianism, communism, westernization etc. are derided, holding them responsible for social disintegration. In the narratives the golden Islamic age is contrasted with the darkness of second Arabian Jahilliya, the age of ignorance before the rise of the *Wahhabi* movement[1].

Epitomizing the Al-Saud's appeal to Muslim faith, are the upholding of Islam as state religion, the *Quran* and the *Sunna* of the Prophet as the state's Constitution and the implementation of a strict *Hanbali* interpretation of *Sharia* law. These hallmarks of the state have been recently re-affirmed officially (Basic Law of Government, 1992: Article 1, 7, 8)[2]. The Saudi Monarch is routinely referred to in the kingdom and in its public relations material internationally as 'the Servant' or the "Custodians of the two Holy Places or the 'Two Holy Mosques', a title which plays overtly on the dynasty's religious legitimacy and is aimed particularly at the Muslim Population across the world. Indeed James P. Piscatori has referred to this special status as the Al Saud's 'primary claim to govern'[3]. As an extension of this role, the Saudi regime has been careful to promote itself as a benefactor of Muslim communities globally, typically by sponsoring the buildings of mosques, Quranic schools, and Islamic cultural centers.

The religious character of Al Saud's regime is buttressed by the institutionalization of *Ulema* in the state system. The Al Saud-Wahhabi nexus is historically entrenched relationship, whereby the Saudis foster, recognize and sanction conservative *ulema* in return for official religious approval, and it continues to be the basis of the critical relationship between Saudi royal family and Islam. However it needs to point out here that contrary to the popular modernist perception, the Al Saud—Al Shaikh relationship is not a black and white matter of secular/political-religious alliance. Rather both families are religious, although the religious credentials of the Al Sheikh family are stronger and both of them are prominent tribal families. Though the Al Sauds have long been more powerful—both families are part of the tribal and religious *asabiyya* of Saudi Arabia[4].

The importance of the politico-religious nexus to the power structure created by the Saudis becomes clear when set in the context of the consitutional issues as follows: (a) There is no legally binding written Constitution; (b), the *Quran* and the *Sunnah*, despite centuries of entrenched tradition, are to some extent still subject to interpretation, especially in periods of rapid technological and social development when Quranic principles have to be applied in new situation and circumstances...which means Saudi Arabia's constitution is 'fluid'. And (c), the agents of Quranic and Prophetic exegesis, the *ulama*, are effectively controlled by the Saudi regime...which means the regime in reality also controls the interpretation and application of the kingdom's unwritten 'constitution' on a day-to-day basis. This measure of control, coupled with control of the generally respected religious establishment, and the institutionalization of rule by the royal decree with no popular representation, makes clear the absolute nature of the power of the Saudi monarchy.

Oil Wealth: It was the oil boom of the 1970s that spawned the entire contemporary Saudi bureaucracy and the state institutions; whose primary function it was to distribute oil 'rents' through out society. Massive petroleum revenues have enabled the state to bestow the new fruits of those export earnings upon its population in the form of modern infrastructure development and subsidies which include, for example, free education and health care with ultra-modern facilities; token charges for utility services (including water, electricity, gas) and petrol; subsidized staple foods such as bread, rice and sugar; and the importation of foreign labour for much of the country's heavy manual and menial work; and no income tax[5].

The distributive—welfare state is an important element in what has been termed 'the Saudi Social Contract'; this incorporates the Al Saud's strategy of the 'legitimacy of largesse', which has consistently allowed the regime to 'buy off any potential hostility long before it has time to develop into anything like a serious threat'[6]. The strategy of largesse, however, has developed into a pillar of the regime's legitimacy and now colours every aspect of the Kingdom's political economy, socio-economics and socio-politics. According to one source, the Al Saud rely on two types of legitimacy: ideological, largely through a co-opted *ulema*; and 'functional', through the use of subsidies[7]. In short, Oil wealth enabled the Al Saud to be patriarchs and patrons to their subjects—a kind of social contract...a respected role in Arabian tradition; purchasing a great deal of domestic socio-political stability.

Political Traditions and Social Engineering: This form of legitimacy is claimed in terms of the Al Saud having been instrumental in bringing the country together—a process that achieved some success in the 18th century, experienced both success and setbacks in the 19th century and finally came to fruition in the 20th century. The Al-Sauds are portrayed in weaving the different strands of the country together, preventing it from disintegrating. It is important to note that in the historical narrative of the Saudi state, as reflected in the school textbooks, the term 'unification' rather than 'conquest' is used to describe the military campaigns in Arabia after the capture of Riyadh by Ibn Saud in 1902. Further, the slogan of the centennial celebration of Al-Saud's rule in 1999 was 'a hundred years of unification and construction'[8]. The 'unification' of present day Saudi Arabia is in part due to the Al Saud's political tactness and a policy of the balance of power between the nomadic and settled population, the *badu* and *hadhar*-that requires both 'social engineering' (settlements in agricultural communities—*hujar*) and ideological (sectarian prosleytization). The policy was maintained since the outbreak of *Ikhwan* movement in 1929 with checks and balances, carrot and sticks. Over the Years the House of Al Saud has been transformed into a symbol around which national unity is expected to revolve.

Decision Making Process: The Kingdom of Saudi Arabia provides a paradox: a "post-traditional' absolute monarchy has developed the trappings of modern state institution, but traditional hierarchical, tribal-kinship values largely determine all its procedures, decision making and general conduct[9]. Historically informal and non-institutional, if compared to modern conception of the rule, the process of discussion and consensus building remains an important point of legitimacy and stability for the regime that precede any significant policy changes. The opportunity to participate in such discussion is limited to major tribal and other social elites of the Saudi society. It gave weight to specific decision, the royal decision-making process in general, and Al Saud legitimacy overall, by nurturing an image of consultation, discussion and consensus and providing the king and senior royals with the opportunity to act as benevolent patrons and patriarchs[10].

The Najdiisation of the State: Saudi historiography emphasizes the central role of Najd in the unification of the country. Not only was Najd the homeland of the *Wahhabi* reform movement, but also the traditional homeland of the Al Saud. In historical memory, Najd is projected as the region responsible for the delivery of salvation. The formation of modern Saudi state was accompanied by gradual social, political and economic domination of the Najd. By 1969 the Najdis occupied 61 per cent of senior bureaucratic positions—a process that continued over the course of the 1970s[11]. By 1973 Najdis commanded the collective Saudi bureaucracy and were in a position to favour kin and the new 'cluster of clients' during the boom era[12]. The formation of Najdi dominated Saudi Confederation of Chambers of Commerce, Industry and Agriculture in 1981 marked the end of Hijazi dominated Jeddah Chamber of Commerce. Although Najdis made up just 26 per cent of the total urban population in 1981, they accounted for 44 per cent of the top household income bracket...the largest single percentage according to the region[13]. The Najdiisation of the public culture was also evident from the beginning of the formation of Saudi state:..." The founder of the Saudi Arabian Kingdom, Abdul Aziz al-Saud, decreed that all men serving in government position must wear the Najdi Bedouin dress, the clothing seen widely in Saudi Arabia today"[14]. The domination of Najd in the Saudi state system has historically served the interest of Al Saud regime.

Gauging Public Opinion: The Al Saud government keeps a vigilant eye on the pulse of people's thinking. In the absence of scientific methods of gauging public opinion, such as surveys and polls, the royal family utilizes informal networks of informers 'with links to academics, businessmen, tribesmen and other sections of the community' to keep in touch with the feelings at a grass-root level. The state security apparatus is also involved in monitoring public opinion, with a special branch of the professional intelligence dedicated to gathering information on anything that may have connotations, including whatever is said in general discourse including...jokes about the king and (senior) princes[15].

Oppositions in Saudi Arabia

A multitude of factors converged in the last quarter of twentieth century to produce the diffused, but effective oppositions to the Saudi regime, beginning with the seizure of Grand Mosque of Mecca in 1979. First, the impact of declining oil prices that remained throughout the major period of the 1980s and 1990s was felt throughout the kingdom. During this period the average price of crude oil remained below $20, failing to a low point of $12.7 in 1998. The era of high budget deficits actually began in 1983 with the onset of recession, and has continued into the 1990s. In addition to weak oil prices, the direct and indirect expenses of 10 years of war—Iran—Iraq and Gulf—both financially costly to Saudi Arabia, and of military and security expenditures in general, took their toll on the Saudi economy[16]. Of the 71 billion worth of arms agreement between the United States and Saudi Arabia from 1950 to 1993, and 17 billion worth were concluded between 1991 and 1993[17]. The US Department of Defence estimated the cost of the 1991 Gulf War at $61 billion, but of this $54 billion was offset by contribution from 'other members of the Coalition'. Saudi Arabia was responsible for some $30 billion of the contribution to the United States, in addition to its own expenditure of the war. The total cost of the war to Saudi Arabia came to about $60 billion[18].

Given that oil revenues made up the major part of government revenues, ranging between 60 percent and 90 percent of the total revenues, the impact of the changing price levels on Saudi Arabia's economic development and stability was substantial. In the light of growing population (currently running at 3.4% to 3.8% annually) the effect on per capita income was even more dramatic. Whereas Saudi Arabia in 1981 had a per capita GDP of $28, 600 (roughly equivalent to that of the United States), in 2000 per capita GDP came to less than $7,000. In the United States, per capita income in 2000 had reached $35,027[19]. A recent survey of the major cities of Riyadh, Jedda, Medina, Mecca, Dhahran, Khobar and Abha carried out by the Saudi Ministry of Public Works and Housing revealed that the income of 40 per cent of the households in these cities is less than 6,000 riyals…approximately US $,602…and that around 51 per cent of the household had no fixed income[20]. On the other hand, it has been reported that less than 1 per cent of the Saudi population had more than US $500 billion in liquid portfolio investments held in Western equity markets by September 1999[21]. In nutshell, the 'Asabbiyah capitalism'[22] with its associated features of growing inequality and corruptions in the high places created a belief that the inequalities were unjustified and damaging to society. The problem was further compounded, given the rising graph of unemployment among the Saudis youth[23]. Daryl Champion, while surveying sources of the instability of Al Saud regime concluded: "The Saudi regime is presiding over rising unemployment, falling living standards, increasing poverty and the withdrawal of social services and benefits. An increasing pool of educated, unemployed youth with no political voice can only add to the ranks of the discontented as the forces of social transformation gather momentum"[24].

Second, a significant agent of social change with political implications is the cultural intrusion of the Western world. This non-physical Western presence is increasingly being felt in Saudi Arabia, as it is in other countries of the globe. Debate verging on social conflict is already occurring in the kingdom over what is undoubtedly becoming an onslaught of Western cultural influence. The Great Mosque rebels of 1979 were very much concerned with the Western influence; their first demand was: "The adoption of socio-cultural values which are based on just Islamic values rather than corrupt Western emulations, and the breaking of diplomatic relations with Western states which are exploitative in nature". Anthropological research on the Saudi middle and upper class youth of Jeddah is revealing that behaviour common everywhere in the developed world is beginning to be seen in the Kingdom[25], too. Lisa Wynn has indicated the direction in which a significant segment of Saudi youth is already moving: 'Using a commodity—mediated space to evade or resist the control of the state, religious and familial authorities, upper and middle class urban youth thus expand their social networks from groups primarily determined by kin contacts and school friends to those around a class-based consumerism. In the act of creating a youth which subverts dominant gender, generational and moral norms, the elite youth in Jeddah affirm their loyalty to a culture of commodity consumption[26]." Thus the call for a return to more simple and authentic Islamic values therefore carried weight in the developing socio-economic environment.

Third, the Iranian revolution (1979) challenged the Islamic legitimacy of the Saudi state. The Kingdom was portrayed as outdated, corrupt, compromised by its relationship with the United States and (for all these reasons) unfit for a leadership role in global Islam. Iran was now promoting change within the Islamic world, seeking the establishment of regimes based on radical Islamic principles. There was no doubting the appeal, which this approach held for many Muslim around the world.

Fourth, the close security relationship with the United States posed further problems. The value of this relationship was perhaps understandable to many Saudis for as long as the Soviet Union was in existence. Saudi Arabia and the United States could be portrayed as engaged in a joint struggle against the forces of atheism. US-Saudi support for the Islamic resistance to the Soviet-backed regime in Afghanistan constituted the high point, and most alluring symbol, of this joint struggle. But with retreat of Soviet Power in the late 1980s, and the subsequent collapse of the Soviet Union, the relationship with the United States could no longer be perceived in the same light. The focus of the US concern was now directed towards the Islamic world, and the military actions and economic retaliation undertaken by the United States after 1990 were largely against Muslim countries. The failure of the United States to use its power to curb Israeli settlement in the occupied territories deepened the perception of US antagonism towards the Islamic World. To the more radical trends in *Wahhabism*, then, the collaborative US-Saudi relationship was becoming a symbol of Saudi subservience to an anti-Islamic agenda. International developments combined with the domestic policies to broaden the support for oppositions, mostly Islamic, within country.

Finally it was the Gulf war (1991) that provided the political context of massive, but diffuse opposition to the Saudi state. The stationing of American troops in the country during the Gulf War in early 1990s transformed an inchoate resurgence of Islamic identity into an organized opposition movement. Dekmejian, for example, believes the opposition to the presence of foreigners and foreign influence reached a level of 'heightened xenophobia' after the Gulf War, a symptom of an 'identity warp' caused by, among other factors, declining living standards, eroded socio-economic standing, rapid modernization, Western cultural influences, conflicting al Saud policies, and the military weakness of the kingdom[27]. Fandy also refers to 'moral and patriotic—xenophobia' in the discourse of Islamist dissent that rose with the Gulf Crisis: a fusion of "Saudi nationalism' and wounded *muwahhidi* religious sentiment[28]. Saad al-Fagih, in his history of dissent against the al-Saud, presents a fuller historical perspective. Fagih depicts a socio-cultural and political landscape in which the Islamist discourse was dominant but low profile, a situation which led to the 'alienation—of the political leadership from the nation', creating tensions between society and the state. Thus the Gulf Crisis was able to provide 'the cultural shock' and the 'historic event' which pushed (these) tensions—to manifest (themselves)—politically in an open manner[29]. In fact, at the time of 1990-91 crisis, the majority of Saudis believed the propaganda 'that Iraq would have invaded Saudi Arabia, but this belief had worn thin by 1993. Now 'ninety five percent' of Saudi citizens believe the war was a 'well staged plan' for the United States to insert a greater presence in the Kingdom and the Gulf region generally. Common terms for the Gulf War inside the kingdom today are 'the Gulf Show' and 'the Gulf Massacre'[30].

These internal and external factors shaped the ground for the political discontent, which was to achieve expression in the 1990s, both in violent and non-violent forms.

Siezure of Grand Mosque, 1979

The first serious threat to the Saudi regime, after Ikwan rebellion in late 1920s, took place on 20 November, 1979 in the form of seizure of Grand mosque in Mecca by a small band of Islamic militants led by Juhayaman al-Qtaibi. While with the help of French assistance, the Saudi government crushed the rebellion, but the act was symbolically significant: Al Saud was being challenged on their own ground, accused of having betrayed the *Wahhabi* basis on which the Kingdom had been founded. Second, Juhayman's origins, and the context in which his beliefs had developed, however, gave a dimension of significance to his action. Both by virtue of belonging to one of the main tribes of Najd, which had been a mainstay of support for the Al Saud, and coming from the religious tradition, which was the ideological backbone of the Kingdom, he was by no means a peripheral figure. Though the action taken by Juhayaman and his companions appears to have enjoyed very little support among Saudis, especially as it involved the desecration of the holiest religious site in the country. It did, however, exert a powerful influence on the development of government policy through the two decades, which followed.

Shii Assertion in the Eastern Province

The seizure of the Great Mosque was rapidly followed by a further element of religio-political unrest: demonstration, leading to riots, among the Shiites of the Eastern Province. As a community, the *Shiis* still suffered from a lack of public recognition or acceptance. On 28 November, 1979 *Shii* leaders in the eastern region staged '*ashurah* ceremonies with processions marking the event. Public celebration of the major Shiite ceremonies, such as the '*ashurah* mourning rituals in memory of the martyrs of Shiism, Hasan and Husain, and the buildings of new *Shii* mosques, had been banned by the temporal authorities in the eastern region even since the al-Hasa region had come under Saudi rule in 1913[31]. The *Ashura* processions reflected a wider politicization including the demands to bring about a fairer distribution of wealth in the country, end discrimination against Shiites, support the Islamic revolution in Iran and stop supplying oil to the United States. During the clash with security forces in Qatif, 17 Shiites lost their lives.

The Social origins of those who took a lead in demonstrations and who formed the nucleus of the Organization of the Islamic Revolution which was established secretly following the November events, was significant. Most were ARAMCO workers and students at the University of Minerals and Technology in Dhahran[32]. A technically skilled and professionally oriented sector of the population was mobilizing a more widely based popular movement on the basis of Shiite identity. After 1992, the Organization of the Islamic Revolution became known as the Reform Movement. From London, the organization published a monthly periodical, *Al-Jazirah al-Arabiyyah*, which pursued a well-informed critique of Saudi government policies[33]. The main target of criticism from the Shiite opposition, then, was the Saudi state and its repression of the Shiite community. However in August 1996 the Reform Movement reached an agreement with the government. *Shii* prisoners in Saudi prisons would be released, there would be a review of the ban on travel for 2,000 *Shiis*, passports would be issued to those *Shii* who wanted to return to Saudi Arabia, and the *Shii* community would be allowed cultural and religious expression (with permission to import books on *Shiism*, an agreement that negative references about the Shiite community in official documents would be removed and acceptance that the *Shii*'s constituted one of the sects of Islam)[34]. Despite this agreement and the spurt of government's developmental activities in the region, the *Islah* Islamic movement in the Arabian Peninsula is calling attention to the continuing discrimination against, and neglect of Saudi Shiites[35]. The more hierarchical structure of Shiite Islam and the greater independence and autonomy of Saudi Shiites forced on the community by state discrimination have made the Saudi Shiites more effective clandestine organizers of dissent than their Sunni counterparts

Mainstream Islamic Opposition: The Petition(s) Movement

The massive presence of western forces in the kingdom provided the opportunity for both—the oppositional voice within the Saudi state system that was seeking for the greater reform within the kingdom and the oppositional forces outside the system that challenged the very legitimacy of the Al-Saud to rule. The most powerful expression of liberal middle class (in relative sense) pressure for change was the demonstration organized by 45 Saudi women to press for the right of Saudi Women to drive to be recognized. The demonstration took place on the 6 November, 1990, with 45 women driving into the center of al-Riyadh[36]. This incident was followed by the submission of a petition, signed by 43 moderate liberal business and intellectuals—including the former Minister of Information, Ahmad Abdu Yamani, to the King in late January 1991. The petitioned demanded limited political reform within the kingdom. However its significance lies in the fact that it was widely circulated within the kingdom and published in the Arab world[37]. From this point onwards, the lead in petitioning the state for political change was taken by liberal Islamist reformers. One reason for these petitions by the reform minded *ulema* was to ensure that younger and more militant religious teachers and preachers did not outflank them.

The petition, known as the 'Letter of Demands', was signed by 400 *ulema* including the senior and establishment *ulema*, judges, university professors, lawyers and other leading persons in society[38]. Even the state's *alim*, Shaikh Abd al-Aziz bin Baz, endorsed a draft version of the letter[39] though the latter distanced himself from it once the text had become public and controversial. The Letter of Demands was the first major document of the Saudi Islamist reform movement, and was the basis of the more comprehensive petition, the 'Memorandum of Advice', which was delivered to *Shiekh* Baz in July 1992. The letter bore the signature of more than 100 petitioners: *ulema*, university professors and the prominent figures (al-Fagih, 1998: ch. 9). In 2003 and 2004 thee was a renewed petition movement by liberal Islamists/modernizers within the Kingdom, calling for political reform and the expansion of human rights

In terms of subject matters the petitions focused on and called for reform in the Kingdom's socio-economic and political-economic structure that includes the issue of establishment of a Majlis al-Shura (Consultative Council) to handle the state's domestic and foreign policies, according to the Islamic law, the revision of all state regulations and laws in the political, economic and administrative sectors, to make them consistent with Islamic law, the acceptance of principle of accountability for all state officials, just distribution of public funds and prevention of the waste and exploitation of resources, adoption of Islamic economic system, reform of military and unfair state bureaucracy, tackling rising unemployment, ensuring the rights of the individual and society in accordance with the *Sharia*, dealing firmly with cases of nepotism, bribery, corruption and unfair practices associated with commission farming among many others[40]. Thus it was an attack on the regime's structures which 'legitimated administrative and financial corruption—sanctioned injustice, despotism, wide spread corruption and nepotism. In other words, it was largely an assault against the Saudi system of *asabiyya* capitalism, which was condemned broadly as anti-Islamic.

The significance of these petitions lies in three things. Firstly a large number of signatories to both these petitions were affiliated with the conservative Najd region[41], the traditional stronghold of Al Sauds. Second, these petitions reflected a perceived decline in the moral and Islamic stature of Saudi state, seen as signs of the even more complete 'corruption' of the Al Saud regime. In these respects, the demands put by these petitions evoke Juhaiman al-Utaibi's capture of the Great Mosque 12 years earlier. Thirdly, according to Abir, "On the surface it seemed that the King had opted to follow the time honoured Saudi practice of doing nothing… Yet, the '400 *ulema*'s petition seriously shook the monarch and most Sauds because it signified the emergence of a broad-based coalition between the different streams in the ranks of the *ulema*. It also represented a departure from the traditional alliance between 'state and church' within the framework established by Ibn Saud after 1930 and therefore, a threat to regime's authority and legitimacy".[42]

The Gulf war also witnessed the emergence of more radical Islamic criticism of Al Saud rule from within the establishment. At the core of the radical group which was making critique were religious personalities with positions at religious universities in Saudi Arabia: Safar al-Hawali, Salman al-' Auda and Nasir al "Umar. Their criticism had been initiated within a week of the Board of Senior 'Ulama's *fatwa* in support of the government's position. Safar al-Hawali, head of the '*aqidah* department at Umm al-Qura university, described the reliance on the United States to deal with the Iraqi invasion of Kuwait as a violation of Islamic law, asking 'how can the *ummah* of the faith and *tawhid* accept reliance on America to solve the problem instead of Almighty Allah?"[43] Salman al' Auda, a member of staff at the Imam Muhammad Ibn Saud University, broadened the criticism to suggest that neither Iraq nor Kuwait were operating on Islamic principles, with the conclusion that no Islamiic obligation could arise in the conflict between them. Nasir al 'Umar, a professor at the same university, asserted that the United States was motivated by the desire to gain hegemonic control in the Gulf.[44]

The CDLR and MIRA

From these early days of post-Gulf War calls for reform sprang the attempts of a more serious and organized dissent beginning in mid 1990s. A number of dissident organizations were formed, some of which achieved a relatively high profile and gained some notoriety both inside and outside the Kingdom, including the Advice and Reformation Committee (ARC) associated with Osma bin Laden. But foremost among these organizations was the Committee for the Defence of Legitimate Rights (CDLR). The CDLR was formed in May 1993 in Riyadh. The six signatories of the initial declaration of the Committee were senior academics and legal personalities. One of the signatories was Abdullah al-Jibrin, a member of the highly important *Ifta* Committee which was responsible for issuing *fatwas* on behalf of the senior *Ulama*. Another was a retired judge and former head of the dawn of Ombudsmen, Abdullah al-Masari, whose son, Muhammad al-Masari, acted as the spokesperson of the group. Within few days of the announcement of the formation of CDLR, the government outlawed the organization, arrested those, including Saad al-Fagih and Muhammad al-Masari, associated with the organization and later released.

Fagih and Masari fled the Kingdom and re-established the CDLR in London in April 1994. CDLR propaganda activity was prolific and became a source of agitation for both the al-Saud and the British establishment. The Economist reported that the CDLR faxed 800 copies of its newsletter to the Kingdom on a weekly basis, to be further copied and distributed there[45]. Through fax as well as website—they spread information on the situation within Saudi Arabia, mostly dealing with the issue of political reform and human rights violation. While not all of the information was accurate, it did open up internal as well as external discourse on developments in the Kingdom. Further, Masari adopted a very high profile and proved adept at conducting a clever public relations campaign in the (mainly British) media. The CDLR thus quickly came to represent two things, the Saudi regime both feared and loathed: organized opposition, and publicity. Responding to heavy pressure from the Saudi government, the British government sought to deport Muhammad al-Masari, but the Court rejected the ground for the deportation. In fact the issue of deportation of al-Masari developed into near scandal in which, among other revelations, 'the symbiotic relationship between the British arms firms and various branches of the (the British) government' was exposed.[46]

However, a split occurred in 1996, which effectively destroyed the CDLR in the form in which it had existed before. Saad al-Fagih left the organization to found a new grouping, the Movement for Islamic Reform in Saudi Arabia (MIRA). MIRA kept the focus on Saudi Arabia, running an effective web site, which gave, continued publicity to the developments within Saudi Arabia and the campaign to bring about political change in the country. A publication, which it initiated, *Arabia Unveiled*, focused on such issues as the independence of the judiciary, the accountability of the government and royal family, the oil and defence policies pursued by the regime and the socio-economic problems facing the population. Both of the organizations tended to direct their criticism more against the King, Prince Nayif (Minister of Interior), Prince Sultan (Minister of Defence) and Prince Salman (Governer of al-Riyadh,) than against Crown Prince "Abdullah. In December 2004 MIRA opened a radio station called Sawt al-Islah, broadcasting from an undisclosed European country to Saudi Arabia[47].

The CACSA

There has also been another kind of opposition to the Al Saud, the presence of which has been felt only on the Internet. The only organized Saudi opposition that has existed exclusively in this form was the Committee Against Corruption in Saudi Arabia (CACSA). CACSA's website certainly gave the impression of being a collective effort with resource behind it, as opposed to the fleeting cyber-presence of individuals hostile toward the al-Saud. Article 1 of the CACSA's mission statement[48] made clear the orientation of the US-based organization: "CACSA is a peaceful organization whose sole purpose is to change the Saudi Arabian status quo using the Internet as a worldwide campaign tool. CACSA is not associated or affiliated with any political or religious group. CACSA condemns violence, fundamentalism, and extremism and supports the interest of both the United States and "Saudi Arabia". Article 2 of CACSA further state: 'CACSA is committed to identifying alternative leadership in Saudi Arabia that will govern the country without corruption and malice. This alternative leadership needs to include independently minded businessmen, intellectuals, and other Saudis who wish to bring Saudi Arabia into the twenty-first century without disrupting either the Saudi societal mores or its Islamic roots. CACSA appears to be 'an example of the so-called virtual opposition to the Al Saud. It appears to be a relatively rare example of an (apparently) organized and highly visible (in Internet terms) group of dissidents, which was opposed, to the current Saudi leadership but not to the United States.

Islamic Militants: The Violent Dimension of Oppositions

The Gulf War and its aftermath left the Saudi population 'simmering' and provided the environment for the radical-militant views, either of Bin Laden and his al-Qaida or of domestic organizations, to gain acceptance among the common Saudi population. Opposition to the 'US occupation' of the land of the two holy mosques and, by extension, opposition to the Al-Saud, was not confined to the Kingdom but soon took on an international dimension, making itself known and spreading throughout the Muslim world, via the new media technologies[49]. The Bin Landen's group and other unidentified, underground domestic groups posed the severest terrorist challenge to the security of Saudi state. Between 1995 and February 2006, more than hundred lives including civilians, foreigners and state personnels have been lost and wounded in the terrorist attack inside the Saudi Arabia[50]. Some of the major terrorist operation within the Kingdom that attracted world-wide attention are: attack on Saudi National Guard (13 November, 1995), Khobar Tower Bombing (25 June, 1996), Riyadh Compound Bombing (12 May, 2003) Black Saturday (1 May 2004) and Al-Khobar Massacre (29 May, 2004). Although the mainstream Saudis did not endorse the violent actions, many openly professed that they 'liked the message'[51].

Further, post Gulf war militant political opposition, in a broad sense, enjoys a good deal more popular sympathy than did Juhaiman's narrowly based rebellion and, by comparison, the radicals among today's dissenters are choosing the right targets[52]. Jamal Khashoggi, a Saudi Political analyst and the deputy editor of Saudi Arabia's Arab News daily newspaper, wrote that 'there are very few people in Saudi Arabia who are prepared to criticize Bin Laden, especially among the more religious after all, he had become a symbol of confrontation with the United States"[53]. In one remarkable report from Riyadh, the director of Saudi intelligence, Prince Nawaf bin Abd al-Aziz, 'acknowledge that the vast majority of young Saudi adults felt sympathy for the cause of (Bin Laden) after September 11, even though they rejected the attacks in New York and Washington'[54]. Evidence was also presented in this report that, of the Kingdom's nationals aged between 24 and 41 surveyed by Saudi intelligence, 95 per cent were found to be supportive of Bin Laden's cause[55].

Nature and Strength of Oppositions

What is the nature of emerging oppositions to the Al Saud regime in Saudi Arabia? How effective is this internal opposition? It has been observed that the mainstream oppositions in Saudi Arabia since the Gulf Crisis has, with the possible exception of the Kingdom's *Shii* minority, been heterogeneous, fragmented, disorganized and unprepared[56]. The Saudi neo-Ikhwan ideology epitomized by Juhaiman al-Utaibi's movement was described as 'classical Wahhabism, but revolutionary and as 'rejectionist', with no programme—no clear ideas' about a constitution, human rights and the like, they were 'a little bit better than the present government, but not much". This description also holds true for other militant outfits and individuals who lack moral legitimacy and positive agenda to pose a serious threat to the regime. In fact such violent groups and their attended actions provide good rationale to enhance the state's coercive apparatus and use them against any emerging opposition that pose a serious threat to the stability of the regime.

Mainstream Islamists are by far more coherent, powerful, and organized than any other social force in Saudi Arabia, including those based on nationalism, regional identity, or business activity. It provided the vocabulary, symbols and historic reference points that resonated with the population. The mainstream Islamism is the only movement that is able to cut across multiple cleavages in Saudi Arabia. It has tapped into two forces: a convergence of dissent, and socio-economic distress. In fact, Wahhabism itself is now increasingly divided into two trends: one of which drew closer to the ruling clique, and the other was conducting a political-religious propaganda for a change of regime, mostly by young Wahhabi *ulema*. Despite significant differences in ultimate agenda, many sources of discontent now focus on three central points: call for redistribution of wealth, procedural social justice and regime's (Islamic) accountability.

This convergence cuts across cleavages of region, gender, class, school of Islam, ethnicity, ideology, and rural-urban settings. Private business persons and civil bureaucrats, industrialists and small-shop owners, university teachers, young religious scholars and establishment *ulema,* men and women share core grievances. All strands of the diverse Islamist movement share three key attributes. First, their critique of the regime is both symbolic and material. Second, all are aware of the power of the embedded social structure in which they operate. Third, all contest the dominant historical narrative on the founding of the Kingdom, particularly the *Shii* opposition[57]. Fourth, a bulk of social support to the emerging opposition-both violent and non-violent came from the region of Najd, the traditional stronghold of Al Saud regime. Finally the very dialogue of political intercourse changed. Before the war, criticism could be offered only in private and on a one-to-one verbal basis. Now it was transformed into a public discussion—much of it written, signed and documented. The most influential petition came were from a section of *Sunni ulema*. It is this non-violent dimension of Islamic oppositions, rather than the violent ones, that the Al Saud regime worried most.

Regime's Response

How and in what manner the Al Saud regime has responded to these emerging internal challenges? One recent analysis that group's Saudi Arabia, Kuwait, Bahrain, Qatar, the UAE and Oman, as a monarchial collective, presents the following reasons for their overall stability: "—Social peace in the Gulf—is maintained by the clever, and consistent use of a variety of government strategies to promote social order. Gulf governments use a combination of six strategies: strong security services; the cooptation of potential dissidents; divide-and-rule measures, ideological flexibility; token participation; and accommodative diplomacy. Taken together, these strategies preserve islands of social peace in an area of turbulence"[58]. In the specific context of Saudi Arabia, the response of Al-Saud regime ranges simultaneously from denying the existence of opposition movement, particularly of *Sunni-Wahhabi*, to the mobilization of establishment *ulema*, to the gesture of political reform, to co-optation of moderate Islamists and semi-loyalists, to the socio-economic package, to asserting its religious legitimacy and finally to unleash repression on the Islamic militants.

The allocation of state funding for the support of religious activities increased rapidly. In the Second Development Plan (1975-80) this stood at SR 1.26 billion, while in the Third Development Plan (1980-85) SR 9.04 billion was allocated. An intensive programme for the construction of new mosques was put in place. Additional funding was put into the country's structures of Islamic education, with a substantial increase in the numbers of students who were admitted into the Islamic universities and provision of more generous grants than before to encourage this participation. A member of Al al Shaikh was appointed Minister of Justice, reinforcing the traditional alliance between the religious and temporal leadership, and restoring control of judiciary to a member of the Al al Shaikh-Shaeikh Bin Baz was made Grand Mufti, giving him a clear leadership position in the country's religious infrastructure. The religious leadership was given a wider role than before in directing the country's social life: the Committees for the Promotion of Good and the Forbidding of Evil were re-vitalized and encouraged to play more active roles, education was put under tighter religious control, and the view of the religious leaders on restricting the role of women in the work place and in the educational sector given more attention[59].

There was, in addition, a socio-economic dimension. Despite the cutting back of expenditure in many fields during the 1980s, the level of subsidies and support for the more marginalized parts of the population increased. There was a sharp increase in the funding going into social security, as also in the subsidies paid to those in the rural sector. More funding than before was put into the development of the areas where Shiites were predominant[60]. The government has also launched the policy of *Saudiization* to deal with the problem of growing unemployment, but without much success[61].

The gesture of political reform, a long promise since the reign of King Faisal (1964-75), with a clear agenda of accommodation and cooptation of moderate political dissidents was made public in March 1992. It took the form of a Basic Law of Government setting out the responsibilities and process of the governing institutions, a Law of the Consultative Council (*Majlis*) and a Law of the Provinces. Without going into the details of the provisions of these laws, it would be sufficient here to indicate that these laws aim at the formalization, regularization and institutionalization of traditional pattern of Al Saud rule. In July 1997 the number of members of Majlis was increased from 60 to 90 and again in May 2001 when it was further increased to 120. Many moderate Islamists critique as well as the member of Shii community along with increasing number of professionals found the place in the Consultative Council. Further the Crown Prince Abdullah in 2002 announced that the 50 per cent of total seats of Provincial Council would be elected from the local community members. Notwithstanding the delay, in due course the elections were held in February 2005. The election of Municipal Council also took place in October 2005 amid charge of victimization, manipulation and discrimination by the government agencies.

The gesture of political reform was in part to co-opt the moderate Islamic opponents, to wage the gulf between the various factions of Islamicist, to demonstrate its commitment to the agenda of democratic reform, particularly to the Western world and was also in part a reflection of power struggle within the al-Saud regime. However when the primary mechanisms of state security fail to achieve the desired result and grievances become open protest, dissent, sometimes violent, the Al Saud resort to direct, physical methods of coercion and repression. At this stage, the more overt organs of population control such as the police, *mutawwaeen* (religious police), National Guard and the various domestic security intelligence are called to unleashed the state repression. Amnesty International (AI) has noted a steady rise in the number of executions since the 1991 Gulf War: 15 executions were recovered for 1990, 29 for 1991, 66 for 1992, 88 for 1993 and at least 53 for 1994, and the trend appears to be continuing. The highest execution in recent years was recorded in 1995: that year at least 192 people put to death. Incidentally the year also coincided with the election of Provincial Council as well as Municipal Council. In 1999, AI recorded at least 103 executions; by December 2001, at least 75 people had been executed in that year. In the past 20 years 1,163 people are known to have been executed[62].

Apart from public executions, detention and arrest are common, particularly in socio-political cases. For example, 1994 saw unprecedented public displays of support for young, dissenting '*Ulama* and dissatisfaction with the regime—events that precipitated a series of massive security crackdowns and resulted in thousands of arrest including stripping of Saudi nationality of Osama Bin Laden[63]. But a significant milestone in the history of Saudi dissent was passed on 12 August, 1995 with the execution of Abdullah al-Hudhaif, a political prisoner. Hudhaif was accused of attacking a security officer with acid and sentenced to 20 years imprisonment. Saudi state security operations are not necessarily restricted to home soil. Even if Saudi dissidents resident in Western countries may be relatively safe, their families in the kingdom are not, and persecution or the threat of persecution of dissidents' families has been a tactic employed by the regime[64].

Since the September 11 attacks, Saudi Arabia has issued numerous decrees and created new institutions designed to tighten controls over the flow of funds in or through the kingdom, with particular emphasis on increasing the effectiveness of governmental supervision over charitable donations and collections. Since mid-2003, the Saudi government has set up a joint task force with the United States to investigate terrorist financing in Saudi Arabia; shuttered charitable organizations suspected of terrorist ties; passed anti-money laundering legislation; banned cash collections at mosques; centralized control over charitable collections; closed unlicensed money exchanges; and scrutinized clerics involved in charitable collections[65].

In addition to these, the Al-Saud regime further tightens its censorship laws and overall control over the channels of mass communication. The Supreme Information Council was established in 1981. Among many other task, the Council is 'authorized to supervise all the materials presented by radio and TV and the contents of books, magazines, newspaper, films, cassettes, bulletins and announcements and all government and private related information inside and outside the Kingdom[66]. All domestic radio and television stations are owned and directly controlled by the government. While satellite television—one aspect of the globalization of information and entertainment—is on the way to being tamed in Saudi Arabia, the Internet, introduced in the kingdom in early 1999, is proving to be more difficult to handle with. Nevertheless unlike other Internet-restricting countries, which filter access to Internet sites, such as the UAE and Singapore, Saudi Arabia has effectively banned every site until officially approved[67].

Conclusion

What emerge out of the above analysis are a few political trends that appear to underline the emerging discourse that is shaping the relationship of the state and the rainbow of Islamic oppositions in Saudi Arabia. The dominant discourse today in Saudi Arabia is about the issue of equity, representation and about the development of more inclusive society. The larger debates in Saudi Arabia today are about the construction of meaning of a nation. People are taking about the terms and content of their belonging together, and about the right to talk about such sensitive topics. The contemporary debate is about what it means to be "Saudi" that is, the meaning of citizenship. The Islamic oppositions, whether within or outside of the regime, began a national conversation about what it means to belong and about the relationship of state and citizen, and region and state.

Despite the vast resources—both material and ideological—at the disposal of the Al Saud regime, it lacks today, compare to pre-Gulf war period, the moral capital and (Islamic) legitimacy to contain the moral and political appeals of the oppositions. The fact that the principle of representation has been accepted by the regime, paving the way for the development of *Majlis* and other bodies, with an element of 'election' being introduced at the provincial and municipal level (on the individual basis) at the later stage, clearly indicates the success of oppositions, if success is measured in terms of discourse and meaning. However if the success of a movement is measured by regime change, then the rainbow of Islamic oppositions, as narrated above, has failed in Saudi Arabia.

Reference

1. Al-Rasheed, Madawi, *A History of Saudi Arabia*, Cambridge University Press, 2000, p. 195.
2. See, Basic Law of Government (1992). Royal Order of King Fahd No. A/90,

dated 27/81412H (29 February/1 March, 1992). Reproduced in *Highlights of Development in Saudi Arabia*. Riyadh: Dar al-Ufuq/Saudi Ministry of Information (n.d), pp. 91-110.

3. Piscaotri, James P., 'Ideological Politics in Saudi Arabia' in J.P. Piscatori, ed., *Islam in the Political Process*, Cambridge University Press, 1983, p. 61.
4. Fandy, Mamoun, 1999, *Saudi Arabia and the Politics of Dissent*. New York: St. Martin Press, 1999, pp. 22, 36, 22.
5. Amuzegar, Jahangir, *Managing the Oil Wealth OPEC's Windfalls and Pitfalls*, London: I.B. Tauris, 1999, p. 98. Also, *The Kingdom of Saudi Arabia: A Welfare State*, Publication of the Royal Embassy of Saudi Arabia (London, 1997).
6. Wilson, Peter W. and Graham, Douglas F., *Saudi Arabia: The Coming Storm*. New York: M.E. Sharpe, 1994, pp. 81, 178, 185. Also Amuzegar, no. 5, p. 99.
7. Champion, Daryl, *The Paradoxical Kingdom: Saudi Arabia and the Momentum of Reform*, Hurst & Company, London, 2003. p. 82, quoting his/her personal communication with Piscatori, J.
8. Al-Rasheed, no. 1, p. 208.
9. See, for example, Hudson, Michael C., *Arab Politics: The Search for Legitimacy*, New Haven: Yale University Press, 1977, pp. 17, 165-82, Kostiner, Joseph, 'Transforming Dualities: State Formations in Saudi Arabia' in P.S. Khoury and J. Kostiner, ed., *Tribes and State Formation in the Middle East*, Berkely and Los Angeles: University of California Press, 1990.
10. See, Niblock, Tim, 1982. 'Social Structure and the Development of the Saudi Arabian Political System' in Tim Niblock, ed., *State, Society and Economy in Saudi Arabia*. London and Exeter: Croom Helm/Centre for Arab Gulf Studies, 1982, pp. 88-91; also, Wilson and Graham, no. 6, pp. 86n. 13n, al-Rasheed, Madawi, 1996. 'God, the King and the Nation: Political Rhetoric in Saudi Arabia in the 1990s', *The Middle East Journal*, pp. 359-71).
11. See, Chaudhry, Kiren Aziz, *The Price of Wealth: Economics and Institutions in the Middle East*, Ithaca NY: Cornell University Press, 1997, pp. 94, 170.
12. *Ibid.*, pp. 170-71.
13. *Ibid.*, p. 158.
14. Quoting al Yamini, *Al-Rasheed*, no. 1, p. 201.
15. Quoting al-Fagih, Champion, no. 7, p. 125.
16. Mohamedi, Fareed, 'The Saudi Economy: A few years yet till doomsday', *Middle East Report*, November-December, 1993, p. 14.
17. Niblock, Tim, *Saudi Arabia: Power, Legitimacy and Survival*. Routledge: London and New York, 2006 p. 151.
18. *Ibid.*
19. *Ibid.*, p. 74.
20. *Saudi Economic Survey*, 2000.
21. See Allen, Robin, 'Secretive Saudis start to admit realities', *Financial Times*, 1 Dec, 1999, p. 13.

22. Assibya capitalism refers to the process of formation of dominant social elite on the basis of kinship and family networks, a practice widely prevalent in the Arab world. For details on Assibya Capitalism in Saudi Arabia, see, *Champion*, no.7, ch. 3 'The Oil Boom and Modernization: The Rise of Asabiyya Capitalism and Social Stress', pp. 76-140.
23. In the absence of any official figure the various estimates about the percentage of unemployment in Saudi Arabia are purely speculative. The Saudi American Bank Publication (SAMBA) 2001, estimated the 2000 unemployment rate for Saudi males at 14 per cent, rising to 15 per cent in 2001 (sources: htpp://www.samba.com.sa/sindex.htm). Using Saudi Figures from the Fifth Development Plan (1990-05), Wilson and Graham (no. 6, pp. 254-55) reveal unemployment rates of 45.6 per cent for men and 94.7 per cent for women, while Chaudhry (no. 11, pp. 275, 297) puts around 40 per cent.
24. *Champion*, no. 7, pp. 305-06.
25. Wynn, Lisa, 1997. 'The Romance of Tahliyya Street: Youth Culture, Commodities and the Use of Public Space in Jiddah', *Middle East Report*, July-Sept., 1997, pp. 30-31.
26. *Ibid.*
27. Dekmejian, R. Hrair, 1994, 'The Rise of Political Islamism in Saudi Arabia', *The Middle East Journal*, 48(4) (Autumn) pp. 629-30, 627-43.
28. *Fandy*, no. 4, p. 102.
29. *Champion*, no. 7, p. 219, quoting al-Fagih.
30. *Ibid.*, p. 233.
31. Al-Rasheed, Madawi, 'The Shia of Saudi Arabia: A Minority in Search of Cultural Authenticity', *British Journal of Middle Eastern Studies*, 25(1), 1998, pp. 122-23, 121-38.
32. *Ibid.*, pp. 122-25.
33. *Ibid.*, pp. 125-30.
34. Galinsdo-Marines, Alejandra, *The Relationship between the Ulama and the Government in the Contemporary Saudi Arabian Kingdom: An Interdependent Relationship*. Ph.D. Dissertation, University of Durham, 2001:228, cited in Niblock, no. 17, p. 102.
35. *Champion*, no. 7, p. 256.
36. *Niblock*, no. 17, p. 93.
37. *Champion*, no. 7, p. 220.
38. Abir, Mordechai, *Saudi Arabia: Government, Society and the Gulf Crisis*. London: Routledtge, 1993, pp. 189-90, Also, *Dekmejian*, no. 27, pp. 635-36.
39. *Ibid.*, p. 192.
40. See, *Fandy*, no. 4, pp. 50-60, *Champion*, no. 7, pp. 220-24, *Niblock*, no. 17, pp. 93-96.
41. See, *Dekmejian*, no. 27, and *Fandy*, no. 4, pp. 59, 65, 43.
42. *Abir*, no. 38, p. 191.

43. Alshamsi, Mansoor J., The Discourse and Performance of the Saudi Sunni Islamic Reformist Leadership 1981-2003. Ph.D. Dissertation, University of Exeter 2003: 130, cited in Niblock, no. 17, p. 127.
44. *Ibid.*, p. 136.
45. *The Economist*, 1994, p. 71.
46. Milne, Seumas and Black, Ian, 1996. 'Arms Bosses' secret plot', *Guardian Weekly*, 14 January, 1996, p. 10.
47. *Nimblock*, no. 17 p. 100.
48. CACSA, 'Our Mission'. Committee Against Corruption in Saudi Arabia, 1999. htpp:// www.saudhouse.com/stories/article.as?idr= 24
49. See, www.muslimmedia.com/archives/oaw98/oaw98.htm.
50. See, http://en.wikipedia.org/wiki List_of_terrorist_attacks_in_Saudi_Arabia, retrieved on 13.06.2006.
51. See Hirst, David 'Dangers of supping with the Americans', *Guardian Weekly*, 7 July, 1996, p. 12.
52. *Champion*, no. 7, p. 237.
53. Jamal Khashoggi, 'Once Again Ramdhan gives Muslims something to lament', *Daily Star*, (Beirut), 23 November, 2001, p. 6.
54. Quoted in *Champion*, no, p. 237.
55. See Sciolino, Elaine, 'Saudi warns US to Respect Arafat', *International Herald Tribune,* 28 June, 2002, p. 1.
56. Byman, Daniel L. and Jerrold D. Green, Jerrold D., 'The enigma of Political Stability in the Persian Gulf Monarchies", *Middle East Review of International Affairs*, Vol. 3, No. 3, Sept, 1999, pp. 48-53.
57. See, *Al Rasheed*, no. 1 ch. 7, 'Narratives of the state, narratives of the people.
58. Byman & Green, no. 56.
59. For details, see, *Niblock*, no. 17, pp. 83-85.
60. *Ibid.*, p. 84.
61. Although Saudiization has been presented as a major socio-economic goal for more than 15 years—ushered in with the words 'a reduction—in the number of non-Saudi workers—is one of the most important targets of the (fourth) Plan' (Ministry of Planning, (1984). Fourth Development Plan: 1405-1410 A.H./1985-1990 AD. Riyadh: Ministry of Planning press; cited in Champion, p. 256)—progress has been non-existence or, at best, 'piecemeal'. There is as yet no firm evidence that this pattern is changing, despite official speeches and the convening of 'conference and debates held to address the issue' (Bashir, Abdul Wahab, 'Creating Jobs is a Challenge for Planers', Arab News, 23 July, 1999).
62. These IA figures were quoted from *Champion*, p. 279.
63. The arrest of two celebrated detainees—Safar al-Hawali and Salman al-Auda sparked a large protest demonstration in the Shaikh's home town of Buraida, about 350 km north west of Riyadh, on 13 September, 1994. The demonstration was the first of its kind in recent Saudi history.

64. *Cordesman*, 'Saudi Arabia: Guarding the Desert Kingdom', Boulder, Co: Westview Press, 1997, p. 40,
65. For details see, http://www.fas.org/irp/crs/RL32499.pdf dated 13.6.2006.
66. Ministry of Information, *The Saudi Media: Evolution and Progress*, Riyadh: Dept of Information, Saudi Ministry of Information, 1993, p. 123).
67. Preisler, Ulf, 'Saudi Arabia braces for Internet revolution", *Gulf Business*, 3(8) Dec., 1998.

3

Saudi Arabia
From Oil Kingdom to Market

GIRIJESH PANT

After twelve years of negotiations Saudi Arabia joined the membership of WTO in December 2005.[1] With the accession begins a new phase of economic management where state has to retreat and market has to step in, where the social contract between the state and society has to be revised, where the interface between domestic and global has to be made transparent, accountable and rule based. This in more than many ways a leap forward over the rentier mode of governance and organization that the kingdom has been based on. Clearly the transition is not going to be pain less, it is bound to be rough and tough. It is challenging with very wide ramifications beyond the economy. It will be impacting the polity and society. How the process is unfolding in economic domain is an interesting account that this essay intends to profile.

Rent and the Economic Regime

Rent based economies tend to be highly centralized in terms of their organization and ownership. The fiscal strength provides the state with power to write the script of social contract on its own terms. Consequently the economic regime becomes state centered. Since the state does not derive its fiscal strength from taxation, on the contrary distributes the rent to underwrite the fiscal needs of the society and under no obligation it finds to be accountable and transparent in its transactions. Apparently such an autonomous fiscal regime creates a corresponding authoritarian political regime. What is most striking in the context of transition that the rent promotes distributive/allocative economy hence the structures around it are said to have anti production bias. The trajectory of Saudi Arabian economy has been dictated by the huge rent amassed by the system during the oil price boom of the seventies. This is reflected in the contribution of oil in the GDP, its contribution in state revenue, in export account. Oil transformed the Bedouin-tribal economy into rentier mode.

Saudi Arabia is the kingdom of oil, with the proven reserves of 260 billion barrels, about 25 per cent of global share, thus with largest oil reserves it is the leading oil exporting country of the world. Oil contributes 65.8 per cent of the GDP, ratio of oil exports to total exports is estimated 99.9 per cent and of oil exports to GDP 87.8 per cent. Oil revenue ratio to total Government revenue is estimated at 91.2 per cent[2] On behalf of the State, ARAMCO produces more than 90 per cent of oil. Empowerment of the State of Saudi Arabia could be seen in the dramatic rise in public expenditure from $2.6 million in 1972-73 to $43.7 billion in 1978-79. The financial solvency enabled the state to underwrite the structure the economy, polity and society. The state and society found the allocative fiscal arrangement mutually beneficial. The state did not tax its citizens and in the bargain retained full control over the economy with very little accountability. In fact the state subsidized the utilities besides rewarding through a range of mechanisms like free loans, free education, fabulous fellowship to go abroad etc. The state pursued massive civil infrastructure construction leading to construction boom. Overwhelmed by the gravitational pulls of the hydrocarbon, the economy became the victim of Dutch disease. The structural shifts towards the oil sector ironically lead to the underdevelopment of the non-oil sector and made the economy dependent on oil prices determined by the international market. The vulnerability of this dependence was experienced in the mid eighties when oil prices started crashing.

Though the economy did make recovery in the nineties with oil prices firming up but it was no more as buoyant as in the late seventies. The deteriorating fiscal health of the state could be gazed by the fact that during the decade of 1983 to 1992 the cumulative deficit reached to $141 billion in contrast to the cumulative surplus of $107 billion in the preceding decade. This was also reflected in balance of payment account from cumulative surplus of $163 billion to cumulative deficit of $138 billion.[3] Most disturbing was the five years projection made by IMF in mid 1993, stating the budgetary deficit to move from $6 biilion in 1993 to $11 billion in 1997 necessitating the public borrowings to move to 77 per cent of GDP in 1997 compared to 56 per cent in 1993. The public domestic debt went up from zero in 1987 to $74 billion in 1993 and the external

Saudi Oil Export Revenues (1995-2005)

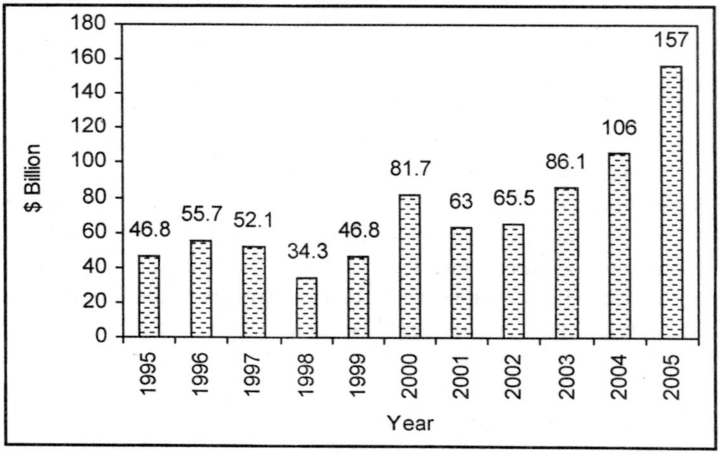

Source: Samba Saudi Economy at Mid Year 2005.

debt to $20 billion.[4] The annual interest on debt was expected to go to 11.8 per cent of government expenditure in 1997 as against of 7.3 per cent in 1992. The per capita income having reached to $1,7000 in the eighties plumped to $8200 in 2003. If adjusted by prices and declining dollar exchange rate, it would be much less.

Saudi Government Debt

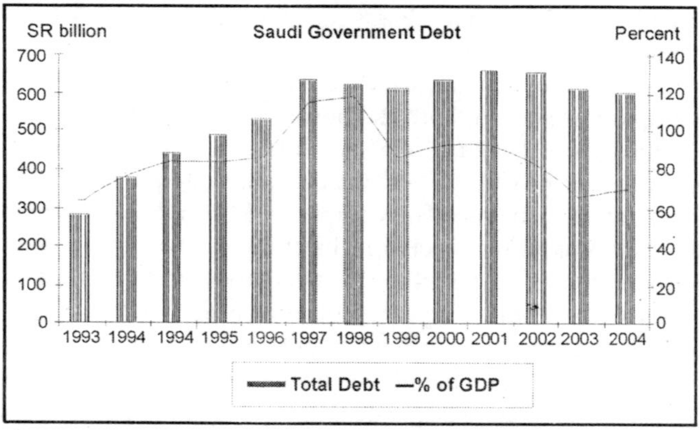

Source: Samba; The Saudi Economy 2004 performance 2005 Forcast..

Significantly, the rentier economy discovered its structural limitation when it failed to create employment opportunities for the growing young population. The growing unemployment and the unemployability of the Saudi nationals brought the central question of the capacity of the rent based economy particularly when these youngsters started becoming the constituency of protest including the recruiting grounds for militant groups. The Central Department of Statistics data first ever published in 2002 shows that while overall unemployment was 8.1 per cent, it was 28 per cent for Saudis in the age group of 20-24, 9.8 per cent for 25-29 and 0.9 per cent for 35 and above.[5] But as observed by Saudi Human Development Report 2003,

> that unemployment in Saudi society is not attributable to deficiency in aggregate effective demand as it is the case with deflationary unemployment. Evidence to the contrary presents itself in the excess demand for labour and the presence of large numbers of foreign labour. The un-employment that exists is of the structural type which results from the fact that job seekers' qualifications and training levels do not match the requirements of the jobs on offer. In other instances, job seekers' occupational and training characteristics may conform to the requirements of the jobs on offer, but the mismatch, or non-conformity, lies in the conditions acceptable to job applicants.[6]

Thus if Saudi Arabian state is failing to provide its population gainfully employed not because of slow motion economy but due to the mismatch then problem is not managerial in nature. It is structural. Saudi economy has to undertake structural changes. The economic reform processes initiated by the government is the recognition of the need of moving away from the rentier mode.

Road to reforms: Like most other countries Saudi Arabia too embarked on the economic reform under fiscal stress. It is premised on neoliberal understanding of liberalization, privatization and globalisation of the economy. The WTO membership is the admission that the future trajectory of the Saudi Arabian economy is going to be determined by the new set of parameters redefining the social contract.

The State which has been the prime mover on the strength oil rent is gradually recasting its place by working as facilitator in the reform process. It is opening up the economy for the external players, expanding the space for private initiatives, retreating from a few important segments and inducing the market to step in. The Supreme Economic Council (1999) has been bestowed with the responsibility to steer the reform programme. In 2001 it was assigned the task to supervise the implementation of privatization process.[7] It has spelled out objectives, policies and strategies. According to it the programme has two major objectives,[8]

"Improving the efficiency of the national economy and enhancing its competitive ability to meet the challenges of regional and international competition. The Economic efficiency of the economy can be strengthened by subjecting projects to market forces. Enhancing competitiveness is closely linked to the general strategy of developing the private sector in Saudi Arabia. Important measures taken so far to create a favourable climate for investments, such as developing the capital and labour markets will help achieve this objective. It is important that all enterprises in a single sector be required to operate under the same conditions of competition.

Encouraging private sector investment and effective participation in the national economy, and increasing its share of domestic production to achieve growth in the national economy. Mature and strong private sectors participation is essential for Saudi Arabia, as the private sector is able to develop comparative advantage and provides a better opportunity for diversifying the economic base away from the dependence on oil."

Among the sectors and services moving into the domain of private sector in stages include the following,[9]:

1. Water and sewerage.
2. Saline water conversion (Desalination).
3. Telecommunications.
4. Aviation and its services.
5. Railroads.
6. Airport services.
7. Postal services.
8. Grain silos and flour mills.
9. Seaport services.
10. Industrial cities services.
11. Municipalities services.
12. Educational services.
13. Social services.
14. Agriculture services.
15. Medical services.

The face of Saudi private sector is changing. It has been a significant contributor to the national wealth but it too has been growing in the shadow of the state. "In the pre-1973-74 period, private sector activity accounted for around 30 percent of the country's output. This fell slightly following the 1973-74 oil price increases, only to increase to 60 percent by 1985. Since then, private sector output has declined gradually, leveling off at around 48 percent of output."[10] However with privatization process unfolding it is gaining back its significance. The first major move in this direction was the 30 per cent share of the state telecommunications. Saudi Telecom went for public offering subsequently leading to government's ambitious plans to open 20 major sectors for private sector participation, which includes "water and drainage, saline water conversion, air transport and aviation services, railways, roads, seaport services, postal services, municipal services such as cleaning and waste disposal and collection of revenues, building schools, printing of educational books and the management of social welfare organisations, health facilities including some hospitals, government-owned hotels and the future railway network."[11]

Along the line the government established the Saudi Arabian General Investment Authority SAGIA in April 2000, primarily to mobilize foreign investment, reportedly the country has been able to attract foreign economic investment as reflected in 30 fold increase in FDI in 2005 over the previous year. On the strength of its energy endowment giving it the advantage of cost effective feed stock and geographical location, it intends to become "one of the top ten foreign investment locations in the world by 2010."[12] IFC study "Doing Business in 2006" rated the Kingdom as the best investment location in the Arab World and 38th out of 155 locations worldwide. It is observed that by September 2004, SAGIA issued licenses for projects worth $15.9 billion of these $10.5 billion were 100 per cent foreign-owned.[13] According to the Council of Saudi Chambers of Commerce and Industry, after joining WTO the Kingdom is targeting $623 billion investment in the fields of "$90.7 billion in electricity, $88 billion in water, $60 billion in telecoms, $140.7 billion in infrastructure, and $92 billion in petrochemicals, $50 billion in natural gas, $28.3 billion in agriculture, $10.7 billion in information technologies, $53.3 billion in tourism and $10.7 billion in education."[14]

From the perspective of future of oil economy, it would be relevant to factor the shift in Saudi decision to enhance its oil production capacity. In 2004 the kingdom took the decision to expand oil production capacity which was not changed since 1981 though configuration did change, in a phased manner. "In the first phase, last year Saudi Arabia expanded capacity from 10.5 to 11 million barrels per day with the expansion of production from two fields, Abu Safah and Qatif, at a cost of $4 billion. Aramco will expand capacity by another net addition of 1.5 million barrels per day, at a cost of about $10 billion, between now and 2009, to bring total production capacity to 12.5 million b/d."[15] Apparently the Kingdom is redefining the parameter of development by expanding its strength from hydrocarbon towards a more diversified and globalised system. The Vision 2020 spells it out by identifying five thrust area, Economic diversification; Development of human resources; Expansion of public services needed to support these objectives; Promoting the expansion of the private sector as a key partner in the implementation of Vision 2020 and Streamlining and modernizing the governance structures of the public sector to meet the challenges of implementation.[16] Accordingly the 8th Five-Year Development Plan (2005-10) has placed importance on increasing oil and gas production, creating new sources of income, developing service institutions, encouraging new joint stock companies and the merger of existing firms and promoting manpower development programmes.[17]

WTO Regime: the Bumpy Road!

According to the Saudi Commerce and Industry Minister, Hashim Yamani: 'The accession will further integrate the Kingdom's economy into the world economy. It will also deepen the universality of the multilateral trading system. It will enhance the business environment in Saudi Arabia by adding more transparency and predictability. Thus we expect to lead to more investment and job creation.'[18] Opening of the closed economy under WTO meant reduction in tariff, access to services sectors, greater foreign participation, and to implement to adhere to regime regarding intellectual property rights, transparency in trade issues, legal recourse for trade partners, and elimination of technical barriers to trade etc. According to the WTO sources among the leading commitments and the obligation that the state has to fulfill include the followings:[19]

- Elimination of exports subsidies on agricultural products.
- At the end of the ten year implementation period, average bound tariff levels will decrease to 12.4 and 10.5 per cent for agricultural and non-agricultural products respectively. The individual tariff rates for agricultural products will range from 5 to 200 per cent, with the highest rates being applied to tobacco products and dates. Some 11 per cent of non-agricultural products will be imported duty-free whereas the highest tariff rate will affect wood, as well as iron and steel products. Most tariffs (92.6 per cent) will be set at their final bound rates at the date of accession. The remainder will mostly be implemented in 2008 and 2010, but in no case later than 2015.

- Foreign insurance companies will be permitted to open and operate direct branches in Saudi Arabia. A three year transition period will be given to existing foreign insurance providers to convert to either a Saudi cooperative insurance company or to a direct branch of a foreign insurance company. During this transition period, existing foreign insurance providers will be able to continue existing business operations, as well as offer new products and service new client.
- Within three years from accession, Saudi Arabia's commitments will allow up to 70 per cent foreign equity ownership in the telecommunications sector. These commitments apply to both basic telecommunication services and value-added telecom services.
- Some restrictions on the distribution of goods inside the country are allowed but will be phased out over a three-year transition period.
- Implementation of the Agreement on Trade-Related Aspects of Intellectual Property Rights, the Agreement on Technical Barriers to Trade and the Agreement on the Application of Sanitary and Physosanitary Measures.

The road to WTO regime is not going to be smooth. The central question remains whether the Saudi political social cultural milieu is ready to accept the norms and practices of globalising market. This produces a number of paradoxical situations. The country has enough financial resources but bulk of it is still parked in foreign countries. This could be due to two reasons namely, the limited absorptive capacity or poor investment climate including lack of confidence. It is observed that "that the investment climate and the accompanying infrastructure (in Saudi Arabia) do not inspire confidence among local investors. Most companies are run either by individuals or families. Their combined capacity will only absorb 50 per cent of the available liquidity and the remaining 50 per cent is taken to markets in the neighbouring countries where they have been exposed to all sorts of exploitations and indignities. Is it not strange that a country such as ours with large tracts of land, a large population, rich mineral resources and a rapid growth rate does not have sufficient capitalisation channels while the tiny emirates surrounding us offer a congenial investment climate? The long and short of it is that the regulations governing our capital market do not reflect the huge investment potential. This situation has created a glaring imbalance between available liquidity and the investment facilities. It is, however, within the power of the government to rectify the imbalance and provide a favourable investment climate with priority to private companies and a significant reduction in bureaucratic and administrative bottlenecks."[20]

Similarly in moving towards the ICT based service economy, the country faces serious deficit of trained manpower hence, despite its policy of Saudisation, it has to increasingly depend on the expatriates. What is more critical that under WTO regime the Kingdom looses the freedom of maneuverability: be it wages, service conditions and the property rights. It is observed that there has been concern in the kingdom about the loss of sovereignty which certainly, "do form part of both the political culture and decision making context of trade and investment liberalization in the Kingdom"[21]

Challenges of Corporate Business Culture

Most of the private business in Saudi Arabia has so far been family owned and managed where the decision making is controlled by the founder and owner with quick profit as the only consideration confined to limited time horizon. The long term planning is not the part of business culture. WTO regime expects this business to run on corporate basis taking into account the global linkages as the local market is going to be integrated to the world market. Similarly it has to be dynamic enough to meet the challenges and competition going to be coming from next generation. The transition amounts to transformation with social consequences because family still remains the important social institution empowered by business traditions. The apprehensions of erosion of local culture is expressed in public debate on WTO. The 7th Jeddah Economic Forum reportedly discussed issue under the title "Saudi Arabia Beyond the WTO".[22] According to Saudi economist Dr. Fahd Al-Etani "Multinational companies and international companies will affect small and medium businesses that still work in a traditional way,".[23] It has been recognized that Saudi business have to learn hard lessons.

> "First it must figure out how to survive without captive markets. At the very same time, it has to find out how to face competition from international companies which themselves long ago learned how to survive in highly competitive markets. During the transitional period of WTO membership, some Saudi companies will have no difficulty in transforming themselves into world-class businesses, if they are not so already. Others will take foreign partners. Still others will merge to strengthen their capital and operational bases. There will however be many who will simply

> not manage the transformation. Part of their problem may be that they will not persuade middle management and other employees to review the way they work, tighten their discipline and look always to the best way to increase efficiency and profitability. With an increasing flow of graduates coming into the job market, existing workers will also begin to realize that if they fail to deliver, there will be others eager to take their places."[24]

It is argued that to graduate to new ethos Saudi business will have to "to develop their abilities and production quality, to merge with other similar companies, to go in partnership with foreign companies, to balance the business financial needs and the family financial needs, to arrange for a smooth power transition within the family, to allow for more than one owner and to involve women in the business to guarantee a continuation of ownership."[25]

A closer peep into the political economy of Saudi Arabia tends to suggest that the Oil monarchy is engaged in propping up a kind of corporatism which could possibly facilitate the transition to the market mode. It is argued that top down institution making is inevitable in the context of Saudi Arabia where the social political and business interests have been tied-up to patronage distribution under the rentier mode. The State has, of late, been encouraging these interest groups through National Dialogue to be engaged in the transition processes beyond but away from the state networking. This is noticed more clearly with reference to the business community because the state needs it to take over some of its burden like generating jobs building new infrastructure. Indeed the Saudi business class is graduating from mere accumulator of rent, also described as 'lumpan bourgeoisie', it has "possibly reached the higher stage of economic maturity in all of the Middle East. Although it is a class largely created by the state, through years of massive rent accumulation it has developed its own dynamics and capacities. It is internationally integrated, and a sizeable share of business leaders is highly educated. Although Saudi business players are still tied up in cronyist structures, their policy demands have become more complex, as their managerial and production structures are much more advanced than 20 or 30 years ago."[26]

Clearly moving to market regime, the rentier mode of social contract where the State used financial resources to distributive purpose have to be given in favours of optimal investment in the production-based activities. Looking from the perspective of power matrix, it would mean State sharing the power for resource allocation to the market thereby loosing its control over the system. Can Saudi Arabia at this stage of its evolution sustain a major retreat of the State or even softening of the state is central question? More so when it is faced with external and internal security challenges. While the question is settled that Saudi Arabia cannot survive on rentier mode but it seems still to be resolved conclusively that neoliberal trajectory would be the best way out. It is argued that the Oil monarchies are passing through a phase where the relation between the state and the market is being redefined. State might be abducting some of its responsibilities but it continues to steer the reform process.[27] The devolution of economic power would indeed have its political ramifications but it needs to be underlined that state despite fragile institutional makeup is fairly embedded in the society hence the political culture would continue to be influenced if not determined by the local context. Further the oil economies are moving to market mode in the phase of globalization. Whether the national market would wield the economic clout to restrain the state or the state would gain as managerial state to maneuver between national and global players is going to be significant factor in the political economy of the oil kingdom.

The Economy Bounces Back

Since 2003 with the oil prices firming up the economy has once again been bouncing back. Though apprehensions are expressed that with the fiscal buoyancy reforms may be deferred but as the trends indicate the possibilities are more in favour of their continuation. On the contrary it can be argued that with the fiscal facility the State could define the terms of reforms more effectively. According to SAMBA:

> The Saudi economy performed exceptionally in 2004, with historic oil performance augmented by the strongest growth in 22 years in the non-oil private sector. With the breadth and balance of the performance, we believe 2004 was the best year in history for the economy. The 1974-82 oil boom years were relatively one-dimensional by comparison. Growth then was almost all government spending of oil revenues to build infrastructure. The next period of high growth, 1990-91, was war-driven. In 2004, oil revenues were exceptional, resulting in large twin surpluses for the budget and the current account, GDP growth was high, inflation was tame, the stock market boomed, real estate continued strong, and the private sector across the board had a good year.[28]

The synoptic view of the economy is given in the table below:.

($ billion unless noted otherwise)

	1994	1995	1996	1997	1998	1999	2000	2001	2002	2003	2004	2005
Nominal GDP (billion SR)	503.06	533.50	590.75	617.90	546.64	603.59	706.66	686.30	707.00	797.00	939.59	1185.00
$Billion Equivalent	134.15	142.27	157.53	164.77	145.77	160.96	188.44	183.44	188.53	212.53	250.53	250.56
% Change	14	6.1	10.7	4.6	41.5	10.4	17.1	–2.9	3.0	12.7	17.9	26.1
Real GDP (% change)	0.10	0.00	1.40	2.60	2.90	–0.80	4.90	120	0.74	6.40	5.30	6.50
Oil	0.20	0.27	2.10	–1.40	3.20	–7.50	6.90	–1.20	–5.00	14.30	5.90	7.10
Non-Oil Private Sector	0.70	0.30	1.10	4.60	2.60	4.20	4.30	3.50	4.20	3.40	5.70	7.40
Government	0.00	–0.30	1.30	6.10	1.90	0.90	3.20	170	1.00	1.50	4.00	3.80
Male Unemployment (% or Saudi labor force)	n/a	n/a	n/a	n/a	n/a	6.66	6.54	6.82	7.57	8.20	8.50	8.80
Population (million persons)	17.79	18.23	18.67	19.13	19.60	20.08	20.57	21.08	21.60	22.13	22.67	23.23
Saudi	12.98	13.25	13.58	13.92	14.26	14.62	14.98	15.35	15.74	16.13	16.53	16.94
Non-Saudi	4.86	4.98	5.09	5.21	5.34	5.46	5.59	5.73	5.86	6.00	6.14	6.29
GDP/Capita (US $)	7,541	7,804	8,438	8,613	7,437	8,016	9,161	8,682	8,728	9,604	11,052	13,603
Oil Price (S/barrel)												
West Taxes intermediate	17.25	18.43	22.14	20.67	14.00	19.62	30.61	25.76	26.57	29.00	41.33	51.00
Saudi Average	14.50	16.05	19.08	17.75	11.30	16.88	26.81	21.84	23.72	27.00	35.17	45.00
Current Account Balance	40.40	–5.33	0.68	0.31	–13.15	0.41	14.32	9.36	11.87	29.66	51.50	96.00
As percent of GDP	–7.82	–3.74	0.43	0.19	–9.02	0.26	7.60	5.11	6.30	13.96	20.55	30.38
Government Budget Balance (billion SR)	–34.79	–27.44	–19.03	–15.77	–48.45	–36.39	22.74	–26.98	–20.50	36.00	98.00	191.00
Revenues	128.99	146.50	179.09	205.50	141.61	147.45	258.07	228.16	213.00	293.00	393.00	527.00
Expenditures	163.78	173.94	198.12	221.27	190.06	183.84	235.32	255.14	233.50	257.00	295.00	336.00
Budget balance as percent of GDP	–6.9	–5.1	–3.2	–2.6	–8.9	–6.0	3.2	–3.9	–2.9	4.5	10.5	16.1

Source: Samba: The Saudi Economy at Mid Year 2005.

It is argued that the present upward swing despite triggered by the oil price boom is qualitatively distinct as "It is private sector-led and government supported, versus government spending-led in the past. The private sector, especially financial markets, have depth and absorptive capacity that were lacking in earlier periods of strength. As a result, channels of wealth distribution exist now that did not before, such as through local firms winning major pieces of new business, and IPO's in the stock market spreading wealth to individual Saudis."[29]

Comparing Oil Booms: Then and Now

The second oil boom which the kingdom is currently beginning to experience differs in many respects from the oil boom of the early and late 1970s:

Then	*Now*
Oil Prices: Crisis driven and short-lived lights	Demand driven and sustained high prices
Domestic Economy: Government led-growth through high expansion of government budget	Private sector-led growth government spending grows incrementally
Private Sector: Limited absorptive capacity, contracts to foreign firms	Depth and diversity: Contracts go mostly to local companies
Wealth Distribution: Limited channels for distributing oil wealth. No stock market	Stock market is major channel for wealth distribution
Institutional Depth: Constrained institutional infrastructure to handle oil windfall	Enlarged government institutional base, especially regulatory to manage growth
Capital Markets: Limited access to funding other than bank borrowing	Deeper and developing sources of capital in stock and bond markets
Infrastructure: Very limited, oil windfall devoted to government bulking of basic infrastructure	Qualitative update of infrastructure with public and private participation

Source: Samba: Saudi Economy at Mid Year 2005.

However the expanding profile if the state underlines that public expenditure still setting the pace as the following Fig. 3.1.

Following the initiatives of the State, the economic landscape is changing radically. Some of the significant developments include:

King Abdullah Mega Economic City with proposed investment of $26.6 billion, it is located at Rabigh, north of Jeddah. It is designed to put the country on global investment hub. It will have six distinct components namely—seaport, industrial district, educational zone,

Saudi Arabic Budgeted Spending 2000-2006

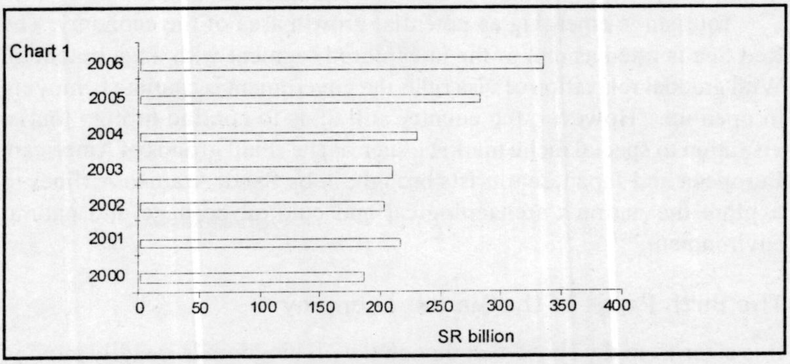

Source: Sambu: Saudi Arabias 2006 Budget, 2005 Performance.

financial island, resorts and the residential area. The port will have a dedicated Haj terminal. It will have the facility to enable world's largest super vessels to drop anchor. Its strategic location on the Red Sea with integrated transport system, seamless high speed transition from sea to rail, road and air, will make the city main gateway to the Central and Eastern Provinces and to the entire Kingdom.

New Export Refinery at Yanbu on the Red Sea to produce 4,00,000 bpd of clean fuels involving a $5 billion-$8 billion investment is going to reassert Saudi role in the global energy market. The country is keen to strengthen the global refining net work to boost global capacity. Yanbu is strategically located and the new refinery could supply the US East Coast with high-quality gasoline, low-sulfur diesel to Europe and naphtha to East Asia.

Saudi Arabian Natural Gas Initiative, with estimated investment of $40 billion is said to be the largest opening to foreigners in Saudi Arabia since the early 1970s. The three core projects to be developed by consortia made up of various partnerships. Two projects are in the area of the great Rub' al Khali desert, or "Empty Quarter," and the third is along the Red Sea coast in the northwest part of the country. The project has been facing opposition both from within and outside. It is reported, "Internally a powerful lobby led by oil minister Ali Al Naimi is maneuvering to maintain the status quo. Mr. Al Naimi apparently wishes that the oil companies had never been offered the SGI, and has declared all gas reserves to be part of Saudi ARAMCO's birthright, therefore denying the oil companies access to gas without buying it from Saudi ARAMCO."[30] The compamies were not happy due to rate of returns. However it was revised subsequently in July 2003. Negotiations between the eight International

Tourism is emerging as potential growth area of the economy. The Red Sea is rated as one of the unexplored segment with huge potential. With gradual relaxation of visa rules the government is cautiously moving to open up. "However, the country still aims to confine foreign tourist visitation to special niche markets, such as the small groups of American, European and Japanese tourists brought in by Saudi Arabian Airlines to explore the nation's archaeological and cultural heritage and natural environment."[31]

The Birth Pangs of the Market Economy

It is clear from the above that though the oil kingdom is steadily moving to market, yet it is encountering formidable challenges which apart from institutional are attitudinal in nature, as well. The recent experience of stock market crash exposed the new obsession of the Saudi society with the stock market. It is estimated that around six million, about one third of the natives, are engaged in stock wealth directly or indirectly. "People are in a frenzy to become involved in the ebb and flow of capital. They are even buying in other people's names (by offering commission for the use of their family ID cards so they can buy higher quantities of stock, which in Saudi Arabia are capped for investors based on their family size and the level of demand for the particular stock) to increase their profits."[32] What is significant that the impact has been felt across the society from big players to small savers like the taxi drivers. The deepening of Saudi society with stocks could be appreciated by the observation that, "The sight of school teachers using laptops or mobile phones to monitor the stock market or give instructions to sell and buy shares during class breaks, which would have once been unthinkable in Saudi Arabia, became part of the landscape."[33]

The market lead boom has escalated the land prices leading to "disappearing from within the limits of these once-pastoral cities as farmers discover that selling the land for development is more lucrative than selling dates."[34] In fact with the altering of terms of trade it became more profitable to sell the land particularly when the watering them is becoming costly. This has very obvious bearing on Saudi policy of food security. Similarly the economy is experiencing pressure on urban infrastructure. No doubt the Saudi state is expanding infrastructure support to meet the growing demand yet the issues of subsidized services has to be addressed under new policy orientation. The issue acquires serious proportion when the numbers are rising dramatically. The size of young population with the aspirations of new generation of globalizing information regime does not allow the state the degree of freedom it enjoyed even if it has the sufficient rent derived resources. Further with the sharpening of the contradictions of regional-global interface, Saudi Arabia, being the vital player in defining the terms of the interface, has to reinvent a regime though embedded in the society yet negotiating with the global changes. The state has initiated a political and social agenda to correspond with the economic transformation but the threshold where the state would be expected to make leap forward to able to the needs of the market economy still remains a matter of conjecture. It critically depends upon how Saudi state is going to pursue the delicate task of revising the social contract of the rentier economy without jeopardising the legitimacy.

References

1. This was rectified on 11 December, 2005 when Saudi Arabia became the 149th member of the WTO after over 12 years of negotiations. In the process of preparing for membership, Saudi Arabia enacted 42 new trade-related laws, created nine new regulatory bodies, and signed 38 bilateral trade agreements. When the Kingdom first applied for membership in the WTO's predecessor, the General Agreement on Tariffs and Trade (GATT) in 1993, 75 percent of the Kingdom's tariffs on imported goods were at 12 percent. By 2003, 85 percent of tariffs were 5 percent or less, and the commitments made for WTO membership will now bring tariffs down further." SUSRIS-Samba Report Saudi Arabia and the WTO.htm
2. ESCWA, Economic Diversification in the Oil Producing Countries. The case of the Gulf Cooperation Council Economies, GENERALE/ESCWA/ED/2001/110 January 2001.
3. Eliyahu Kanovsky The Woeful State of Saudi Finances. www.jcpa.org/jl/vp308.htm-42k.
4. *ibid.*
5. Saudi Arabia's Employment Profile Saudi American Bank October 2002
6. UNDP, Saudi Arabia Human Development Report 2003
7. http://www.sagia.gov.sa/innerpage.asp?ContentID=185&Lang=en
8. http://www.sec.gov.sa/english/list.asp?s_contentid =22&s_title=&ContentType=&CatTypeld=&Category=3&Step=1
9. http://www.sec.gov.sa/english/list.asp?s_contentid =21&s_title=&ContentType=&CatTypeld=&Category=3&Step=1.
10. Robert Looney Can Saudi Arabia Reform its Economy in Time to Head Off Disaster?*Strategic Insights*, Volume III, Issue 1 (January 2004).

11. Saudi privatisation get into top gear Saudi privatisation get into top gear Saudi Arabia Focus.htm
12. http://www.arabnews.com/?page=6&section=0&article=71477&d=10&m=10&y=2005.
13. http://www.state.gov/e/eb/ifd/2005/43038.htm
14. http://www.gulfindustryonline.com/bkArticlesF.asp?Article=4126&Section=675&IssueID=234.
15. The Saudi Economy at Mid-Year 2005. SAMBA August 2005.
16. Strategic Positioning and Industrial Development VisionFor the Kingdom of Saudi Arabiahttp://www.commerce.gov.sa/industrial/1.%20Report%20on%20Vision%202020.doc
17. http://www.saudinf.com/main/y9035.htm.
18. Saudi WTO success heralds economic expansion Saudi Arabia Focus.htm.
19. WTO 2005 Press Releases-WTO General Council successfully adopts Saudi Arabia's terms of Accession-Press 420.htm.
20. Khaleej Times Online >> News >> BUSINESS Saudi's poor investment climate leads to capital outflow to other Gulf stateshttp://www.khaleejtimes.com/Displayarticle.asp?section= business&xfile= data/business/ 2005/October/business_october536.xml.
21. M. Chemingui and Safadi, Saudi Arabia Long Road to WTO Membership: The Potential Payoffs. Economic Research Forum Cairo.
22. Saudi Economy and Culture Can Withstand WTO Challengeshttp://www.arabnews.com/?page=6&section=0&article= 77736&d=13&m=2&y=2006.
23. http://www.menafn.com/qn_news_story_s.asp?StoryId=89258.
24. Editorial: WTO Membership*Arab News*http://www.ArabNews.com 30 October, 2005.
25. Future of Family Businesses Under WTO Maha Akeel & Razan Baker, Arab News.
26. Steffen Hertog, Making Economic Policy in Saudi Arabia: An Emerging Corporatism http://www.ceri-sciences-po.org. 2
27. Luciani and Neugart ed. The EU and the GCCA new Partnership. http://www.bertelsmann-stiftung. de/bst/de/media/The_EU_and_the_GCC. pdf.
28. The Saudi Economy 2004 Performance, 2005 Forecast SAMBA February 2005.
29. The Saudi Economyat Mid-Year 2005. SAMBA Report August 2005.
30. Can the Saudi Gas Initiative survive? http://www.ameinfo.com/16473.html.
31. P.K. Abdul Ghafour 'Kingdom Going Global With Tourism Plan.' http://www.arabialink.com/Archive/GWPersp/GWP2001/GWP_2001_08_27.htm#4.
32. "Many parents are now busy monitoring the stock market at the expense of quality time with their children. The sight of stocks going up or down is to them a lot better than watching their children go up and down on playground seesaws. We see people on TV talking about this stock and that IPO. Even Sheikhs are getting involved in the market dynamics.

33. "Dr. Laith al-Anani of the King Fahd Medical City in Riyadh said "there had been an increase in the number of cases of heart failure and drop in blood pressure since Tadawul All-Shares Index (TASI) started its nosedive last month."
34. In Holy Cities, Farmers See Profits in Killing Crops http://www.arabnews.com/?page=1&section=0&article=85175&d= 11&m=7&y=2006.

4

Population and Society in Saudi Arabia

PRAKASH C. JAIN

Saudi Arabia, a member of the Gulf Cooperation Council, is the largest country in terms of population as well as area in the Arabian Peninsula. The area of Saudi Arabia is 2,150 sq. km. However, there are no precise estimates of Saudi Arabia's past or current population for the simple reason that there has never been any comprehensive census in the Kingdom; instead estimates are made on the basis of advance sampling techniques. Thus the Saudi Ministry of Planning reckoned the Kingdom's population at 21.4 million in 1999; the Saudi Central Department of Statistics enumerated the same at 22.01 million in 2000. The World Bank's comparable figure of 20.7 million and that of US State Department's of 21.7 million are underestimates compared to that of the US Census Bureau Statistics that indicated that Saudi Arabia had a population of 22.02 million in 2000. Notwithstanding different estimates even if we take the lowest estimate of 20.7 million, Saudi Arabia's population would increase to 32.1 million in 2015 and 46.0 million in 2030 as per World Bank estimates. These trends are compared to those in other Gulf States in Table 4.1.

Demographic Profile

Population Growth Rate

Saudi Arabia had a population of about 3.8 million in 1950, about 4.7 million in 1960 and about 5.4 million in 1970 which almost doubled in 1980 and tripled in 1990. Saudi Arabia's population in the past grew at the rate of 4.9 per cent per annum during the 1970s, 4.0 per cent during the 1980s and 3.3 per cent during the 1990s. Currently it is still growing at the rate of about 3 per cent per annum which is high even by Third World standards. These figures tend to show that Saudi Arabia's

Table 4.1: Population of Saudi Arabia and other GCC countries, 1970-2015

	1970	1980	1990	2000	2015
Bahrain	0.22	0.4	0.5	0.6	NA
Qatar	0.09	0.3	0.4	0.7	NA
Kuwait	0.8	1.4	2.1	2	2.7
Oman	0.7	1.1	1.5	2.3	3.3
UAE	0.3	1.0	1.6	2.7	3.8
Yemen	7.2	8.5	8.4	16.6	27.0
Saudi Arabia	**5.4**	**9.4**	**13.2**	**20.7**	**32.1**
Iraq	9.4	13	15.7	22.3	31.2
Iran	30.1	39.1	47.6	61.9	80.4

Source: Cordesman (2003: 233).

population growth rate is not declining steadily with time. "Demographic shifts towards a lower birth rate are common in developing states, particularly as urbanization increases, women enter the labour force, and economic pressures lead to smaller families. So far, however, the impact of such shifts on Saudi Arabia has been limited"[1]. Thus taken together with sharply declined mortality rates from 18 per 1,000 population in 1970 to 5 in 1991 and to 4 in 2003, it is clear that extremely rapid population growth has taken place in Saudi Arabia during the past four decades or so. The other major indicators of demographic and social changes in Saudi Arabia are briefly discussed below.

Table 4.2: Saudi Arabia: Socio-Economic Indicators, 2003

Population	*Area*	*Population Density*	*GNI per capita*	*PPP Gross National Income*
23 m.	2,150 sq. km	10 persons/sq.km	$9,240	$13,230

Source: *World Development Indicators*, 2005.
PPP = Purchasing Power Parity.

Youthful Profile

Among the GCC countries Saudi Arabia is conspicuous in having higher proportion of young population, particularly in 0-9 and 10-19 age groups (Table 4.4). These two cohorts consisting of over 56 per cent of the total population of Saudi Arabia clearly reveal the youthful profile of Saudi society. The unique youthful profile of the Saudi population is further heightened if we add the next higher age-cohort of 20-29 years. Taken

Table 4.3: Varying Estimates of Saudi Population, 1950-2050 (million)

Year	*World Bank*	*US Census Bureau*
1950	NA	3.8
1960	NA	4.7
1970	5.4	6.1
1980	9.4	9.9
1990	15.9	15.8
2000	20.7	22.0
2010	28.3	30.5
2020	36.4	41.9
2030	46.0	55.8
2040	NA	72.3
2050	NA	91.1

Source: Cordesman (2003: 233).

together more than 73 per cent of the Saudi population is below 29 years of age—a fact that has serious repercussions not only on the population dynamics of the country but also on socio-economic and political aspects of Saudi society as well.

Table 4.4: Distribution of the Saudi Population according to Age-Groups, 2001-03

A		*B*	
Age Groups	*Percentage*	*Age Groups*	*Percentage*
0-9	32.3	0-14	40.2
10-19	24.1	15-64	56.9
20-29	16.9	65+	2.9
30-39	11.0		
40-49	7.2		
50-59	4.2		
60 +	4.4		
Total	100.00		100.0

Source: *World Development Indicators* 2005.

Urbanisation

On the urbanisation front changes in Saudi Arabia have been startling. Thus in 1902 less than 10 per cent of the country's population was living in urban areas. "As late as 1948 Riyadh was estimated to hold 25,000 souls. Mecca's population was put at 40,000 while Medina's was 20,000".[2] Even in the early 1960s Saudi Arabia had only 30 per cent of its population living in towns and cities.

In subsequent decades this scenario quickly changed mainly due to oil price boom in 1973-74. "Increased petrodollars accelerated the development process and the rush to the cities. Also having an effect was the late king Faisal bin Abdulaziz's emphasis on electrification, which made air-conditioning possible. The advent of the latter changed the rhythm of Saudi life, which heretofore had been based on mid-day inactivity due to the unbearable heat. Petrodollars paid for the construction of thousands of apartments and villas, as well as making loans available for the kingdom's burgeoning middle and upper classes. Oil money allowed the government to offer massive subsidies and to create thousands of jobs in its own bureaucracy"[3].

These measures led to accelerated rural-urban migration within Saudi Arabia. Foreign workers too were largely employed in Saudi towns and cities swelling the urban population. Thus by 1980 Saudi Arabia's urbanisation had touched 66 per cent in 1980 and 75 per cent in 1990. The World Bank estimates only slightly vary from these estimates: 39 per cent of the Saudi population lived in cities and towns in 1965, 49 per cent in 1970, 67 per cent in 1980 and 77 per cent in 1990.

Defined in terms of a certain number of persons (2000 plus) living in urban areas, Saudi Arabia, with 86 per cent of its people in cities and towns in 2002, is today highly urbanised by any standards. Thus from a Bedouin, nomadic, rural and isolated society, divided into regional and tribal groups, today Saudi Arabia is mainly an urban society, although tribal links still remain powerful. Again, whereas only 12 per cent of the Saudi population lived in cities with a population of one million or more, this figure had reached 25 per cent by the year 2000. During the past forty years the average annual growth rate of Saudi urban population was recorded as follows: 1965-80: 8.5 per cent, 1980-90: 6.3 per cent, 1990-2000: 5.5 per cent.

Progress in Education

Education is the key to human resource development and eventually to economic development. It is also an important indicator as well as means of social change. Judged from this angle, Saudi Arabia has seen unprecedented development in education. There has been a dramatic increase in access to education during past half a century in Saudi Arabia. Thus school enrollment has increased more than 160 times since 1952 from 25,000 to over four million in 2002. Gross enrollment ratio as percent of relevant age group in 2002-03 at various stages of education was as follows: Primary 67, Secondary 67 and Tertiary 25. These figures, particularly at the primary level, are far below the world average of 103,71 and 26 respectively[4]. But on the other hand, there has been considerable progress in adult literacy among 15 years and older population in Saudi Arabia from 33 per cent in 1970 to 62 per cent in 1990 and 77 per cent in 2002. Female literacy however continues to lag behind at 69 per cent in 2002 vis-a-vis the male literacy at 84 per cent.

In spite of unprecedented expansion in student enrollments, Saudi education system has been suffering from a number of problems. These include high dropout rates at primary and secondary levels, rote learning, poor quality of education, emphasis on Islamic Studies, problems regarding medium of instruction in higher education, and lack of interest in science subjects. The relatively high dropout rate in the GCC countries is also reflected in the secondary school level entollment rates: 48 per cent in Saudi Arabia, 54 per cent in Oman, 64 per cent in UAE and 90 per cent in Kuwait. The female enrollment at this stage, too, is lower compared to the male enrollment. Moreover, the standard of education in these countries is generally not high. Owing to stigma attached to manual work in Saudi society, vocational schools have also not been able to attract sufficient number of students[5].

The emphasis on the Islamic Studies in terms of time-consumption and their contents has also been problematic. Thus, for example, "in Saudi Arabia it consumes 32 per cent of class time for grades 1-3, 30 per cent in grades 4-6, 24 per cent in grades 7-9, and then 15 per cent or more for grades 10-12. "These Statistics do not give the whole picture, however, because other parts of the curriculum, such as history, Social Studies and Arabic, have a fair amount of Islamic content"[6]. At the higher educational level in 1990 the Religious Studies major accounted for more than 15 per cent of all Saudi graduates[7].

The negative implications of low enrolment in higher education are further exacerbated by the fact that the majority of students opt for the less demanding humanities and social sciences subjects where the teaching and textbooks are in Arabic; only a minority choose sciences, engineering and medicine disciplines where the medium of instruction is English and the admission requirements are tough. Available data for the early 1980s clearly highlight this trend in the GCC countries (Table 4.5).

The under supply of students in science and engineering subjects needs to be addressed at post-secondary level of education where on an average less than 30 per cent of students were pursuing these subjects in the Arab World in 1996. Moreover, Saudi educational system further suffers from the more serious problem, that is lack of quality research and knowledge production with the result that "Arab business leaders are concerned that Arab education institutions are not providing graduates with the skills needed to work effectively in private sector"[8]. In the words of another Arab observer[9]: "despite such vast quantitative growth of education in the Arab world, the balance sheet reveals impediments and substandard outcomes. Arab educational systems have not prepared their students to meet the requirements and demands of contemporary societies. The analytical skills, sciences, mathematics, reasoning, and ability to apply knowledge are inadequately articulated in the curriculum and poorly taught in the classroom." Not surprisingly, Saudi private sector tends to prefer expatriate skilled manpower to nationals who are also not expensive to hire at the same time.

Table 4.5: Higher Education in GCC Countries, 1980-82

Country	*20-24 Age Group*	*Humanities*	*Social Sciences*	*Applied and Pure Sciences*
Bahrain (1980)	5.3	–	58.4	41.6
Kuwait (1982)	15.4	11.2	58.9	29.9
Qatar (1982)	16.5	21.8	64.4	13.8
Saudi Arabia (1980)	7.8	44.3	32.9	22.7
UAE	6.8	25.5	49.4	25.2

Source: *Statistical Yearbooks for 1984 and 1985*, UNESCO, Paris.

Public Health

Saudi Arabia has made an all round progress in the field of public health since the early 1970s. During the past three decades extensive and state of the art public health infrastructure has been set up in place. Much of this was already achieved by the early 1990s. Various indictors relating to public health clearly reflect this point. Thus by 1990 90 per cent of the Saudi population had access to improved water sources. The number of government hospitals increased from 47 in 1970 to 290 in 1998 and medical and paramedical staff from 4,500 to about 100,000. Hospital beds per 1,000 populations were 2.5 in 1990; corresponding figure for the period 1995-2002 was 2.3. The availability of physicians per 1,000 people was 1.4 in 2004, which is slightly less than the world average. Life expectancy at birth for Saudi population in 1990 was 69 years and 73 years in 2003. Infant mortality rate per 1,000 live births was 34 and 22 respectively for 1990 and 2003, and under-five mortality rate per 1,000 was 44 and 26. Prevalence of diabetes in 2001 in adult population (20-79 years) was 12.3 per cent, whereas in 2003, 40 per 1,00,000 people had incidence of tuberculosis.

Implications of Demographic Transition

The peculiarity of 'demographic transition' taking place in Gulf countries, which is characterised by the high birth rate and the low death rate, is also reflected in the age structure of the Gulf population. In most Gulf countries about half of the total native population is under 15 years. This is understandable given the fact that the population of these countries is growing at a rate of about 3 per cent per annum. As would be seen shortly this 'young' population profile of the Saudi Arabian population has significant sociological implications for the well being of the Saudi society.

Rapid population growth and youthful profile of Saudi population have serious implications for not only economic development but also for the Saudi labour market and the social sector (education, health, social security and allied subjects). Besides housing, education and health the Kingdom must spend more on infrastructure, transport, water, sewers and power. It has also to address the question of direct and indirect subsidies in social security, food stuff, electricity, and agricultural products. "Existing population momentum will place massive pressure on the Saudi budget, and suitable infrastructure and services will probably require better sources of revenue, such as a real income tax, reductions in entitlements, and prices much closer to market levels. Saudi Arabia simply cannot afford a patriarchal solution to its youth explosion or cumulative under-funding of key services and infrastructure"[10]. Some idea of this expenditure on housing projects in Saudi Arabia can be had from the fact that estimatedly "since 1974 more than 5,00,000 housing units have been constructed throughout the kingdom: about half by the Government and half by the private sector. All adult Saudi Arabians, if not independently wealthy, are entitled to a plot of land and a loan of $80,000 with which to build a home[11].

One of the most pressing problems that have been persisting in Saudi Arabia relates to creation of new jobs for the young Saudis. The seventh Development Plan calls for the creation of 3,28,000 new jobs of which 3,11,000 (about 85%) were projected to come from the private sector. A rough estimate of various job categories are as follows: sales. services, and clerical–91,100; construction–81,400; manufacturing–72,000; agriculture–24,400; management, administration etc: 9,000; professional and technical–15,500. Overwhelming majority of these projected new josbs are not of the liking of Saudi young men and women. Moreover, whether appropriately skilled Saudis are available to man these jobs is another issue.

In order to overcome these challenges Saudi government has been putting emphasis on Saudisation—a programme that is in force since 1986. Under the programme the private sector that employs most of the expatriate labour is required to employ more Saudi citizens. Thus in 1996 a quota system was enforced whereby Saudis ranging from 5 per cent to 40 per cent of the company workforce of various job categories were required to be employed. This resulted in the private sector employers adopting standard contracts of employment and standard salary ranges for different occupations, with a rider, of course, that the Saudi citizens should continue to get significantly higher salaries than their expatriate counterparts doing similar work.

In 1997 the targeted sectors for Saudisation included transport and commerce and financial services. "In July 1998 the Saudi Government restricted the duration of public-sector employment contracts for expatriates to a maximum of 10 years in most categories of employment. In July 2002 the Ministry of Labour and Social Affairs instructed recruitment agencies to stop issuing new visas to non-Saudis seeking employment in 22 professions, including administration and procurement managers, car salesmen, public relations officers and secretaries. The policy of Saudiization of the workforce brought to 36 the total number of occupations to which expatriate access was restricted or denied. The Manpower Development Fund, financed partly by more expensive expatriate work permits and visas, was launched in April 2002 to subsidize skills training for nationals. In February 2003 the Ministry of the Interior announced plans to reduce the number of expatriate workers and their dependants in the Kingdom to 20 per cent of the population by 2013"[12].

Unfortunately, Saudisation has not been successful in real terms for the simple reason that the majority of jobs in which foreigners are employed are not preferred by the Saudis. These include about 1.7 million foreign females, most of whom worked as servants. Similarly, about 8,00,000 foreign workers are employed in menial or low status jobs. Replacing about 2.0 million such workers would neither be practical nor desirable. On the contrary, expatriate population has been increasing steadily in Saudi Arabia from 4.6 million in 1993 to 4.9 million in 1999 to 5.9 million in 2002.

Table 4.6: Saudi Arabia: National and Non-National Population, 2001

Item	*Sex*		*Percentage*
Nationals	Male	8,432,177	
	Female	8,338,379	
	Total	16,770,556	**73.7**
Non-Nationals	Total	5,919,346	**26.3**
Total Population		**22,689,903**	**100.0**

Source: *Gulf in the Year 2003*, Gulf Research Centre, Dubai, 2004.

Saudisation suffers from patriarchy as well as rentier state and economy syndrome. Not only the saudisation process, the entire social formation and its dynamics in Saudi Arabia underscore the aptness of these concepts. Let me briefly explain. According to the noted Arab scholar Hisham Sharabi, patriarchy is a social formation that centres around family, kinship, tribalism and sectarianism. Rentier state is essentially an allocative state rather than productive one, and as such it tends to promote only rentier mentality and ethics, which is essentially an ethics of idleness and easy life. In such a situation there is no relationship between work and reward, except in the case of expatriates. Citizenship of the rentier state thus becomes both a privilege and a source of income.[13] In the context of Sandisation the following points need to be highlighted.

1. Differential salary scales and other employment regulations for natives is major deterrent for Saudi employers to hire Saudi workers. Thus for example, if an expatriate gets a salary of 600 to 800 riyals, Saudi national for the same job must get 1500 to 2000 riyals. Moreover many Saudis are appointed on unneeded government jobs or unproductive jobs in the private sector.
2. Low work ethics and productivity on the part of Saudi citizens goes against the grain of Saudisation.
3. Saudi females with same level of education earn about half the salary of their male counterparts.
4. Employment conditions and regulations are highly discriminatory for expatriates. In the case of working class these regulations amount to human rights violations.
5. Social segregation for the middle class expatriates in Saudi Arabia is more pronounced than elsewhere in the Gulf. The well-known compound living in Saudi Arabia is typical of social and residential segregation. According to one description:

   What is this famous Saudi "compound life" all about? For

starters let me explain. Conceived exclusively for expatriates for all nationalities, each compound is a restricted, walled-off residential area for a few dozen to several hundred families. Totally self-contained little townships, each has its own recreational facilities—swimming pools, tennis courts, gym, restaurants, book and video libraries, super market and beauty parlours. Within these confines, one has all the freedom one needs. Yet, just one step outside the gates and one faces the sharp reality of a restricted life in Suadi Arabia[14].

6. In spite of significant educational progress made by women, particularly at secondary and tertiary levels in recent years, Saudi women constituted only 20.2 per cent of the labour force in 2003 compared to 33 per cent of Saudi men (the world average being 40.8%). But only 14 per cent of women are paid workers in non-agricultural sector (World average 36.6%). Again, 9.1 per cent of the total female labour force remained unemployed in 2000-02. These factors directly emanating from patriarchal social structure seriously hamper Saudisation policy and its implementation and would continue to do so in future if women are not allowed to get involved in the development process.

Saudi Arabia: Status of Women Indicators, 2003

Female Population	:	46.0 per cent.
Life expectancy at Birth	:	75 Years; for males 72 years.
Female Literacy: (15 plus)	:	69.4 per cent.
Total Fertility Rate	:	5.3 per cent (World average 2.6).
Adolescent fertility rate	:	(per 1,000 women aged 15-19): 89 per cent (world average 63 %).
Pregnant women receiving prenatal care	:	90 per cent.
Women paid work in non-agricultural sector	:	14.0 per cent.
Women in parliament	:	0 per cent.

Implications of urbanization in Saudi Arabia have been even far more serious than rapid population growth and/or its youthful profile. To begin with traditional tribal life and associated values and norms have suffered a grievous blow in the face of sudden affluence and 'modernisation'. This is particularly true in the case of post-oil boom generation that has different values and world-view than their parents. "Born into an easy subsidized lifestyle, many see no reason to work. Others, who have seen different ways of life during their travels or via satellite dish have grown increasingly restive by the limited options they see in the country".[15] Except sports clubs there are no other alternative recreational outlets such as cinemas, theatre and parks, etc. in Saudi Arabia.

As a result in the post oil boom period crime, divorce, alcoholism and drug abuse have continued to grow. Thus according to the Ministry of Interior report, 16,343 crimes were committed in Saudi Arabia in 1984. "Of that number, alcohol-related crimes accounted for 3,319, or nearly 20 per cent of all offenses. Thefts comprise 33.6 per cent of all crimes reported to the police, and of that number car thefts accounted for a hefty quarter. Immorality offences accounted for 11.8 per cent of all crimes. The Ministry added that 523 capital crimes were committed during the year of which 115 were murders (up from 1983's total of 44). Attempted murder accounted for 161 cases, while murder threats numbered 105"[16].

The incidence of drug abuse has become so alarming in Saudi Arabia that a *fatwa* had to be issued in 1987 that prescribed death penalty for drug dealers. In 1993 more than 100 such dealers had been arrested and 50 of them (mostly Pakistanis) publicly beheaded. Other problems associated with the rapid pace of development in Saudi Arabia relate to increasing anxiety, depression and allied psychopathological symptoms among the youth.

Political Reforms and Social Change

Oil economy in Saudi Arabia has induced tremendous changes in the field of public health, education, urbanization and infrastructural developments. In these terms at least the country has emerged as a modern society. Unfortunately the same can not be said about its political system, human rights practices and social values which are still embedded in conservatism. Thus according to Country Reports on Human Rights Practices, 2004, the Saudi Arabian "Government's human rights record remained poor overall with continuing serious problems, despite some progress. Citizens did not have the right to change their government. Security forces continued to abuse detainees and prisoners, arbitrarily arrest and hold persons in incommunicado detention. There were cases in which Mutawwain continued to intimidate, abuse, and detain citizens and foreigners. Most trials were closed, and defendants usually appeared before judges without legal counsel. Security forces arrested and detained reformers, some of whom continued at year's end to seek an open trial. The Government reportedly infringed on individuals' privacy rights. The Government continued to restrict freedom of speech and press, assembly, association, religion, and movement. There was widespread public perception that corruption by some members of the royal family and in the executive branch of the Government was a serious problem. There was little government transparency, especially notable in official budgets, and with no laws providing the right to access government information. The Government continued to discriminate against women, ethnic and religious minorities and to impose strict limitations on worker rights."[17]

Therefore for several decades now there has been an on-going movement for political reforms towards democracy and liberalism. During the last 15 years the following seven major petitions for political reform have been submitted by various groups of the Saudi people comprising intellectuals, clergy and academics to the Saudi authorities: (1) Petition for Change (December 1990), (2) Memorandum of Advice (February 1991), (3) fax Message of the Islamic Movement for Change-Jihad Wing (1995), (4) National Reform Document (January 2003), (5) The Shia Petition (April 2003), (6) Petition for Reforms (September 2003), and (7) Communiqué of the Second National Dialogue (January 2004).[18] But unfortunately nothing came out of these petitions. On the part of the regime the history of Saudi Arabia from this perspective has been a history of missed opportunities.

Cultural sociologists often conceptualize such a situation in terms of a lag between material and non-material aspects of culture. Thus the Saudi Arabian regime is willing to accept the most modern and contemporary technology, mostly from the West, but is unwilling to accept its concomitant socio-political value system, that is democracy, liberalism, competitiveness, multiculturalism etc. Even if these are not regarded as concomitant values they are certainty the emergent ones at a global scale.[19] Thus the Saudi society suffers from major contradictions in that its conservative non-material socio-political superstructure is not in correspondence with the modern, liberal base or structure. The fact that fifteen of the nineteen terrorists who attacked the World Trade Centre and the Pentagon on 11 September, 2001 were Saudi citizens seriously underline the prevailing social structure and value system in Saudi Arabia that produced such violent personalities. The crisis is akin to those in *pre-perestroika* or *pre-glasnost* communist societies. Presently the indigenous forces of religious dogmatism, patriarchy and rentier state and economy loom large on the horizon and a balance has to be achieved with liberalism in order for Saudi Arabia to emerge as a knowledge-based modern society. Needless to say, wide-spread educational reform is needed to inculcate these values among the young and future generations beside political reforms.

Can Saudis do it? No one knows, because the Saudi society is generally perceived to be an intolerant and conservative society with corrupt and authoritarian political system. Some recent studies however provide a slightly more optimistic view of Saudi society and culture. This was particularly revealed in a values orientations survey of Saudi citizens toward such key issues as the form of government, religion, religious tolerance, gender relations, marriage and western culture that was carried out in 2003. It was based on a sample of 1,526 Saudi adults that included 1,026 Saudi citizens, 500 foreign residents and equal number of men and women. Using a multistage probability sampling procedure the respondents were selected from all the regions of Saudi Arabia, including the major cities. "The households were the final sampling units, from which respondents were randomly selected. In terms of age, 29 percent were 15-24 years old, 29 percent were 25-34, 27 percent were 35-44, 11 percent were 45-54, and 4 percent were 55 or older. The majority of respondents identified themselves as members of either the upper-middle class (48 percent) or the lower middle class (34 percent); the rest identified themselves as upper class (10 percent) or working class (8 percent). In terms of education, 80 percent of respondents had less than a university education whereas 20 percent had a university education.[20]

It must be pointed out here that somewhat identical surveys of national representative samples of 3,000 Egyptians, 2,532 Iranians and 1,224 Jordanians were carried out in 2001. With a sample of 1,200 American adults a similar survey was carried out in the US in 2000. All the surveys used interview schedule (face to face interview) technique. The following was the major findings of the Saudi survey that are presented here in a comparative perspective by a sociologist:[21]

"Although by Western standards Saudi Arabia is a conservative society, compared with other Islamic countries like Egypt and Jordan, Saudis are not as conservative as one might expect. In fact they are less religious than either Egyptians or Jordanians. In terms of their attitudes towards marriage, almost half of the Saudis prefer love rather than parental approval, as the basis of marriage. A large percentage of Saudis than either Egyptians or Jordanians consider marriage to be an outdated institution. On such issues as those related with religiosity, marriage, women, and work and children, Saudis are close to Iranians than to Egyptians or Jordanian Arabs. The similarities between the Saudi and Iranian citizens in terms of religiosity and their differences from Egyptians or Jordanians may indicate the effect of state's culture on people's attitudes. It appears that the religiosity of the Iranian and Saudi states have made the publics of these societies less religious instead of making them more so."

Indians in Saudi Arabia

Some of the Muslims from India going on *haj* must have settled in Saudi Arabia in ancient and medieval times but we do not know much about them. Probably all of them got assimilated. Indian migration to Saudi Arabia in recent time begins with Indians' employment in the Arabian-American Oil Company (ARAMCO). Saudi Arabia was most restrictive in employing Indian labour in the oil industry than other Gulf countries. Thus in the case of all-American-operated ARAMCO only 37 Indians were employed in 1940. Two factors were responsible for this situation: (i) absence of British control on Saudi oil industry, and (ii) the relative lack of traditional links between Saudi Arabia and the Indian subcontinent.

The Saudi government was reluctant to allow large numbers of British Indians into the country and indeed expressly prohibited the entry of Jews, Hindus (after 1937) and *Shia Muslims*. In the early 1940s a strict quota limit was imposed on the number of Indians which the company could employ. The few Indians who were recruited gave the company much trouble indulging the first organised strike in Saudi Arabia in March 1943 after which the Saudis threatened to prohibit further Indian immigration.[22]

Eventually this did not happen and after World War II when ARAMCO began to expand operations the numbers of Indians working for the company had increased substantially; 599 in November 1945. After substantial decline in 1946, this figure remained steady in 1947 and continued to increase significantly in subsequent years. These data also included Indians who were working for the company in Bahrain.

The migration of Indian workers to Saudi continued to take place at moderate pace during the 1950s and 1960s, or more precisely until the oil boom of 1973-74 following which it accelerated substantially. Consequently the Indian population in "Saudi Arabia increased from about 35,000 in 1975 to 2,70,000 in 1983 (Table 4.8). Figures of migration of Indian contract workers are presented in Table 4.7. The data clearly suggest that since the early 1980s Saudi Arabia has been an important destination for Indian contract workers. During the past quarter of a century Saudi intake of Indian contract workers ranged from about 24 per cent annually to just over 66 per cent of total Indian migration to the Gulf countries. The only exception was the year 1999 when only 13.61

per cent of the total Indian contract workers immigrated into Saudi Arabia. Since then the situation has improved considerably.

Table 4.7: Number of Indian Migrant Workers to Saudi Arabia, 1982-2004

Year	*Total Migration to West Asia*	*Number of Migrants to Saudi Arabia*	*Percentage of Total Migration*
1982	2,39,545	78,297	32.68
1983	2,49,952	83,235	33.30
1984	2,05,922	88,079	42.77
1985	1,63,035	68,938	42.28
1986	1,13,649	41,854	36.88
1987	1,25,356	57,243	45.66
1988	1,69,888	85,289	50.20
1989	1,25,786	49,710	39.52
1990	1,43,565	79,473	55.36
1991	1,97,889	1,30,928	66.16
1992	4,16,784	2,65,180	63.63
1993	4,38,338	2,69,639	61.51
1994	4,25,385	2,65,875	62.50
1995	4,15,334	2,56,782	61.83
1996	4,14,214	2,41,068	51.68
1997	4,16,424	2,14,420	51.49
1998	3,55,164	1,05,239	29.63
1999	1,99,552	27,160	13.61
2000	2,43,182	58,722	24.15
2001	2,78,664	78,048	28.00
2002	3,67,663	99,453	27.05
2003	4,66,456	1,21,431	26.03
2004	4,74,960	1,23,522	26.00

Source: Ministry of Labour, Government of India, Annual Reports (Different years).

Among the major sociological characteristics of Indian migrants to Saudi Arabia, as also to the other GCC countries, the following ones are important to keep in mind. Most such migrants originate in Kerala and other South Indian states, and happen to be male, young, unmarried and unemployed or under-employed. This migration is also "circular" in nature—migrants stay only for a few years at a time and look for an opportunity to migrate again. Thus a study in Bihar had found that about two-thirds of the migrants to the Gulf stayed there between 2 to 6 years.[23] In another study of return migrants in Kerala it was found that about two-thirds of them had worked in the Gulf countries "for less than 5 years; nearly 30 per cent had worked for less than 2 years. The average length of work experience abroad for the entire group was 7 years and 3 months"[24]. Studies have also found a high degree of circularity among the Gulf migrants: 25 per cent were once migrants, 42 per cent twice migrants, 21 per cent thrice migrants and the rest had migrated four-times or more[25]. Thus short-term stay and circularity keep the "community" in a flux.

Table 4.8: Indian Community in Saudi Arabia, 1975-2005

Year	*Number of Indians*
1975	34,500
1979	1,00,000
1983	2,70,000
1987	3,80,000
1991	6,00,000
1999	12,00,000
2005	16,00,000

Source: Author's own estimates based on a number of academic sources.

The number of Indians in Saudi Arabia rose to 6,50,000 in 1990. During the Kuwait crisis of 1990-91 about a million Yemen workers employed in Saudi Arabia and other Gulf countries were forced to go back to Yemen. This resulted in Saudi employers recruiting Indians in large numbers to replace them. Consequently, the size of the Indians expatriate community in Saudi Arabia grew to about 1.2 million in 1999 and to about 1.6 million in 2005.

The Indian Diaspora in Saudi Arabia consists of three broad categories of people: (1) professionals working for the government and the private sector. They constitute about 5 per cent of the Indian community. (2) "A somewhat larger non-professional group of 10 per cent includes white collar staff employed as clerks, secretaries, accountants, store keepers, booking clerks etc." (3) Finally there is the remaining 85 per cent consisting of oraganised labour and technicians working on project sites and industrial establishments, as well as on operations and maintenance jobs. Outside these three main groups, there is the unorganised labour which includes a small number of illegal entrants who are either working in the country without legal sponsors or who had come to the kingdom on *Haj* or *Umrah* visas and then stayed on to work there. Periodically the Saudi Government declares amnesty to flush out and deports only such illegal residents.[26]

As elsewhere in the Gulf, in Saudi Arabia too Indians' socio-cultural life center around regional identity: Keralite, Tamil, Gujarati, etc. There are a number of senior secondary schools in major Saudi cities and towns like Jeddah, Damman, Jubrail, Taif, Banaridah and Tabuk. Over 32,000 students are enrolled in these schools most of which follow the Central Board of Secondary Education (CBSE, Delhi) pattern.

As in other Gulf countries, in Saudi Arabia, too, the foreign workers suffer from a number of disabilities—economic, political and socio-cultural. Indian expatriate workers, too, share the same fate. Legally, there is no question of permament resident status, naturalization or citizenship for the Indian migrants in the Gulf. Politically, the Gulf regimes are authoritarian. There are no political and civic rights for expatriates. Contract substitution and lower wages, delayed payments, confiscation of work permits, long working hours, deportation and police brutality are some of the common downsides to the Saudi labour markets. Female domestic helpers particularly suffer the worst labour abuses, including rape and physical violence. As already pointed out, the expatriates live an extremely segregated life in Saudi Arabia. As Weiner puts it, "Migrants are incorporated into the economic structure, but are excluded from the social structure. Separation, not integration or assimilation, is the goal.... Social contacts between Arabs and expatriates are minimized.... An increasing number of migrants stay for extended periods, and some may remain legally 'temporary' resident, with little notice they can be asked by the government to leave".[27]

Non-Muslims conspicuously lack any freedom to practice their religion. The Hindu immigrants in Saudi Arabia are not allowed to carry with them any of their religious books, idols or photographs of gods or goddesses. "They must observe their festivals in less conspicuous locations or in private".[28] In Saudi Arabia and elsewhere in the Gulf Islam is a state religion and any criticism—direct or indirect—is absolutely prohibited and can be severely punished.

Socially, Saudi Arabia is highly patriarchal in ethos and practice. A certain amount of duality in terms of Arab vs non-Arab is there. Fortunately, there is no racism in the Gulf region as a whole but ethnic articulation in terms of *watni vs* non-*watni* (native vs non-native) and Muslim *vs* non-Muslim are rather strong. Even South Asian Muslims are ranked a bit below the Arab Muslims.

Death is a nightmare for Indians working in Saudi Arabia. The biggest problem of course is bringing home the body by the next of kin for funeral rites. In 1996, for example, 2,877 Indians had died in the GCC countries including 1,461 in Saudi Arabia and 785 in the United Arab Emirates. In Saudi Arabia non-Muslims are not allowed to be buried. Their bodies cannot be claimed until the responsibilities of death (in the case of an unnatural one) had been fixed, and the wages and death compensation due to the deceased have been paid to the next of kin. The whole procedure takes usually one to two months, and in complicated cases even more.

Presently the Indians in Saudi Arabia annually remit to India about four billion US dollars which is "the largest amount inward flow of foreign exchange from any single country".[29] Earlier they significantly contributed to the Resurgent India Bond of 1998 and the India Millenium Deposit Bonds of the year 2001, besides substantial donations to relief works for floods in Orissa, earthquake in Gujarat and Tsunami in Tamil Nadu, etc.

Concluding Remarks

Rapidly expanding and young population profile poses a major challenge to the existing socio-political set up in Saudi Arabia. Born in the era of information revolution, this segment of Saudi population is increasingly educated, urbanized and modern in its outlook. It will not easily be "contained" by Saudi patriarchy and rentier state. As such the Saudi society suffers from a crisis of rising expectations which cannot be met by authoritarian Saudi regime.

Saudi Arabia is no longer an isolated society. With 260 TV sets per 1,000 population, 117 television stations, widespread availability of radios and fax machines, access to internet and satellite dishes, contemporary Saudi Arabia has truly entered into electronic and information age. According to Saudi Government's own estimates, an average Saudi spends 50 per cent to 100 per cent more time watching television than his or her European counterpart. Thus in spite of censorship and control on the media, the inflow of information into the Saudi society has gone beyond the government and clergy's control. But at the same time the Saudi society is not keeping pace with the emergent global liberal socio-political ethos.

References

1. Cordesman, Anthony H., *Saudi Arabia Enters the Twenty-First Century: The Political, Foreign Policy, Economic and Energy Dimensions*", Praeger Publishers, New York, 2003, p. 237.
2. Wilson, Peter W. and Doughlas F. Graham, *Saudi Arabia: The Coming Storm*, M.E. Sharp, Armonk, New York, 1994, p. 235.
3. *Ibid.*
4. World Bank, *World Development Indicators 2005*, World Bank, Washington DC, 2005, p. 90.

5. Abir, Mordechai, *Saudi Arabia: Government, Society and the Gulf Crisis*, Routledge, London, 1993, pp. 16-17.
6. Rugh, William A., "Arab Education: Tradition, Growth and Reform", *Middle East Journal*, 2002, 56(3): 397-414.
7. Wilson and Graham, n. 2, p. 258.
8. Rugh, n. 6.
9. Jreisat, Jamil E., Politics *without Process*: *Administering Development in the Arab World*, Lynne Reinner Publishers, Boulder, 1997, p. 53.
10. Cordesman, n. 1, p. 307.
11. *Europa Yearbook 2005*, p. 1014.
12. *Ibid.*, p. 1007.
13. Sharabi, Hisham, *Neo-Patriarchy: A Theory of Distorted Change in Arab Society*, Oxford University, Press, 1988. Beblawi, Hazem, "Rentier State in the Arab World", in Giacomo Luciani (ed.), *The Arab State,* Routledge, London 1990.
14. Ramaswami, Bhanu, "Living the good life in a Saudi Expat Compound", *The International Indian*, 2003, p. 22.
15. Wilson and Graham, n. 2, p. 238.
16. *Ibid.,* n. 2, p. 237.
17. http://www.state.gov/g/drl/rls/hrrpt/2004/41731.htm.
18. Ansari, M.H., *Islamic Boomerang in Saudi Arabia*, Samskriti Publications, New Delhi, 2004.
19. Murden, Simon W., *Islam, The Middle East and the New Global Hegemony,* Lynne Rienner Publishers, London, 2002.
20. Moaddel, Mansoor, "The Saudi Public Speaks: Religion, Gender, and Politics", *International Journal of Middle East Studies,* Vol. 38, 2006, p. 82.
21. *Ibid.*, pp. 103-04.
22. Seccombe, I.J. and R.I. Lawless, "Foreign Workers Dependence in the Gulf and the International Oil Companies 1910-50", *International Migration Review*, Vol. 20, No. 3, 1986, p. 570.
23. Rahman, Anisur, *Indian Migration to the Gulf Countries*, Rajat Publications, Delhi, 2003. see also Jain, Prakash C., "An incipient Diaspora: Indians in the Persian Gulf Region", in Bhiku Parekh *et al.* (eds.) *Culture and Economy in the Indian Diaspora,* Rutledge, London, 2003.
24. Zachariah, K.C., P.R. Gopinathan Nair and S. Irudaya Rajan, *Return Emigrants in Kerala: Welfare, Rehabilitation and Development,* Manohar Publishers and Distributors, Delhi, 2006, p. 40.
25. *Rahman*, n. 23.
26. High Level Committee, *High Level Committee Report on the Indian Diaspora*, Indian Council of World Affairs, New Delhi, 2001, p. 40.
27. Weiner, Myron, "International Migration and Development: Indians in the Persian Gulf", *Population and Development Review*, 1982, Vol. 8, No. 1, p. 26.
28. *Ibid.*
29. High Level Committee, n. 26.

5

Iranian Nuclear Programme
Saudi Concerns and Responses

GULSHAN DIETL

The Iranian nuclear issue has dominated the global agenda for the past few years. The question has largely been perceived as a stand-off between Iran and the United States. It is the states in the immediate neighbourhood of Iran, however, which will be most seriously impacted in all possible scenarios in which the situation may evolve. Their perceptions, policies and preventive measures have largely been discussed only on the periphery of the great debate over Iran's nuclearisation. The paper proposes to scrutinise the Saudi concerns and responses to this development on their eastern flank across the Gulf waters.

Quest for Nuclear Capability: Saudi Arabia and Iran

Muhammad Reza Shah Pahlavi signed a nuclear co-operation agreement with the US under the Atoms for Peace proposal in 1957. Within two years thereafter, the Shah constituted the Atomic Energy Organisation and established the Tehran Nuclear Research Centre. The US supplied the latter with a small 5-megawatt nuclear research reactor. In 1968, Iran became a signatory of the Nuclear Non-Proliferation Treaty (NPT).

By 1974, Iran had established the Atomic Energy Organisation of Iran and announced the plan to build twenty-three nuclear power plants in the next twenty years. Besides US, Germany and France assisted the Iranian programme by way of providing enriched uranium, nuclear reactors and research centres. The German firms of Siemens and Kraftwerk Union entered into an agreement to build two nuclear reactors in Bushehr, a port city on the Gulf coast.

After the revolution, the Iranians put a complete freeze on nuclear programme, as Ayatollah Khomeini declared the Weapons of Mass Destruction unislamic and immoral. The country found itself at the receiving end of Saddam Hussein's chemical weapons during the Iran-Iraq war. The world was silent and indifferent. Khomeini was dead. Its own reactors had been damaged. That probably was the time, when Iran revived and resumed its nuclear activities.

In 1995, it entered into an agreement with Russia to complete the construction of its nuclear power plant in Bushehr and to provide it with low-enriched uranium. The deal was worth $800 million. China also agreed to supply Iran with two nuclear reactors, which were to be installed in Isfahan. It later cancelled the deal. The US was determined to stop the Iranian programme; and the successive US administrations sought to put pressure on Russia and economic sanctions on Iran to terminate it.

The Saudis were late arrivals on the nuclear scene. In June 1981, the Israelis attacked and destroyed Iraq's Osirak nuclear reactor. That seemed to convince Saudi Arabia that an Islamic bomb to counter the weapons held by Israel was indispensable. Despite their denials, their funding of Pakistan's nuclear programme was an integral part of the Saudi foreign policy in the eighties.[1] The Saudis might have approached the US for assistance in nuclear field as well. The close covert partnership between Washington and Riyadh inspired Prince Bandar to confide to a journalist in 1981 that "if you knew what we were really doing for America, you wouldn't just give us AWACS, you would give us nuclear weapons."[2]

The Iran-Iraq war was going on at that time. There were times during its long span of eight years, when it threatened to spill over into the neighbouring countries. The Saudis felt vulnerable to air, naval and missile attacks from Iran, though a land offensive was not expected. In fact, There was a direct clash between the two as the Saudi jets, guided by the AWACS, intercepted and destroyed an Iranian F-4 fighter-bomber in mid-1984. According to the Saudi Prince Khaled bin Sultan:

> It was against this background that, I assume, King Fahd decided that we needed a weapon to improve the morale of our armed services and our people; a deterrent weapon not intended to be used, except as a last resort when it should be able to demoralize the enemy by delivering a painful and decisive blow; a weapon which, once launched, could not be jammed or intercepted; a weapon which could make an enemy think twice before attacking us.[3]

The Prince continues his narrative to describe his mission to China.

In March 1988, there were disclosures that the Saudis had taken delivery of an unspecified number of Chinese DF-3, (CSS-2) medium-range missiles with an estimated range of 3,000 kilometres. Amidst reports of threats from Israel and protests from the US, King Fahd stuck to his refusal to permit their inspection. Instead, he requested the US government for a replacement of Hume Horan, the American ambassador who had delivered an official protest note from his government. In May, the US Senate voted to ban sales of military equipment to Saudi Arabia unless the President could specify that the missiles had no chemical, biological or nuclear warheads with which to equip them.

The Chinese missiles were believed to be deployed at two sites from where they could fire at both Iran and Israel. The sites were about 400 kilometres apart in the desert south of Riyadh. The missiles were considered inaccurate and therefore ineffective for pinpoint strikes using high explosive warheads.

The Saudi ambitions in the nuclear field had, in the meanwhile, generated a lot of curiosity. The Saudi Arabian National Centre for Science and Technology (SANCST) was reported to be negotiating with West Germany's Interatom, a subsidiary of the Siemens concern, for the supply of two small reactors: one with a 10 MW capacity, for the production of isotopes for medical purposes. The Interatom said that the two-year old talks were at "a very preliminary stage," with the two sides "exchanging ideas." The Bonn government, however, which was required to license all West German nuclear exports, was asked to approve the deal in principle, and the Interatom was optimistic of a positive response.[4] No further development took place on this deal. In fact, in October 1988, Saudi Arabia signed the Non-proliferation Treaty to alleviate apprehensions on this score. In due course, the US President George Bush certified that Saudi Arabia did not possess nuclear, chemical or biological warheads for its CSS-2 missiles.

Interestingly, it was a defector/dissidents in each case, who blew the whistle on the clandestine programme of his/their respective country. Thus, in June 1991, the Iranian dissident movement Mojahedin-e Khalq Organisation (MKO) operating from bases inside Iraq, claimed that Iran was engaged in an ultra-secret nuclear weapons project under the direction of the Revolutionary Guards corps. It singled out a purported nuclear research centre in Mo'allem Kelayeh in the north-west mountainous region near the city of Qazwin as the centrepiece of Iran's nuclear weapons project.[5] The International Atomic Energy Commission (IAEA) refuted the MKO claim. After a long hiatus, in August 2002, the MKO announced that its sources had discovered two secret facilities in Iran built to produce fissile material for nuclear weapons: the gas centrifuse plants at Natanz to enrich uranium and a heavy water production facility at Arak to extract plutonium.

In the Saudi case, it was Mohammad al-Khilevi, the Saudi defector who was the First Secretary in Saudi mission to UN till 1994. According to him, Riyadh had sought a bomb since 1975.[6] He produced documents in support of his charges that between 1985 and 1990, Saudi government paid upto $5billion to Saddam Hussein to build a nuclear weapon. These payments were made on condition that some of the bombs be transferred to Saudi arsenal if the Iraqi project were successful. He also claimed that Saudi Arabia provided financial contribution to the Pakistani nuclear programme, and had signed a secret agreement that obligated the Pakistani government to provide positive security assurances to Saudi Arabia.[7]

Bilateral Relations: US Pillars to Wings of Islam?

Iran and Saudi Arabia were the "Two Pillars" of the US military posture in the Gulf in 1970s. After the Iranian revolution, the two became the chief protagonists all through the eighties. In 1987, there was an unprecedented tragedy at the time of the hajj, when the Saudi security guards and the Iranian demonstrators engaged in a confrontation that, according to Iran, left more than six hundred dead as a result of fifty thousand bullets fired on them.

The situation changed again in the wake of Iraqi invasion, occupation and annexation of Kuwait. Diplomatic relationship between the two resumed after a brief break. Presenting his credentials, Gholam Ali Najafabadi, the new Iranian ambassador to the Kingdom, said, "The Islamic world has two wings, and it is not possible to fly without its two wings of the Islamic Republic of Iran and the Kingdom of Saudi Arabia. Both have their weight and place in the Islamic world."[8]

The process of reconciliation between the two was thus set in motion. During President Khatami's tenure, there was a proliferation of ties in various fields. The year 1997 witnessed a flurry of visits between the two countries. In March, the Iranian foreign minister Ali Akbar Velayeti visited the Kingdom to invite its leaders to the Organisation of Islamic Conferences Summit to be held in Tehran at the end of the year. In April, president Hashemi Rafsanjani visited Saudi Arabia; ostensibly in a private capacity to perform the hajj. In December, the Saudi Crown Prince Abdullah participated in the OIC Summit in Tehran.

After having paid an unofficial visit as the President, Rafsanjani paid an official visit as the former President in February 1998. In May, the Saudi Foreign Minister Prince Saud al-Feisal visited Tehran in order to "reinforce and expand" bilateral ties.

In March 1999, the Iranian president Muhammad Khatami paid an official visit to Tehran; the first Iranian president since the revolution. The visit marked the culmination of a steady upswing in the ties.

Two years later, one more stride was made during the visit of Prince Nayef to Tehran. A security pact was signed for co-operation against drug trafficking and money laundering, and for border surveillance, administration of water and territorial matters. Conspicuously missing in the text was any mention of extradition—especially as the US had accused Iran of involvement in the 1996 blasts in al-Khobar. A clause on extradition would have resulted in the return of the accused to Saudi Arabia. Khatami visited the country in September 2002 to discuss the impending war on Iraq.

The Iranians sought to build on the pact to make it comprehensive in scope and multilateral in membership. The Iranian Defence Minister Ali Shamkhani, during one of his visits to the Kingdom, pursued the matter by offering an arrangement to eliminate Western military presence in the Gulf. In response to a question on the issue in a joint press conference with Shamkhani, the Saudi Defence Minister Prince Sultan put an end to the speculation. He said categorically, "We cannot neglect Iran's security or say that it is not a country present by our side and our neighbour and a great Islamic country. But direct co-operation with Iran to protect the Gulf is out of the question."[9]

The security ties remained within the boundaries specified in the pact. There was a regular follow-up in the form of the joint meetings. The Iranians, though, did not give up on upgrading the security relationship. "I hope the agreement marks the first step towards a general and comprehensive security agreement between the countries of the region, so that these states can live in peace," Khatami said in an interview with the Kingdom's daily newspaper *al-Watan.*[10]

An upswing in relationship was clearly manifest in economic sphere. A joint Economic Commission was instituted, which met annually in Tehran and Riyadh alternatively. Trade went up from $95 million in 1999 to $133 million in 2000 and $248.5 million in 2001.[11] Iran improved its position from running a trade deficit to accumulating a surplus, as a result. There were exhibitions of Iranian trade products in Riyadh and Jeddah. The first Saudi Airlines flight in twenty-one years arrived in Tehran with

Ali Shamkhani on board.[12] Iran waived the visa requirement for the GCC states for a maximum stay of three months.[13] And, finally, Iran upgraded its hajj quota to 90,000 pilgrims.

There were feeble moves even in the political arena as the parliamentary delegations exchanged visits. In December 2001, the speaker of Iranian Majlis Mehdi Karrubi led a group of fellow Majlis members to Riyadh and met the members of the Saudi Shura Council. At the end of the visit, there was a joint Shura-Majlis statement: "The two countries condemn the vicious media campaign against the lofty principles and values of Islam and consider it a conspiracy to deface the image of Islam and to weaken the Islamic and Arab nations."[14] The Saudi Shura Council Chairman Saleh bin Abdullah bin Hamid paid a return visit with a parliamentary delegation next year.[15]

Contentious Issues: Old and New

The relations between Saudi Arabia and Iran were never devoid of suspicion and rivalry. Even as they constituted the complementary pillars of the US Gulf strategy, the two were competitors for regional leadership and Islamic credentials. According to the Saudi Air Force Colonel Alsudairy, the two-pillar approach was "more a descriptive rationalisation in Washington than an actual operational model."[16] It was the common broad goal of maintaining status quo in the Gulf that contained their rivalries.

With the revolution in Iran, the situation changed drastically. The Iranian calls for the emulation of its example were direct threats to the rulers in the Gulf. There were instances of challenge to the hereditary rule in Saudi Arabia itself. The Iraqi aggression on Iran in 1980 was widely perceived as a Saudi-inspired diversionary move to keep Iran occupied away from itself. The formation of the GCC was similarly seen to be a Saudi design to stem the tide of Iranian revolution. The Saudi involvement in Afghanistan was as much to counter the influence of revolutionary Iran as that of the Soviet Union.[17]

When Iraq attacked Kuwait, Iran found itself in the most comfortable situation in the triangular power balance, as two of its adversaries—Iraq and Saudi Arabia—became enemies of each other. The Saudis began to lose their grip on the GCC, as a consequence. As the Iraqi threat persisted, the Kuwaitis were forced to show more deference to the Iranian wishes. A border dispute between Saudi Arabia and Qatar provided Iran with a unique opportunity to assume the posture of an honest broker and to offer to mediate. The Saudi-Omani rivalry propelled King Qaboos to adopt a more conciliatory policy towards Iran.

In April 1992, Iran chose to capture and claim the entire island of Abu Musa. Situated 56 kilometres from Sharjah and 70 kilometres from the Iranian coastline, the island had come under the co-sovereignty of the two in 1971. The Iranians used their side of the island as a base for the naval forces of the Iranian Revolutionary Guards Corps. It was one of a string of islands that was used for attacks on international shipping during the war between Iran and Iraq. Apart from its military significance, it is rich in resources. It contains half a billion barrel of oil in addition to substantial deposits of gas and red iron oxide.

It was only in December 1993 that the GCC Summit endorsed the United Arab Emirate's proposal to refer the case to the International Court of Justice. The dispute has remained on the GCC agenda ever since and is routinely included in its resolutions. By the end of the decade, the UAE had lost patience. It was additionally aggravated by the Saudi-Iranian rapprochement. In 1999, it threatened to quit the GCC on the issue. A committee of the Saudi, Omani and Qatari foreign ministers was formed to resolve the issue.

As the committee met and called upon Iran to co-operate with its efforts, Iran conducted military manoeuvres around the disputed area. The committee's call to desist met with defiance. Hamid-Reza Asefi, the Iranian government spokesman, repeated the official Iranian position: "Holding manoeuvres is part of our general policy aimed at strengthening and defending security and stability in the Persian Gulf. We expect that policy to be supported by the countries of the region. The islands have been Iranian territory and will remain to be."[18] The two have captured each other's boats at bad points in their relations, and the UAE has sent relief supplies at the time of earthquake in Iran at not so bad points in their relations. The island issue is unresolved, so far. As the leader of the GCC, Saudi Arabia bears a huge share of responsibility in the matter.

In May 2000, Saudi Arabia became a direct party to a territorial dispute with Iran, when the latter started drilling in the Dorra offshore field. Saudi Arabia and Kuwait both have claims on the area and lodged an immediate protest. Iran stopped the work and took down the installations as a response; but reiterated its claim to the site. The issue can re-emerge.[19] If the issue of Abu Musa challenges Saudi position within the GCC, the issue of the Dorra fields poses a direct threat to its territory.

As noted earlier, the Saudis did not implicate Iran into the bombing at Khobar, even after the formal US indictment. Whether it was due to a lack of credible evidence in the matter, or due to the fear of unveiling domestic dissent network[20], or simply due to a desire to maintain cordiality with Iran; would remain in the sphere of speculation. Almost a decade after the Khobar incident, there was another espionage case involving Iran. This time, Mohammad Reza Maher, a former Iranian diplomat in Cairo and Mahmoud Dabbous, who worked in Saudi Arabia were said to have supplied information to the IRGC that helped carry out an attack on a petrochemical site in the Saudi city of Yanbu. Dabbous admitted having received $50,000 in cash from IRGC to spy for Iran and to kill unnamed targets in Egypt.[21]

After the Khatami presidency ended, the strains in the bilateral relations worsened.[22] President Mahmoud Ahmadinejad created world-wide outrage by his remarks calling for wiping Israel off the map of the world and denying the Holocaust. What irked the Saudis was that he reiterated his views on the Saudi soil, while participating in an OIC Summit in December last.

Saudi Response: Statements

The official Saudi pronouncements on Iran's nuclear programme, especially from the royals, are unexceptionable. Even diplomatese is not resorted to in conveying a message. To sample a few:

Prince Sultan, the Minister of Defence, dismissed a possible Iranian nuclear attack calling it a "friendly state". He did not think Iran "will think one day of jeopardising the security of the peoples of the GCC states."[23]

Prince Nayef, the Minister of Interior, said during his visit to Tunisia that he believed the Iranian nuclear programme to be for peaceful end while one could not say the same for Israel, which continues to develop and maintain a nuclear arsenal.[24]

Gradually, the comparison with Israel crept into the princely pronouncements. In a lecture in Phoenix, the Saudi Ambassador to the US expanded the comparison to take in two more cases. The people, he said, "see the US government negotiating with North Korea…and they see the US signing a nuclear peace agreement with India…and they see the US turning a blind eye completely to Israel, although Israel has the most nuclear weapons in our part of the world.[25] Singling out Iran for a harsh treatment did not go down well in the region, he concluded. He did not explicitly spell out, but alluded to the threats from the US and Israel against the Iranian nuclear assets. In such a contingency, the anger may not remain confined to the Iranians or the Shii-majority Iraq, but may expand to the people across the region. The reachable target of their anger would be closer to home.

Prince Saud, the Foreign Minister, reiterated the Saudi position in a joint press-conference with the French President Jacques Chirac's visit to the Kingdom:

> Of course as I have said many times before, the double standard in the issue of non-proliferation is being viewed particularly in the Middle East, by giving a blind eye to what is happening in Israel, and giving strong and restrictive policies against everybody else. It is what has unbalanced the issue of non-proliferation in the Middle East. We hope there will be equality in treatment. We hope that the best way to have that resolved is to have no WMD in the Middle East. God knows Israel does not need it. It is the only country that is guaranteed security by almost every country including France so we don't see why they need nuclear weapons in the face of such guarantees of security and territorial integrity.[26]

Saud repeated the same arguments in an interview with the BBC: that the West was partly responsible for the current stand-off because it had helped Israel develop its own nuclear arsenal; that if Iran were ever to use nuclear arms against Israel, it would end up killing the Palestinians; and that Saudi Arabia had no intentions of joining the nuclear arms race.[27]

Turki made one more argument in his Pheonix lecture; that of utter futility of the nuclear weapon. "It escalates the tensions and brings about competition, which is unneeded and unnecessary and uncalled for. If their intention is to bomb Israel, then they will kill Palestinians, Syrians, Jordanians and Saudis as well. If they intend to bomb the US, for example, they will kill other people as well. Where is the value of having a weapon of destruction that people know you are not going to use?"[28]

The Saudi concerns, in the circumstances, are left to the non-government sources to articulate. Abdulaziz Sager, a Saudi national who is the founder-chairman of the Gulf Research Centre, located in Dubai. It works on Gulf-related political, security and economic issues. He is an influential opinion maker with policy influence as well. In an article in the Beirut-based *Daily Star* newspaper, he takes a hard look at the Iranian ambitions. First, he pulls the issue out of the US-EU-Iran context. Since the states directly threatened by the weapons would be members of the Gulf Co-operation Council, the issue should be looked at in the regional context. The Iranian policies intensify foreign military presence in the region and force regional states into an arms race that could adversely affect regional stability, deepen mistrust and obstruct national development plans, he says. It is not in the interest of the GCC states to allow continued animosity between Tehran and Washington because this adversely impacts GCC-Iran relations. "More than ever, the GCC is today required to make Tehran feel that it is an indispensable part of any Gulf security arrangement," he prescribes. On the other hand, he expects Tehran to open a new window of opportunity to address all pending regional issues."[29]

Dawood al-Shirian, another Saudi analyst, adds some more arguments to the case. "A nuclear-armed Iran would be a "justification" for foreign countries to keep their forces in the Gulf longer to protect their oil interests." Any military confrontation between Iran and the West would trigger a response in Iraq that could lead to Shia-Sunni sectarian tensions across the region. His case is that the Iranian weapon would result in a longer stay of the foreign military presence, could trigger a military confrontation between Iran and the West, could precipitate a response in Iraq, and that may, in turn, embroil the entire region in the Shia-Sunni tensions. His prescription is blunt: "Gulf nations utterly refuse any idea that Iran should own a nuclear weapon and they want Iran to stop uranium enrichment...except under international control.[30]

Tariq al-Homayed, a Saudi journalist, points out that the Bushehr reactor is closer to Doha and Manama across the Gulf waters than to Tehran itself; and an accident there would spell a disaster in the Arab lands.[31] Muhammad Abdullah al-Zulfa, a member of the Shura Council of Saudi Arabia, does not want see Iran as a major power in the Gulf and is categorical that "we don't want to see Iran having this nuclear weapon where it will be a major threat to the stability of the Gulf area and even to the Arab world altogether." The Arab countries know what Iran covets "in the region in terms of oil and in terms of the sacred places," says Anwar Majid Eshki, head of the Middle East Center for Strategic and Legal Studies, an independent institute in Saudi Arabia.[32]

There were additional voices on the issue from beyond the Saudi borders. One such deserves to be noted here. Sami al-Farraj of Kuwait Centre for Strategic Studies said, "Iran is seismically unstable, and an earthquake could cause an accident that would be more disastrous for the Gulf countries than for Iran. Any pollution would down six water desalination plants on the Arab shore."[33] That the Bushehr reactor was being built with Russian technology was a cause for worry. What if there was a sequel to Chernobyl accident? Even a civilian nuclear programme was potentially dangerous, in his opinion.

Saudi Response: Policy Initiatives

In September 2003, the London-based *Guardian* newspaper claimed to have unearthed a story about possible Saudi response to the Iranian nuclearisation. In a strategy paper, supposedly considered at the highest level in Riyadh, the Saudis were reported to have chalked out a three-fold policy to counter the Iranian ambitions. These options were set out for maintaining national security: (1) Acquiring a nuclear capability as a deterrent, (2) Maintaining or entering into an alliance with an existing nuclear power that would offer protection, and 3 Trying to reach a regional agreement for a nuclear free West Asia.[34]

Such exercises are routinely undertaken in countries all over the world. In an exceptional situation, they are prolonged; at times continuous. The Saudis, though, are highly secretive and sensitive about the national security issues. The Saudi Embassy in Washington termed the story "baseless and totally false" the next day. The deputy foreign minister Turki bin Muhammad said the Kingdom was noted for its position in support of making the West Asian region free of the WMD.

Inspite of Saudi denials, the three options present a convenient classification to assess the Saudi policy options.

Acquiring a Nuclear Capability

The Saudi follow-up on the first option is clouded in a plethora of unsubstantiated stories. The stories repeat themselves, quote the same unnamed sources, and validate one-another by a systematic self-referential technique.

The Israeli Major General Aharon Zeevi, a senior intelligence officer of the Israeli Defence Forces, suggested a month after the *Guardian* scoop that the Saudis had gone to Islamabad with the intention of buying Pakistani warheads, to be placed on Saudi land-based missiles.[35]

The US-based Defense and Foreign Affairs Daily went so far as to say that Pakistan would station nuclear weapons on Saudi territory. These weapons would be fitted to a new generation of Chinese-supplied long-range missiles with a reach of 4,000 to 5,000 kilometres. The *Jane's* speculated that the then Saudi Crown Prince Abdullah's visit to Moscow in late 2003 indicated an interest in arms trading with Russia and it also raised the possibility of Saudi Arabia buying an entire weapon rather than technology.[36]

Around the same time, the *Washington Times* revealed details of a secret agreement between Saudi Arabia and Pakistan granting Riyadh access to Pakistani nuclear technologies in exchange for cheap, steady supplies of Saudi crude.[37] Ilan Berman cited the story as a public confirmation that the House of Saud — despite all the talk of better relations between Tehran and Riyadh—had begun to actively contemplate the need for a strategic deterrent against Iran.[38]

A story in *New York Times* suggested that it was the generous Saudi funding that had resulted in a successful bomb production in Pakistan as well as its export of nuclear technology to countries like Libya, Iran, and North Korea.[39]

The trading in nuclear technology/hardware happens away from public gaze. Even within the top echelons of the government, very few are privy to the goings-on in this sanctum sanctorum. The Saudi nuclear dealings with Pakistan go back three decades and more. The sum total of that relationship will be understood only when enough details are known.

Alliance with a Nuclear Power

The second option does not need elaboration in view of the fact that there are written and unwritten agreements between Saudi Arabia and the US that would provide protection to the country in the eventuality of threats to its security. The nuclear threats from Iran, in particular, would invite swift and unsolicited intervention; if it ever came to that. The US contingency planning to deter and degrade Iranian advances in nuclear field may yet involve Saudi support.

GWMDFZ

In August 2004, the Gulf Research Centre in Dubai undertook a research project on "Gulf as a Weapons of Mass Destruction Free Zone". A Saudi national Abdulaziz Sager founded the GRC, as previously mentioned. It was made clear that the project would not be a Saudi proposal, but only a Track II initiative. In December, a meeting was held at the GRC to discuss the initiative. The delegates from the region as also the representatives of the UN, EU, and NATO were invited. Iran also sent a delegate. Several arms control experts participated in the meeting.[40] In May 2005, the GRC held a second meeting in Stockholm in collaboration with the Stockholm International Peace Research Institute (SIPRI). Iran participated at this meeting again.

The London-based *International Institute for Strategic Studies* held a conference in Bahrain in December 2004. A unified GCC, a prosperous Yemen, a stable Iraq, and a friendly Iran were on the wish list at this conference. Kamal Kharrazi, the Iranian foreign minister, participated and proposed a new "collective security project" based on independence and self-dependence. Predictably, a quid pro quo between The GWMDFZ and the Gulf Without External Presence failed.[41] The NATO held a conference in Doha a year later. Abdul Rahman Attiya, the GCC Secretary-General, speaking on the role that the NATO can play in the Gulf regional security, called on the NATO to exercise direct pressure to eliminate the WMD from the region. He said, "We do not want to be sandwiched by arms here and arms there."[42] Whether that cryptic sentence referred to the Israeli arsenal was left unsaid.

The 26th GCC Summit was held in Abu Dhabi a few days thereafter. It was preoccupied with the Iranian nuclear ambitions more than any other issue. Attiya said a deal could be brokered between the GCC and Iran, which would prompt the international community to press Israel to open its own sites for inspection.[43]

Amre Musa, the Arab League Secretary-General, stirred up a huge debate and an even greater embarrassment to the delegates by writing a letter requesting that the Summit should also consider the Israeli nuclear capability that posed a threat to all the Arabs. The letter was acknowledged. It was also discussed. But it was ridiculed, in all probabilities. The UAE foreign minister, Rashid Abdullah al-Nuaimi, announced in a press conference, "We appreciate Amre Musa's concern as an Egyptian citizen about the Israeli nuclear programme. In fact, we share that concern with him. However, talking about threats to Arab national security, Musa should have raised concerns about the Iranian programme."[44] Since the GCC states were in the proximity of Iran, rather than Israel, they were legitimately more concerned about the Iranian programme. The Arab League Secretary-General represents the entire Arab world; he speaks for the Arabs across the spectrum. To diminish his stature to that of a private Egyptian citizen was a deliberate and undeserved humiliation.

"It is upto Musa if he is not sharing with us that concern, but we concur with him on the Israeli programme. When the Secretary-General of the Arab League talks about threats posed to the region, he should take into consideration that the Arab security order also covers the six Gulf Arab countries," he concluded. In the concluding statement, the Summit called for co-operation between Iran and the IAEA on the operation of nuclear rectors; reiterated demand to make West Asia, including the Gulf region, free from the WMD.

The GRC Track II initiative graduated to a Track I official position of Saudi Arabia plus five more GCC states with this.

Two months thereafter the US Secretary of State Condoleeza Rice met the GCC foreign ministers in Abu Dhabi. The ministers expressed their fears and serious concerns with regard to the dangers of proliferation. The closing statement reaffirmed the necessity of keeping the Gulf free of the WMD.[45]

The GRC Track II initiative graduated to a Track I consolidated official position of the US and the GCC with this.

During the visit of French President Jacques Chirac to Saudi Arabia, the Saudi foreign minister reworded this position just a little. In a joint press conference with Chirac, he sought to convince the Iranians of "the soundness of the policy of having a Middle East including the Gulf free of WMD."[46]

The French, or the EU, response to the GWMDFZ is not yet in the public domain.

Conclusions

The Iranian nuclear issue has dominated the global agenda for the past few years. The question has largely been perceived as a stand-off between Iran and the United States. It is the states in the immediate neighbourhood of Iran, especially Saudi Arabia, which will be most seriously impacted in all possible scenarios in which the situation may evolve.

Iran and Saudi Arabia have both nourished nuclear ambitions and have sought to fulfil those ambitions. Muhammd Reza Shah Pahlavi signed a nuclear agreement with the US under the Atoms for Peace proposal in 1957. The Saudis were late and surreptitious arrivals on the scene. They have generated speculative stories on this issue; especially in the mid-1970s, late 1980s and early 2000s.

Interestingly, it was a defector/dissidents in each case, who blew the whistle on the clandestine programme of his/their respective country. Thus, in June 1991, the Iranian dissident movement Mojahedin-e Khalq Organisation (MKO) created a media blitz by identifying Iranian nuclear assets. In the Saudi case, it was Mohammad al-Khilevi, the Saudi defector who was the First Secretary in Saudi mission to UN till 1994. According to him, Riyadh has sought a bomb since 1975.

The Saudi response to Iran's nuclearisation can best be understood within the context of the bilateral relations between the two. The "Two Pillars" of the US military posture in the Gulf in the 1970s, the Islamic revolution at the end of the decade brought about a total transformation in their ties. The decade of 1990s did see a turn around; first due to the Iraqi attack on Kuwait that necessitated a friendly—or at least a neutral—Iran, and then due to the moderate foreign policy of President Muhammad Khatami.

Regional powers across the waters of the Gulf, their relations have never been devoid of suspicion and rivalry. Primacy in the Gulf affairs and leadership in the wider Muslim world are the two most contentious issues besides disputes over territory, charges of spying and planting bombs, disagreement on oil policies and several others. But the crucial point of discord is that the Saudis set a great store by their friendship with the US, whereas Iran has been a backlash state, a member of the axis-of-evil and much worse in the US strategic vocabulary.

The Iran issue has acquired a US-Iran dimension more than any other. The Saudis have, as a result, adopted a very cautious and nuanced policy in response to the proliferation in their neighbourhood.

The official Saudi pronouncements on the matter are unexceptionable: we will not join the nuclear race; Iran has assured us that it is not seeking nuclear weapons; there is no possibility of an Iranian attack on Saudi Arabia; the US is partly to blame as it is negotiating with North Korea, signing a nuclear peace agreement with India, and turning a blind eye to Israeli nuclear arsenal.

The unofficial statements from the analysts, journalists and others are very different: the Bushehr reactor on the Gulf is closer to the Arab states of the Gulf than to Tehran and an accident there would spell disaster; the old Soviet technology could result in a Chernobyl-type tragedy; Iran is seismically unstable and an earthquake would cause immense problems; the Iran-US confrontation would destabilise the geopolitics of the region even more.

The Saudis are reported to be working on a three-fold response to the Iranian development; acquiring a nuclear capability of their own, aligning with a nuclear power, and seeking an agreement for a nuclear-free region.

The proposal to declare West Asia as a nuclear-free zone is being discussed at the UN General Assembly since 1974. For the past two years, the Saudis have given it a clever makeover: The Gulf as a Weapons of Mass Destruction Free Zone (GWMDFZ). It has been presented in several formulations: Nuclear-free West Asia including the Gulf; Nuclear-free Gulf as a part of Nuclear-free West Asia; Nuclear-free Gulf to precede Nuclear-free West Asia; Nuclear-free Gulf to generate a momentum from the sub-regional level of the Gulf to the region-wide success. The proposal may, in the final analysis, simply be a substitute for the Nuclear-free West Asia. That would leave Israel out of its purview and focus exclusively on Iran.

References

1. "The Saudi Syndrome", *New York Times*, 1 January 2005. Robert Lacey, *The Kingdom: Arabia and the House of Saud* (Harcourt, Brace, Jovanovich, New York, 1981) pp. 455-56. p. 166.
2. Rachel Bronson, "The US-Saudi Love Affair Predates Bush," *Los Angeles Times* (9 July, 2004) Gerald Posner, *Secrets of the Kingdom: The Inside Story of the Saudi-US Connection* (Random House, New York, 2005) p. 116.
3. HRH Khaled bin Sultan, *Desert Warrior: A Personal View of the Gulf War by the Joint Forces Commander* (Lancer Publishers and Distributors, New Delhi, 1997) p. 145.
4. S. Bhatia, *Nuclear Rivals in the Middle East*, (Routledge International, London, 1988). Quoted in Alan George, "Saudi Arabia: Riyadh's Nuclear Route", *South* (London) May 1988, pp. 41-42.
5. *National Liberation Army Journal* (November 1991) p. 63. Quoted in Nader Entessar, "Realpolitik and Transformation of Iran's Foreign Policy: Coping with the 'Iran Syndrome' in Hamid Zangeneh, ed., *Islam, Iran, and World Stability* (Macmillan, Houndmills, 1994) p. 159.
6. "Saudi Arabia: Country Profile" *www.fas.org/asmp/profiles/saudi_arabia.htm*) Accessed 30 January, 2006.
7. Saudi Arabia Special Weapons *www.globalsecurity.org/wmd/world/saudi/index.html* Accessed 30 January, 2006.
8. *Tehran Times*, 3 June, 1992.
9. *Reuters*, 26 April, 2000.
10. *Reuters*, 19 April, 2001.
11. *AFP*, 8 March, 2003.
12. *AFP*, 3 May, 2000.
13. *IRNA*, 17 January, 2001.
14. *Associated Press*, 1 January, 2001.
15. *IRNA*, 8 June, 2003.
16. Colonel Abdulaziz bin Khalid Alsudairy, "Possible Defense Roles for the Arabian Gulf Co-operation Council", in *International Essays by the International Fellows of the National Defense University* (The National Defense University Press, Washington DC, 1986) p. 166.
17. Champion Daryl, *The Paradoxical Kingdom: Saudi Arabia and the Momentum of Reform* (Hurst and Company, London, 2003), p. 237, ff.
18. *AFP*, 18 April, 2001.
19. *AFP*, 13 May, 2000, *Reuters*, 6 June, 2000.
20. Hani al-Sayegh, the Shiite Saudi arrested in Canada and extradited to the US in connection with the 1996 Khobar bombing, reportedly admitted to having been a member of Saudi Hizbullah. Although other Saudi nationals indicted by the US in June 2001 were allegedly members of Saudi Hizbullah, the Saudi government has denied that such an organisation exists. Champion, n. 17, p. 256. ff.

21. Rasha Saad, "End of the Honeymoon?', *Al-Ahram* (Cairo), Issue 721, 16-22 December, 2004.
22. The Saudis were comfortable in dealing with President Khatami. The latter's reluctance to contest for a second term made them anxious. In a meeting with Iranian Commerce Minister Mohammad Shariatmadari, the Saudi Crown Prince Abdullah is reported to have voiced concern as to whether Khatami would run in a presidential election in June. Shariatmadari "tried to ease his concerns and assured him that Khatami would run for a second term." (*Tehran Times*, quoted in Reuters, 8 February, 2001).
23. *Washington Times*, 10 January, 2005.
24. *http://english.pravda.ru/opinion/columnists/02-02-2006/75036-iran-0* Accessed on 28 March, 2006.
25. *Daily Star*, (Beirut) 10 February, 2006.
26. *www.mofa.gov.sa/Detail.asp?InSectionID=4166&InNews*Item ID=45623 Accessed on 6 March, 2006.
27. *http://news.bbc.co.uk/2/hi/middle_east/4615832.stml* 16 January, 2006 Accessed 27 March, 2006.
28. n. 24.
29. Abdulaziz Sager, Chairman Gulf Research Centre, "For Saudi Arabia and Iran, Searching for Security is a Priority" *Daily Star*, 13 June, 2005
30. (*www.signonsandiego.com/news/world//20060322-0952-arabs-worriedaboutiran.html*).
31. Tariq Al-Homayed, "Iran...'I cry out in the Gulf,' " *Asharq Alawsat*, 13 April, 2006.
    http://aawsat.com/english/news.asp?section=2&id=4523 *Quoted in Emile El-Hokayem and Matteo Legrenzi, "The Arab Gulf States in the Shadow Of the Iranian Nuclear Challenge,"* http://www.stimson.org/swa/pdf/StimsonIranGCCWorkingPaper.pdf *Accessed 26 May, 2006.*
32. Michael Slackman, "Iran the Great Unifier? The Arab World Is Wary", *New York Times*, 5 February, 2006.
33. n. 30.
34. Ewen MacAskill and Ian Traynor, "Saudis Consider Nuclear Bombs," *Guardian Unlimited Online Edition*, 18 September, 2003.
35. David Sands, "Israeli General Says Saudis Seek to Buy Pak Nukes," *Washington Times*, 23 October, 2003. Quoted in Akaki Dwali, "Will Saudi Arabia Acquire Nuclear Weapons?" *www.nti.org/e-research/e3-4oa.html.*
36. Stephen Blank, "Saudi Arabia's Nuclear Gambit" www.atimes.com/atimes/Middle_East/EK07Ak01.html *7 November, 2003.*
37. Arnaud de Borchgrave, "Pakistan, Saudi Arabia in Secret Nuke Pact," *Washington Times*, 22 October, 2003.
38. Ilan Berman, *Tehran Rising: Iran's Challenge to the United States* (Rowman and Littlefield Publishers, Lanham, 2005), p. 51.
39. "The Saudi Syndrome", *New York Times*, 1 January, 2005.
40. Christian Koch, "Gulf Regional Security is Embryonic, but Growing", *Daily Star*, 7 January, 2005.

41. *Ibid*. Roula Khalaf, "Iranian Nuclear Ambitions Worry Gulf Arab States", *Financial Times* (London), 18 December, 2004.
42. *AFP*, 3 December, 2005.
43. *Daily Star*, 19 December, 2005.
44. http://wam.org.ae Accessed 21 December, 2005.
45. AFP, 25 February, 2006. Rasha Saad, "Neighbourly Diplomacy," *Al Ahram Weekly*, Issue 784, 2-8 March, 2006.
46. n. 25.

6

Saudi Arabia and the US

Contextualizing an Uneasy Relationship in the Post-11 September Phase

BANSIDHAR PRADHAN

The year 1945 may well be regarded as a landmark in the history of Saudi-US relationship. In that year, US President Franklin D. Roosevelt invited King Ibn Saud, the founder of modern day Saudi Arabia, to meet him for the first time on board the USS *Quincy* on Great Bitter Lake in the Suez Canal. This first meeting laid the foundation for a strong and durable alliance between an emerging Super Power and an oil giant.[1] It was based on a simple understanding: oil for security. Saudi Arabia, endowed with almost 25 per cent of the world's known oil reserves, has been the world's leading producer and exporter, while the US has been the world's largest oil consumer and importer.[2] Thus, Saudi Arabia became the most reliable source of energy for the US and the larger Western industrial economies and the US in turn ensured the security of the al-Saud regime in the kingdom from potential enemies. This understanding proved both "workable and durable" for more than five decades.[3] Such a stable *energy for security partnership* came under question in the aftermath of the 11 September terrorist attacks on the US mainland. This resulted in an uneasy relationship between what could be described as the two most dependable and strong allies in the history of post-Second World War international relations. What was the context? What were the issues that caused uneasiness in Saudi-US relations? What have been the responses of both the countries towards each other, both at the levels of people's perception and policy measures? What are the challenges that confront them? Will there be a reworking of the terms of Saudi-US partnership? These are some of the questions which the present essay attempts to address.

Before contextualizing the uneasy Saudi-US relations in the post-11 September phase, one needs to take a brief look at the nature of the strong relationship that bounded these two nations before that decisive event.

During his first meeting with the American President, King Ibn Saud "asked FDR for friendship" which was assured unhesitatingly.[4] This assurance was reaffirmed with remarkable continuity by succeeding American Presidents resulting in a robust Saudi-US alliance in the following decades.[5] Both the countries valued their mutually advantageous relationship greatly and nurtured it persistently without any major disagreement despite the huge differences that existed between Saudi Arabia and the US at the systemic level. Unlike other countries in the region, the Saudi oil "was entirely developed" by US companies. Ibn Saud granted the first concession to Standard Oil of California in 1933 leading to the commercial production of Saudi oil in 1938.[6] In 1944, the California Standard-Texaco Operation in Saudi Arabia was rechristened as the Arabian-American Oil Company (ARAMCO).[7] Before its nationalization by the Saudi government in the mid 1970s, ARAMCO was the "largest single American investment in any foreign country".[8] Saudi Arabia played a key role in the energy security of the US and other Western industrial economies by being a regular supplier of oil for the past five decades, except for a brief period during the 1973 Arab-Israel war. It was for the first time that Saudi Arabia sought to use oil as a political weapon in 1973 against the US and the West at large to underline its unhappiness over American support to Israel. The embargo, which lasted only for few months, exposed the US vulnerability even though it did not rupture Saudi-US relationship, thanks to the astute diplomacy of the then Secretary of State, Henry Kissinger.[9] Further, Saudi Arabia's swing production from time to time played a crucial role in stabilizing the world oil market; one need not overemphasize the linkage between stability in oil prices and the world economy at large, not to talk about only economies of the US and its allies. Saudi Arabia is the only producer which has the capacity to produce more when the demand and price are too high and less at a time of glut in the oil market. The "dramatic rise" in Saudi oil exports in the early 1990s to compensate the shortage in the oil market due to the disruption of Iraqi and Kuwait oil exports proved the point graphically. The US import of Saudi oil constituted almost 14 per cent of its total import in 2000. [10]

The US, on its part, remained committed to the security of the al-Saud regime by protecting it from potential threats. This was done through the supply of sophisticated, expensive weaponry to the kingdom from time to time like the AWACS surveillance planes, ultra-sophisticated jets, helicopters, bombers, etc. In addition, US military experts were stationed in the kingdom to train Saudi personnel in manning the imported weaponry.[11] In fact, in the wake of Saddam Hussein's invasion of Kuwait and his subsequent threats to the Saudi ruling family, American troops were stationed in the kingdom. That was a brilliant testimony to US commitment to protect the Saudi regime from potential external threat. The presence of US troops in Saudi Arabia became quite a controversial issue within the country as well as in the larger Islamic world, as we would see later. Over the years, the Saudis emerged as the biggest buyers of US arms.[12] Between 1989-2000, for instance, Saudi Arabia bought US arms worth $45 billion. In that sense, Saudi Arabia and the US had a "symbiotic" relationship, "each feeding and nourishing the other for oil and arms".[13] Further, the Saudi investment in the US ran into billions of dollars, making the kingdom one of the major US creditors.[14] In the larger context, each country enjoyed considerable strategic importance in the other's foreign policy calculations in the Cold War framework.

The 11 September terrorist attacks came as a great shock to the Americans. In what could be termed as the greatest irony in recent history, the mightiest power on earth came under attack by few individuals belonging to a hitherto little known non-State actor, al Qaeda. As is well known, the attacks killed approximately three thousand people, a majority being Americans. From the viewpoint of Saudi-US relationship, what complicated the matter further was the fact that fifteen of the nineteen hijackers were Saudi citizens and Osama bin Laden, the main architect of the attacks, was a Saudi by birth and upbringing. Apart from the enormity of the human tragedy, the involvement of Saudis caused shock and utter disbelief in the US and the West at large. One probably would not have been that surprised had it been the handiwork of some Iranians or Syrians or even by men belonging to the Hamas or Hizboolah. What was more important was that Saudi "private money was used to finance" the attacks.[15] The familiar refrain became: how could the Saudis do it against the US? As one commentator pointed out, "Saudi terrorists have killed more Americans than all those murdered by Iranians, Syrians, Libyans, and Iraqis put together".[16] This psychological dimension assumes crucial importance while contextualizing the Saudi-US relationship in the post-11 September phase. Naturally, therefore, relationship with Saudi Arabia came under severe public scrutiny in the US.

The intense debate about the rationality behind continuing a strong alliance with Saudi Arabia took many forms and operated at various levels. The most virulent form manifested itself in the US media and opinion-making circles. One witnessed a "wave of Saudi-bashing" in the US.[17] Saudi Arabia became the subject of heavy criticism by influential think tanks, most prominently the Rand Corporation and the Council on Foreign Relations. A Rand Corporation briefing in July 2002, for instance, stated that the Saudis "are active at every level of the terror chain, from planners to financiers, from cadre to foot-soldier, from ideologist to cheerleader". It described Saudi Arabia as "the kernel of evil, the prime mover, the most dangerous opponent" in the West Asian region.[18] Few months later, an Independent Task Force of the Council on Foreign Relations came out with a report on "*Terrorist Financing*". The report was unsparing in its criticism of Saudi Arabia for providing continuous financial support to al Qaeda. While underlining the "financially robust" nature of al Qaeda, the report said that "it is worth stating clearly and unambiguously what official US government spokespersons have not: For years, individuals and charities based in Saudi Arabia have been the most important source of funds for al Qaeda; and for years Saudi officials have turned a blind eye to this problem". The Task Force made it very clear that as long as "al-Qaeda retains access to a viable financial network, it remains a lethal threat to the United States."[19] In the larger context, Saudi Arabia was accused of providing funds to *madrassas* to "encourage radical anti-Americanism".[20] Further, members of the Congress also criticized Saudi complicity in the terrorist network. Such open criticism of Saudi Arabia by the American civil society and the law makers brought Saudi-US relationship under strain, as never before. The whole debate needs to be seen in the context of two issues that underpinned Saudi-US ties in the post-11 September phase.

War on Terror

The US response to the attacks was swift and decisive in the form of the so-called "war on terror". This US-led war has been a war without end and without any bounds having serious implications for the international system as a whole and for the conduct of bilateral relations between Saudi Arabia and the US in particular.

The Saudi government has been subjected to constant criticism and accusation for not providing enough cooperation to the US in its war on terror. Once again, the US media and some members in the Congress charged that wealthy Saudis and even some members in the royal family "funnel money to terrorist organizations through Islamic charities." The controversy surrounding Princess Haifa al-Faisal—wife of Saudi Ambassador to the US, Prince Bandar bin Sultan—may be cited as an example in this context. In late 2002, it was suspected that the money which Princess Haifa donated to a Saudi family regularly for four years on medical grounds might have ultimately reached two of the alleged 11 September hijackers. Indeed, the Federal Bureau of Investigation (FBI) had to investigate whether part of the donation to the family of Usama Bassnan passed on to one of Bassnan's friends, Umar al-Bayuni, who in turn sought to help the hijackers in 2000. Saudi officials admitted that Princess Haifa donated to the Bassnan family $15,000 in 1998, followed by a regular monthly payment of $2,000. However, they insisted that those donations were nothing new and formed part of the kingdom's policy of providing charity to needy Saudis. Even though, the FBI found no evidence to link Princess Haifa's donations to terrorists, the very investigation itself caused much uneasiness in Saudi-US relations.[21] It provided an opportunity to score a point to those sections in the media world as well as in the Congress who were critical of the Bush administration's policy dealing with terrorist financing. The *Washington Post* sought to sensationalize the issue by carrying a report which suggested that the US National Security Council had a plan to pressurize Saudi Arabia to initiate action against terrorist financiers within three months or face "unilateral US action". According to the plan, Saudi Arabia was expected to take action against those Saudi citizens and business groups which, in the US view, were financing al Qaeda, even without any concrete evidence. The White House ultimately denied the existence of such a plan.[22] As regards Congressmen, Democratic Senator Joseph Lieberman accused the FBI and other branches of the government of trying to "almost defend the Saudis, or not be as aggressive as they should be".[23] Charles Schumer, another Democratic Senator, "questioned whether the FBI had adequately investigated Saudi links" to the 11 September attacks.[24] Even Republican Senator Mitch McConnell made a scathing comment on Saudi Arabia's role in financing terrorist activities. "We, in some ways, have had a good relationship with them (Saudi Arabia) over the years, and in other ways, it appears that they're funding our enemies".[25]

Even though very few believed that the Saudi royal family members donated funds to terrorist outfits knowingly, the issue of financial linkages between Islamic charities and terrorist organizations came under critical scrutiny. Commenting on the ubiquitous relationship between charities and terrorist financing, the Council on Foreign Relations' report commented: "Today al-Qaeda continues to raise funds from both direct solicitations of wealthy supporters and through retail charities. Some whose donations go to al-Qaeda know fully well the terrorist purposes to which their money will be put. In other cases, donors believe their money will help fund legitimate humanitarian efforts, but the money is nonetheless diverted to al-Qaeda."[26] The Saudi government was criticized for not being vigilant and strict enough to prevent money laundering involved in the process. In fact, the US government publicly identified the Saudi-based al-Haramain organization as one of many charities involved in transferring funds to terrorists.[27]

Therefore, the very wisdom of relying on Saudi Arabia as a partner in the war on terrorism is being questioned. This questioning is based on the premise that Saudi Arabia remains the principal source of funding for al-Qaeda and as long as financial resources are available to Osama's network, there is little chance of effectively controlling its terrorist operations across the world in general and the US in particular. The sub-text here is that within Saudi Arabia one probably can still find many sympathizers and supporters of al-Qaeda. This brings us to the second issue.

Democracy Promotion and Political Reforms

Democracy promotion has emerged as one of the key components of US policy towards the Arab-Islamic world in the post-11 September phase. The policy as such is not something very new to the Bush administration in view of the fact that US foreign policy has always "contained a powerful idealist element" and democracy promotion "abroad has been one of its goals, in one way or another".[28] But the manner in which it is being projected as a major anti-terror measure needs to be underlined. This is specially so with regard to the West Asian region which, from an American perspective, has become a fertile ground for the so-called "Islamic fundamentalist terrorism". The underlying assumption has been that it is bad governance and lack of democracy that create favourable conditions for the recruitment of future terrorists.

There are both "ideological and practical reasons" for this. Promotion of democracy constituted one of the basic pillars of the neo-conservative world-view that guided the foreign policy of the Bush administration so forcefully. There has been a policy consensus within the Bush administration that "fostering democracy" in the West Asian region would "drain the pool from which terrorist organization draw recruits in their global struggle against the US". Further, it would also help resolve disputes in the region peacefully as "democracies do not go to war with one another".[29] But the very assumption that democracies do not promote terrorism is open to question. It may not be always true that the "more democratic a country becomes, the less likely it is to produce terrorists and terrorist groups."[30] In fact, political scientists William Eubank and Leonard Weinberg have conducted a study of terrorist events in the 1980s and have found that most terrorist attacks have taken place in democracies and that mostly both the victims and perpetrators belong to democratic countries.[31] Further, the belief in the larger Arab-Islamic world in general and the Gulf region in particular is that Osama launched the attacks against the US not because he disliked the American values like democracy, rule of law, freedom, etc., but because he was strongly opposed to the US domination of the region, most specifically the presence of US troops in Saudi Arabia—that is home to Islam's two holiest places—and the uncritical American support to Israel vis-à-vis the Palestinians.

While there is a continuing debate within the US in opinion and policy making circles about the relationship between "Democracy and Terrorism", the Bush administration, on its part, has adopted a dual policy with regard to democracy promotion in the West Asian region. In respect of the so-called "rogue states" or the "axis of evil" like Iraq, the US has relied upon a hard, aggressive, militaristic policy to promote democracy. The same may become the case with Syria and Iran in the future. Such cases are being dealt usually by the White House and Defense Department. In the case of friendly, pro-US and long-time allies such as the regimes in Saudi Arabia, Egypt, Bahrain, Qatar, Kuwait, etc. a conciliatory and gradualist approach has been preferred under the stewardship of the State Department. In December 2002, for instance, Secretary of State Colin Powell unveiled the "Middle East Partnership Initiative" (MEPI) which envisaged that the process of democratization would be slow and "incremental" which should be "encouraged" by the US through supporting economic development, education and civil society organizations. Powel's initiative laid thrust on four crucial areas: economic, political, educational and women's rights. These were to be developed through a variety of country-specific and region-wide projects.[32] In June 2004, a second initiative to promote democracy was launched at the G-8 Summit in Atlanta, Georgia. Even though it was not exclusively an American project, the US was the main driving force behind it. The initiative was called Broader Middle East and North Africa Partnership Initiative (BMENAPI) and aimed at making democracy promotion "a cooperative enterprise between G8 and Middle Eastern governments". Like the first one, the second initiative also sought to "encourage reform" in the economic, political, social and cultural fields[33].

Even a gradualist approach has created a latent irritant in Saudi-US relations. The issue of political reforms is a very sensitive one as far as Saudi Arabia is concerned. It may work like a double-edged weapon and threaten the interests of both the US as well as the al-Saud family. This will become evident if one takes a brief look at the Saudi system of governance, the deepening domestic crisis and the urge for political reforms by certain segments of the Saudi society in recent years.

Saudi Arabia has been regarded as the most conservative of Gulf Cooperation Council (GCC) states and is more "overtly committed" to the principles of Sharia law than many of its neighbours. The principles of democratic governance in terms of full people's participation in decision-making process, accountability of the rulers to the ruled, periodical elections, etc. do not operate in the kingdom as state authority is concentrated in the al-Saud family. The al-Sauds' claim to rule derives from a convergence of "religious legitimacy and military might" that dated back to the 1744 pact between Muhammad ibn Abd al-Wahhab and Muhammad ibn Saud and the military conquests in the 1920s and 1930s leading to the establishment of modern day Saudi Arabia. In that sense, the al-Saud rule has been an "uneasy symbiosis" with the Muslim clergy, represented largely by the descendents of al-Wahhab.[34] For a reasonably long period, the al-Sauds ruled the kingdom with a combination of absolute authority, the imposition of the Wahhabi brand of faith and an elaborate network of socio-economic benefits to its citizens, thanks to the oil boom of the 1970s. The first major sign of challenge to the rule of the al-Saud family emerged when Juhaiman al-Utaibi seized the grand mosque in Mecca in 1979 in a bid to topple the ruling family.[35] Even though the attempt was foiled with brutal force and al-Utaibi did not enjoy much popular support, the incident "exposed the vulnerability of regime".[36] With the decline in oil revenue—which reduced the state's capability to attend to the huge network of welfare services—and the deepening socio-economic crisis, the dissent became more pronounced and broad-based in the subsequent years.

Population growth and employment are the most important socio-economic concerns. At least 65 per cent of the Saudi population is below the age of 25 and the level of frustration among the youngsters appears to be quite high. Around 30 per cent of Saudi men and 95 per cent of women are unemployed.[37] In one instance, around 40,000 young unemployed Saudis competed for 5 days for 80 new openings in the Ministry of Finance.[38] The rate of unemployment is somewhat linked to the Saudi educational system. Religious education constitutes the foundation of the country's educational system and it is emphasized at all levels. As a result majority of Saudi university graduates "end up more qualified to analyze holy texts" rather than well-trained professionals to take up productive jobs befitting a modern world—like engineers, doctors and information technology experts. This has led to a peculiar situation wherein Saudi Arabia has to depend more on expatriate workers; almost two-thirds of the work force is foreign.[39] The paradoxical situation of huge unemployment and excessive dependence on foreign workers has led to a Saudi intellectual, Askar Enazy, to comment: "We are the only country in the world that imports the unemployed from other countries in order to swell the ranks of the unemployed among its own people."[40] True, to improve the situation and provide employment opportunities to Saudi citizens, the authorities have undertaken the project of "Saudinization" (*Sa'wada*) whereby more and more jobs are offered to Saudis. But this programme has not succeeded much because many Saudis, particularly young males, do not prefer to take up non-white or menial jobs.[41] Further, contrary to common perception, Saudi Arabia, which should be the richest country in the Gulf, "is now far worse off than many of its neighbours". Therefore, the population "overall has become poorer".[42] Yet another concern for the Saudi planners is the population growth rate which remains more than three per cent annually, among the highest in the world.[43]

There is also the problem of social cohesion which remains very tenuous. The people of the southern mountainous region of Asir do not feel quite integrated to the Saudi mainstream; some Asiris believe that they have not benefited from the oil wealth compared to those in the central heartland of the al-Saud, the Najd. It needs to be remembered that Asir, from which ten of the hijackers came "remains a more independent and hostile terrain at the periphery both politically and geographically." Another five hijackers came from the Hejaz, to which Osama also belongs. It is interesting to note that Osama always asserts his Hejaz identity, deliberately avoiding any reference to Saudi Arabia.[44]

This naturally raises a big question: "Are Asiris and Hejazis more receptive to Bin Laden's ideas and if so how conscious are they of their regional and cultural distinctiveness?"[45] A related question can be asked: Are these the potential factors for the destabilization of Saudi Arabia?

The above questions assume importance in view of the increasing violence by Islamic extremists and the kingdom's closed political system. Since 11 September, Saudi reformers, both Islamists and liberals, have been arguing that the lack of "legitimate channels for dissent" compel the aggrieved and agitated sections of the Saudi society to see violence "as the only viable means for bringing about change". Further, since 11 September, many Saudi intellectuals have gained enough courage to assert that the tendency towards religious extremism is, to a great extent, "re-inforced by the predominant Wahhabi religious discourse which espouses a literalist and purist interpretation of Islam, rejecting all difference and judging" everything purely in terms of "belief and unbelief".[46] Some critics have even gone to the extent of arguing that the teachings of Wahhabism have "bred religious extremism and, probably, terrorism on a large scale".[47] In that sense, political extremism is somewhat built into the Saudi religious education. It is interesting to note that the contents of official text books is "heavily influenced" by the Wahhabi ideology.[48] Further, more than 40 per cent of those enrolled in higher education opt for Islamic studies, whereas only 18 per cent prefer science, maths and engineering.[49]

These liberal and reformist trends have become a matter of great concern for the Saudi rulers in view of the fact that bin Laden still remains popular in Saudi Arabia "not for his crimes, but because of the population's reflexive anti-Americanism". He is considered a "hero" for having challenged the mightiest power on earth by targeting two key symbols of its power.[50] In any case, 11 September and the subsequent attacks on Afghanistan and Iraq have generated an intense, rather "angry", debate among all Saudis, liberal, conservative or radical Islamists.[51] Sympathy for Osama is mostly based on a rejection of US dominance in the region and its support for Israel. In other words, many Saudis accept the message of bin Laden, though they may not necessarily agree with his methods. A secret survey by a Saudi intelligence in mid-October 2001, for instance, have found that 95 per cent of educated Saudis in the age group of 25-41 supported the cause espoused by bin Laden.[52] Another source also points out that support for Osama is prevalent throughout Saudi society "from the Pakistani guards at the residential complexes to young Saudis of the upper middle classes", who find "common cause with al-Qaeda's anti-Western stance". In fact thousands of al Qaeda "sleeper cells" have been found in the kingdom.[53] In the larger context, Osama has improved his stature in the Arab streets substantially subsequent to the 11 September attacks, thanks to the inherently undemocratic nature of most of the regimes in the region and their open identification with dependence on the West in general and the US in particular.[54]

Further, the continuing instability in Iraq has its own impact on many Saudis who view the Sunni armed groups as being engaged in a "legitimate" struggle "against infidel occupiers". It is reported that several hundred Saudi youngsters crossed over to Iraq to join the ranks of those fighting against US occupation.[55] Given such a complex and volatile domestic situation the talk of democracy promotion by the US, argue the Saudi rulers, may lead to a situation which could be harmful to the interests of both the sides.

Realizing the risks involved in over-emphasizing the agenda of democracy promotion in Saudi Arabia, the Bush administration has been maintaining a very low-key position in this regard. One example may illustrate the point. In March 2004, three liberal reformers were arrested for advocating a constitutional monarchy, parliamentary elections and an independent judiciary.[56] In April 2005, Crown Prince Abdullah visited the US and met President Bush in Texas. During Abdullah's visit, the New York-based Human Rights Watch urged Bush to persuade the Crown Prince to release the three men and drop all the charges against them. The White House sources did not confirm whether President Bush raised the issue in his meeting with Abdullah. Instead, the US officials were very eager to report that the President "urged" the Crown Prince to "increase oil production" and "praised" Saudi Arabia's "support for the war on terror". When asked pointedly about the subject, National Security Adviser Stephen Hadley stated: "There was a general discussion about the issue of reform in these various conversations. I am not going to get into specifics". All three reformers received prison sentences—ranging from seven to nine years—after Abdullah's return from the US.[57] The three were convicted of "stirring up sedition and disobeying the ruler". The panel of three judges also found them guilty of criticizing the government, its policies and institutions, the judiciary and its official ideology—Wahhabism.[58] The point to be noted here is that the reformers in Saudi Arabia probably cannot rely much on the US support, notwithstanding the rhetoric of democracy promotion by the Bush administration. In fact, the Bush administration has been subjected to strong criticism by the US media for being soft on democratic reforms with regard to pro-American Arab regimes, particularly Saudi Arabia.

Hence it is a paradoxical situation which both the Bush administration and the al-Saud family are confronted with in the aftermath of 11 September attacks.

The Saudi Response and Dilemma

The Saudis strongly resent the US skepticism about their country's determination to fight terrorism. Both the Saudi rulers as well as the people are greatly shocked, even irritated, by the strong accusations leveled against them by the US media and some members of the Congress. While responding to the accusations, the Saudi rulers have engaged themselves in a delicate balancing act. On the one hand, Saudi Arabia does not want to be seen as too closely associated with the US war on terror. On the other hand, the al-Saud family also does not want to create an impression in the West, the US in particular, that it is becoming an obstacle in the fight against terrorism, specifically against Osama bin Laden and his al-Qaeda network. This has been done through a combination of specific actions and diplomacy. To what extent the Saudi rulers have succeeded in this exercise is a debatable point.

First, the Saudis argue that the country has a large contingent of expatriate workers who send money to their respective countries every year. Further, Saudi citizens themselves keep much of their money outside the country, generally in the West and most particularly in the US.[59] Therefore, there is a huge outflow of money—running into billions of dollars—from the kingdom every year and it is difficult to ensure fully that "no money from the country finds its way to al-Qaeda and other terrorist organizations." Moreover, if the Saudi money goes in the wrong direction it is only after it "leaves the kingdom and passes through European and American banks."[60] Second, it is also argued that it is just impossible to impose a ban on charities as *Zakat* constitutes one of the five pillars of Islam.[61] Reacting to the criticism of Saudi Arabia for not responding fully to the US requests to freeze the bank accounts of those individuals and institutions which, the Bush administration alleges, are funding terrorism, Foreign Minister Prince Saud al Faisal once defended the kingdom's "cautious approach" on the issue of bank accounts: "I do not think the intent was to make a list that would be frozen without proof... One must be careful not to damage charitable institutions unjustly".[62] Third, as regards money laundering, the Saudis assert that they have never been lax. In fact, in its website the Saudi Embassy in Washington has posted a list of measures adopted by the government to check money laundering since 11 September. These measures include auditing of all charitable groups to ensure that "there are no links to suspected groups", forming new guidelines and regulations to make sure that "terrorist organizations" do not take "advantage" of various charitable groups in the future, etc.[63] In addition, the Saudi authorities have been claiming that there has been a crack-down on those having suspected links with or even being sympathetic to Osama from time to time.[64] Apart from the response at these specific levels, in general terms the Saudis argue that investigations of both finance and security "must happen within the Saudi system and tradition, and not in response to what is seen as American arrogance and bullying."[65] Further, the Saudi people are agitated over the law suit which the families of 600 people, killed in the 11 September attacks, have filed against Saudi Arabian banks and charities and members of the royal family "accusing them of financially sponsoring" Osama and his terrorist network, al Qaeda.[66] Yet another source of annoyance is the new "procedures imposed" by the State and Justice departments to keep an eye on the visitors to the US from the Arab-Islamic world, including Saudi Arabia.[67] For many Saudis, these steps are not only unnecessary but even unjust aimed at harassing and humiliating them for something in which they had no role at all.

At the level of diplomacy, the Saudi rulers adopted a multi-pronged strategy to blunt the US criticism against the regime and the people. At one level, the al-Saud family launched a massive public relations campaign to improve the image of the kingdom, its religion, its people, its achievements, etc. Crown Prince Abdullah himself took the lead strongly criticizing the Western media for projecting a negative image about Saudi Arabia. He accused major Western newspapers of "waging a smear campaign against Islam, Arabs and Muslims, and 'Saudis in particular'." Abdullah also took strong exception to the attempt by Western media to denigrate the *Qur'an*.[68] The royal family spent millions on advertisements in newspapers and magazines "extolling the achievements and virtues" of the kingdom. Princes, fluent in the languages of the West, defended their country's position and "reassured friends and allies that all was well" in the kingdom.[69]

At another level, the Saudi rulers tried to highlight the fault lines of the US war on terror and thereby underlining their policy differences with their American counterparts, at least in operational aspects. This also related to other aspects of US foreign policy with regard to the West Asian region. For instance, one young prince, while criticizing the unilateralist approach adopted by the US, commented:

> The arrogance of the US is unacceptable. President Bush says that anyone who does not fully support the US war plans is with the terrorists. In other words, we are being asked to board a train without being told where it is going, what route it will follow, or how long the journey will take. And we are told not to ask questions, which are considered inappropriate.[70]

Further, during the US bombing of Afghanistan, Saudi Arabia did not support the military operations on the ground that they were killing innocent civilians, instead of concentrating on al-Qaeda hideouts. But it maintained its "verbal support for the anti-terrorism campaign". Justifying such a stand Prince Naif bin Abd al-Aziz, the Saudi Interior Minister, asserted: "No, the kingdom is not backing the strikes in the real sense of the word. The kingdom has a position on the anti-terror campaign."[71]

Yet another dimension of the Saudi diplomacy in the post-11 September phase related to the Palestinian issue. By focusing on the Israel-Palestine conflict, the Saudi rulers sought to change the very basis of the debate over the causes behind the growth of extremism and anti-Americanism in the region. It was argued that anti-Americanism among the Saudis grew not out of the country's religious education system but out of the US policy towards the Israel-Palestine conflict. Many in the kingdom perceived that the continued suffering of the Palestinians was a result of the blind US support to Israel. Such a perception led to the "erosion of public support for the US in Saudi Arabia", specially during the second *intifada.*[72] Crown Prince Abdullah had a clear understanding of the people's perception when he had urged President Bush to persuade Israel to stop atrocities against the Palestinians and enter into negotiations with them, just a month before the 11 September attacks. Given such a context, Abdullah sought to utilize the Palestine issue as a convenient weapon to use against the critics of the Saudi regime in the US. Subsequent to the 11 September attacks he became increasingly critical and more outspoken against the US on the issue. This became evident from his comments in the *New York Times* and *Washington Post* in January 2002. In view of the situation in the occupied territories of West Bank and Gaza, Abdullah asserted, it was becoming difficult for him to "defend America".[73] Then in mid-February, he somewhat surprised many, specially in the West, by announcing his bold peace initiative to resolve the Israel-Palestine conflict. The Crown Prince announced his plan during a dinner meeting with Thomas Friedman, the *New York Times* foreign affairs columnist, in Riyadh. Based on a simple formulation—"full withdrawal for full peace"—the Abdullah plan offered full Arab recognition and normalization of relations with Israel in exchange for full Israeli withdrawal from all Arab territories it occupied in the 1967 war. It was the most important political initiative since the outbreak of the second *intifada* in September 2000. It also provided the most viable and feasible compromise solution between two maximalist positions: the concept of Greater Israel, as propounded by the Israeli Right, and the Hamas' dream of regaining the historic Palestine. One is not overemphasizing here the Saudi sincerity in resolving the conflict. But the fact remained that the Abdullah plan contained many positive and forward looking features which was greatly appreciated in the Arab world. This became evident from its unanimous endorsement by the 22-member Arab League which met in Beirut in March 2002.[74] In that sense, Abdullah, at least to some extent, succeeded in capturing the imagination of the disenchanted Arab youth and projecting the US and Israel in bad light. In fact, it was believed in some circles that by choosing Friedman, the Crown Prince was trying to use "him as a major Jewish lobby player to send a message to the US media to lay off their anti-Saudi campaign". At home, the Saudi rulers thought that the Abdullah plan might reduce the appeal of Osama who, of late, was championing the Palestinian cause.[75]

As regards the Osama factor and the resilience of al-Qaeda, the Saudi rulers express deep anguish over the US attitude towards the kingdom after 11 September. After all, as Prince Nayef has argued with indignation, al-Qaeda poses more threat to the kingdom than to the US. He has pointed out that the US will "never suffer anything more than physical attacks" which "however devastating and costly they may be" will not pose a systemic threat to the US. "For US, on the other hand", he argues, "the threat is also—and especially—ideological and political, since bin Laden accuses the royal family of betraying Islam and being an accomplice of the United States."[76] The Saudi people think that it is unfair to put the entire blame on their country for what Osama did to the US. How can the Americans, they wonder, forget their own responsibility in the emergence of the al-Qaeda phenomenon and in the upgradation of bin Laden from a *mujahideen* to a terrorist? What about the US role in supporting the Taliban which was the main supporter and protector of bin Laden and his network. Three countries—the US, Saudi Arabia and Pakistan—played key roles in the whole process and, therefore, should be held responsible equally for the al-Qaeda phenomenon.[77] In that sense, while helping Osama to organize the Afghan resistence to Soviet forces the Saudis promoted US national interests as much as theirs. Hence, many Saudis now question whether their country is being made a scapegoat by the US strategic community to cover up its own failure.[78]

So Osama got the military skills and ideological impetus from his years of experience in Afghanistan. Moreover, the al-Sauds fell out with Osama because of the US factor. It needs to be recalled that a year after the victory of the Afghan mujahideen against the Soviet forces, Iraqi President Saddam Hussein invaded Kuwait and posed a security threat to neighbouring Saudi Arabia. At this point, Osama proposed to King Fahd his idea of raising a defence force through popular mobilization—on the lines of the Afghan resistance—to encounter any future threat from the Iraqi President. The proposal was "summarily dismissed" by the Saudi King who, instead, decided to invite American troops despite heavy domestic opposition. Osama was at the forefront of opposing the presence of American troops on Saudi soil. Many senior clerics too supported the Osama viewpoint on the ground that foreign non-Muslim forces should not be stationed in the kingdom which is home to Islam's two holiest places.[79] Discontentment among Saudis increased when the 5,50,000 strong US force did not leave Saudi Arabia even after the complete liberation of Kuwait in March 1991.[80] What angered many Saudis most was the studied silence on the part of the al-Saud family on the issue. However, the Saudi authorities "grudgingly admitted" the presence of 5,000 US troops in the kingdom after the 1996 truck bombing near Dhahran airbase which killed 19 American servicemen.[81] It was at this point that Osama, who had by then already shifted his base to Afghanistan, gave his call for a *jihad* against US troops in his own country.[82] He and his faithful followers articulated the thesis that their country was "occupied" by the US in same way as Afghanistan was by the Soviet Union in the 1980s.[83] The obvious implication of this line of thinking was that it would not be unjust to resist and force the withdrawal of US troops from Saudi Arabia through violent means.

Thus, tackling the problem of al-Qaeda and dealing with the supporters and sympathizers of Osama bin Laden pose a great dilemma for the royal Saudi family. The US accuses the rulers of not doing enough and if they do too much there could be a backlash from the dissidents. As said earlier, al-Qaeda cells are active within Saudi Arabia itself and do carry out spectacular military operations from time to time. Some of these operations include the 12 May, 2003 synchronized attacks on three expatriate residential complexes and an office building in Riyadh on the eve of a visit by US Secretary of State Colin Powell; the 29 May, 2004 ("Black Saturday") bloodshed in al-Khobar; the armed attack on the

American consulate in Jedah; and the simultaneous suicide car bombings on the Interior Ministry building and a training facility for the Special Forces in Riyadh in December 2004, etc.[84] The abortive attack against the Saudi oil complex, a heavily fortified zone, in March 2006 is a reminder that al-Qaeda is still active in the kingdom. Through its operations, al-Qaeda seeks to prove its determination to topple the ruling al-Saud regime and force their American allies to leave the kingdom. From time to time, the Saudi government brings out a list of alleged terrorists since 2003 when the regime publicly acknowledged the presence of armed extremists, having links with al-Qaeda, for the first time. So far, the notable successes for the Saudi security forces have been the killing of Abd al-Aziz al-Muqrin and Yunis Muhammad al-Hayari (a Moroccan), leader of al-Qaeda in the kingdom in June 2004 and June 2005, respectively.[85] Periodically, the Saudi authorities also crack down on the suspected al-Qaeda supporters. But they are being released after the intelligence agencies satisfy themselves to the effect that there is no concrete evidence of any direct link with the group. The regime has to be very careful, lest Osama may be able to capitalize on the widespread anti-Americanism and the general resentment against the al-Saud rule. Hence the policy has been one of cautious gradualism whereby the regime is largely focusing on attending to the socio-economic problems through increased spending in education, health, public welfare projects, etc. This, the authorities believe, may wean away the disgruntled youth from extremism and the ideological influence of Osama bin Laden. In that sense, the Saudi rulers resent that Americans are not sensitive to the delicate balancing exercise which the royal family is engaged in at the moment.

Challenges Ahead

Both the governments have been under pressure from their people to change the pattern of relationship in the aftermath of 11 September. In other words, there is a growing realization on both the sides at the peoples level to relook at the terms of the partnership that had lasted for more than five decades despite fundamental differences between the two at the systemic level: the US firmly committed to democracy, rule of law, free speech, human rights, etc. has always protected Saudi Arabia, a "secretive autocratic monarchy" with neither democratic rights nor free speech and with a "purist, authoritarian brand of Islam".[86] In the US, some have argued that the Saudi-US relationship has transformed itself from strategic partnership to "strategic enmity". "All the old reasons", it is argued, that prevented the US from "breaking away from, Saudi Arabia are no longer compelling".[87] Others have pleaded for an end to the addiction to oil. Because the oil-for-security partnership makes the US too dependant on governments which are basically authoritarian in nature. On the Saudi front, people are becoming increasingly critical of the regime's excessive closeness to the US. Students in Saudi schools are being advised regularly, though unofficially, to boycott US products. Even the lists of products to be boycotted, along with alternatives to be used, are being distributed. Further, anti-US demonstrations have been reported in the aftermath of 11 September. In April 2002, for instance, around 5,000 people protested against the US near the American Consulate in al-Khobar; the demonstration took place despite heavy security measures and a prohibition order by Interior Minister Prince Nayef. Similarly, there were other demonstrations against the US and Israel in al-Hasa, Safwa and Qatif in Eastern Province. As said earlier, there is strong resentment against the US because of its uncritical support to Israel vis-à-vis the Palestinians. Apart from the Palestine issue, the presence of US troops in the kingdom has been another reason for growing discontent among the Saudis, specially the youth.[88] Many Saudis do not trust the US. There is a feeling that the harsh criticism of Saudi Arabia by the US media and Congress is a "tactic to further weaken" the kingdom and to "drive the price of oil even lower". Some even believe that there is a "Zionist plot to divide Saudi Arabia so that America can retain control of the oil rich Ahsa region."[89] In that sense, Osama has been largely successful in "driving a wedge" between two closest allies—at least at the peoples level.[90]

However, despite the calls for change, both the governments have been somehow able to keep the tensions under control so that the negative fall-out of 11 September do not bring a complete rupture in their bilateral relationship. It needs to be mentioned that the White House has always maintained a safe distance from all the domestic criticism of Saudi Arabia. White House spokespersons keep reiterating that "the President is very pleased with the Kingdom's contribution to the war on terrorism".[91] During the controversy surrounding Prince Bandar's wife, for instance, when the members of the legislative branch were very critical of Saudi Arabia, key officials of the Bush administration such as Secretary of State Colin Powell and Defence Secretary Donald Rumsfeld were quite appreciative of Saudi Arabia.[92] Such divergent approaches prompted Prince Bandar to comment that his country was "caught in the crossfire" of a heated domestic debate between the Bush administration and the members of Congress who were very critical of the Administration's handling of the pre-11 September intelligence and the subsequent probe.[93] A pertinent question arises in this context: Why does the US government not take a hard line against the al-Saud regime? Firstly, the US dependence on Saudi oil is not going to be reduced in the near future. For at least the next two decades, Saudi oil will be "critical" to the world economy, and particularly to the "prosperity" of the US, Europe and Japan. Secondly, the protection and promotion of the interests of the American companies forms an important objective of any Administration, specially in view of the fact that in recent years the Saudi regime has shown interest in opening up the country's economy. For instance, the gas sector in Saudi Arabia has been opened up to foreign companies which is an unprecedented step since the nationalization of the ARAMCO in 1976.[94] It is estimated that the opening of the gas sector could bring around $30 billion for Saudi Arabia in the next ten years in terms of foreign investment. Thirdly, by protecting an authoritarian monarchy, the US is also promoting the interests of American arms industry which is very influential in the decision-making process. The more insecure the al-Saud regime becomes, the greater will be the demand for US weapons. Finally, and more crucially, the alternative to the al-Saud regime could be worse in view of growing anti-American feelings in the kingdom as well as the Iraqi quagmire. As regards Saudi Arabia, the royal family cannot but depend on the US for regime security. The very fact that Crown Prince Abdullah has made two visits to the US to meet President Bush in the aftermath of 11 September (April 2002 and April 2005) shows the vulnerability of the regime at home and its excessive reliance on the US for its own protection. Abdullah made these visits in a domestic environment of anti-Americanism. During both the visits the Saudi leader sought to soothe the Americans by assuring the continuous supply of oil and even to increase the oil production when necessary. It needs to be mentioned that any radical change in Saudi Arabia will end the "absolute power" of al-Saud family and the "privileges enjoyed by some 3,000 princes and hundreds of families linked to them".[95] Hence the stakes are too much to call for a fundamental restructuring of the nature of relationship between Saudi Arabia and the US in the immediate future. Whether such a positive assessment will hold good largely depends on the internal dynamics in Saudi Arabia.

Will the socio-economic measures, that the Saudi rulers are attempting, be able to contain political dissent? In other words, can the demand for fundamental political reforms be postponed for long? The Saudi strategy of cracking down on dissidents while back-tracking on major political reforms may not succeed. The al-Saud regime needs to think seriously about this. The rulers need to understand that the people should be given enough space for effective participation in the political process. The demands for political reforms in Saudi Arabia are basically home-grown which began in response to the overall ambiance for political participation in the aftermath of the 1990-91 Iraq-Kuwait crisis.[96] The aftermath of 11 September has made the environment more surcharged with more and more segments of the Saudi society demanding genuine political reforms. In that case, will there be a repetition of the Iranian experience in Saudi Arabia too? If yes, will the US come forward to protect the al-Saud family? These are difficult questions for which I have no answer. Nevertheless, answer to these questions will greatly determine the dynamics of Saudi-US relations in the coming years.

References

1. Parker T. Hart, *Saudi Arabia and the United States: Birth of a Security Partnership* (Bloomington: Indiana University Press, 1998), p. 38.
2. Gawdat Bahgat, "Saudi Arabia and the War on Terrorism", *Arab Studies Quarterly*, vol. 26, no. 1, Winter 2004, p. 51. Taken together, the six countries of the Gulf Cooperation Council—comprising Saudi Arabia, Kuwait, Bahrain, Oman, Qatar and the UAE—account for 65 per cent of world oil reserves and around a third of the world's natural gas reserves. They currently supply around a third of world's oil and, following the coming on stream of Qatar's massive North Dome offshore field, some 25 per cent of its natural gas. See *Middle East International* (Hereafter *MEI*), London, No. 747, 1 April, 2005, p. 23.
3. Hart, p. xi.
4. *Ibid.*, p. 39.
5. The only instance of Saudi disappointment at the initial stage was the US approach towards the Palestine question. See, *Ibid.*, p. 43.
6. Gawdat Bahgat, "Managing Dependence: American-Saudi Oil Relations", *Arab Studies Quarterly*, Vol. 23, No. 1, Winter 2001, p. 2.
7. Edward W. Chester, *United States Oil Policy and Diplomacy* (London: Greenwood Press, 1999), p. 24; cited in *Ibid.*
8. Seth P. Tillman, *The United States in the Middle East* (Bloomington: Indiana University Press, 1982), p. 79.
9. During the 1973 war, the Arab countries, led by Saudi Arabia, put an oil embargo by way of increasing the oil price and reducing the production on the oil-consuming countries of Western Europe, the US, and Japan. The embargo caused a great deal of alarm in the Western world and went a long

way in bringing about a change in American attitude towards the Arab-Israeli conflict. During his "shuttle diplomacy" Kissinger first tried to somehow persuade Saudi Arabia to lift the embargo. See William B. Quadt, *Decade of Decisions: American Policy Toward the Arab-Israeli Conflict* (Berkeley: University of California Press, 1977), p. 160. For Nixon's reaction to the oil embargo, see *New York Times,* 17 November, 1973. For Kissinger's reaction, see *New York Times,* 22 November, 1973.

10. See Bahgat, "Marging Dependencce", pp. 3-4.
11. In fact, the inability of the Saudis to manage the sophisticated weapons was one of the criticisms in the aftermath of 11 September. See Victor Davis Hanson, "Our Enemies, the Saudis", *Commentary,* July- August, 2002, p. 25.
12. Bahgat, "War on Terrorism", p. 51.
13. Caroline Montagu, "Uncertainties in Saudi Arabia", *MEI,* no. 663, 23 November, 2001, p. 24. For instance, Saudi Arabia paid cash for some $45 billion worth of US arms between 1989-2001, while the US imported upto 6 mbd of Saudi oil for domestic requirements.
14. Bahgat, "War on Terrorism", p. 51.
15. *Ibid.*
16. Hanson, "Our Enemies", p. 25.
17. Bahgat, "War on Terrorism", p. 54.
18. Cited in *Ibid.*, p. 54.
19. Maurice R. Greenberg, *Terrorist Financing* (New York: Council on Foreign Relations, 2002), p. 5, 8.
20. Hanson, "Our Enemies", p. 24.
21. Ghada Khouri, "Caught in the Crossfire", *MEI,* No. 689, 6 December, 2002, p. 10.
22. *Ibid.*
23. Cited in *Ibid.*
24. *Ibid.*
25. Cited in *Ibid.*
26. Greenberg, *Terrorist Financing,* p. 7.
27. The other charities identified include the Afghan-based Afghan support committee, the Pakistan-based Al Rashid Trust and Wafa Humanitarian Organization, the Kuwait-based Revival of Islamic Heritage Society and the US-based Holy Land Foundation for relief and Development. See *Ibid.*, p. 8.
28. Katerina Dalacoura, "US Democracy Promotion in the Arab Middle East Since 11 September, 2001: A critique", *International Affairs,* Vol. 81, No. 5, October 2005, p. 963.
29. *Ibid.*
30. Gregory Gause III, "Can Democracy Stop Terrorism", *Foreign Affairs,* Vol. 84, No. 5, September-October, 2005, p. 62.

31. Cited in *Ibid.*, p. 65.
32. So far, the US has devoted more than $293 million so that "democracy can spread, education can thrive, economies can grow, and women can be empowered". See US State Department, "Middle East Partnership Initiative", at http://www.mepi, state.gov/mepi, accessed on 12 August, 2006; Dalacoura, "US Democracy Promotion", p. 964.
33. See Dalacoura, "US democracy promotion", p. 964. The BMENAPI targeted countries beyond West Asia and North Africa like Pakistan and Afghanistan.
34. Gwenn Okruhlik, "Networks of Dissent: Islamism and Reform in Saudi Arabia", *Current History,* January 2002, p. 22. For a critical analysis of 'dissent' in Saudi Arabia, see, Mamoun Fandy, *Saudi Arabia and Political Dissent* (London: MacMillan, 1999).
35. Juhaiman al-Utaibi was the grandson of an Ikhwan (tribal *Muwahidun)* warrior. It may be recalled that in 1929 the Ikhwan had waged a rebellion against the Saudi King.
36. Okruhlik, "Networks of Dissent", p. 23.
37. Eric Rouleau, "Trouble in the Kingdom", *Foreign Affairs,* Vol. 81, No. 4, July-August 2002, p. 83.
38. Nimrod Raphaeli, "Demands for Reforms in Saudi Arabia", *Middle Eastern Studies,* Vol. 41, No. 4, July 2005, p. 519.
39. Rouleau, "Trouble in the Kingdom", p. 83. There are around six to seven million foreign workers in the Kingdom. Fordetails, see Raphaeli, "Demands for Reforms", p. 519.
40. Cited in Rouleau, "Trouble in the Kingdom", pp. 83-84.
41. Raphaeli, "Demands for Reforms", p. 519.
42. Per capita income plunged from $28,600 in 1981 to 6,800 in 2001. By comparison the average per capita revenue in Abu Dhabi was $36,000, and in Qatar it was $26,000. See Rouleau, p. 85. By the year 2005 the Saudi national debt stood at SR 700 billion ($187 billion), approximately equal to the annual GNP; Raphaeli, p. 518.
43. Rouleau, "Trouble in the Kingdom", p. 83.
44. Mai Yamani, "Passing Nightmare?" *The World Today,* January 2002, p. 17.
45. *Ibid.*
46. Heba Saleh, "Saudi Arabia: Jihad on the Wane?" *MEI,* No. 743, 4 February, 2005, p. 32.
47. Raphaeli, "Demands for Reforms", p. 519.
48. See, Michaela Prokop, "Saudi Arabia: The Politics of Education", *International Affairs,* vol. 79, no. 1, January 2003, p. 80.
49. Mohammed Bosbait and Rodney Wilson, "Education, School to Work Transitions and Unemployment in Saudi Arabia", *Middle Eastern Studies,* Vol. 41, No. 4, July 2005, p. 534.
50. Rouleau, "Trouble in the Kingdom", p. 78.

51. Yamani, "Nightmare?", p. 16.
52. Cited in Dilip Hiro, "US-Saudi Relations: time for a rethink?", *MEI,* No. 668, 8 February, 2002, p. 26.
53. Caroline Montagu, "Turf Wars", *MEI,* No. 678, 28 June, 2002, p. 20.
54. See Dale F. Eickelman, "Bin Laden, the Arab "Street", and the Middle East's Democracy Deficit", *Current History,* January 2002, p. 38.
55. See Saleh, "Jihad on the Wane?", pp. 32-33.
56. The reformers included poet and author Ali al-Dumayni, retired academic Abdullah al-Hamid, and political science teacher Matruk al-Faleh. See *MEI,* No. 751, 27 May, 2005, p. 17.
57. *Ibid.*
58. *Ibid.*
59. It is estimated that the Saudi foreign investment, mainly in the US, amounted to $700 billion to a trillion dollars. See Rouleau, "Trouble in the Kingdom", p. 84.
60. Bahgat, "War on Terrorism", p. 56.
61. *Ibid.*, The other four pillars are: *Shahadah* (declaration of faith), prayer, fasting, and pilgrimage (hajj).
62. Cited in Michael Jansen, "Changes afoot", *MEI,* No. 664, 7 December, 2001, pp. 17-18.
63. For details, see Bahgat, "War on Terrorism", p. 56. Also see, Michael Jansen, "Keeping its distance", *MEI,* No. 662, 9 November, 2001, p. 13.
64. See, Saleh, "Jihad on the Wane?", pp. 31-32; Jansen, "Keeping Distance", p. 13.
65. Yamani, "Nightmare?", p. 16.
66. Bahgat, "War on Terrorism", p. 55.
67. For details, see, *Ibid.*
68. Jansen, "Changes afoot", p. 17.
69. Yamani, "Nightmare?", p. 16.
70. Cited in Rouleau, "Trouble in the Kingdom", p. 77.
71. Jansen, "Keeping distance", p. 13. The minister never explained the position.
72. One Saudi leader argued: "Remember, ten years ago people in Saudi Arabia were naming their sons after Bush (senior). And 90 per cent supported the American presence... What change has happened from then to now? It is because of what they see daily on television... the attacks of the Israelis. they associate this with US support and bias towards Israel..." Cited in Jansen, "Changes afoot", p. 18.
73. Caroline Montagu, "A Peace in the Offing?", *MEI,* No. 670, 8 March, 2002, p. 20.
74. For the plan, See *Ibid.* For the Arab League Summit, See Michael Jansen, "Arab Summit: Palestine and Iraq", *MEI,* No. 672, 5 April, 2002, pp. 7-8.
75. See Montagu, "A Peace in the Offing", pp. 20-21.

76. Cited in Rouleau, "Trouble in the Kingdom", p. 78.
77. Prince Turki al-Faisal, the former director of Saudi intelligence, was mainly in charge of dealing with the Afghan situation for almost 25 years. See Jansen, "Keeping distance", p. 13.
78. See Rouleau, "Trouble in the Kingdom", p. 81.
79. The opposition to US troops was linked to a cardinal religious principle: The Saudi Kingdom is considered a mosque, "where two religions cannot co-exist", see Hiro, "US-Saudi relations", p. 26.
80. The deployment of US troops in Saudi Arabia presents an interesting diplomatic story. For details, see, Hiro, "US-Saudi relations", p. 26. Also see *MEI,* No. 757, 2 September, 2005, p. 30.
81. Dilip Hiro, "America's Shifting Middle East Policy", *MEI,* No. 659, 28 September, 2001, p. 28.
82. Osama stated: "The presence of the American crusader forces in Muslim Gulf States...is the greatest danger and poses the most serious harm, threatening the world's largest oil reserves.... The ordinary Saudi knows that his country is the largest producer in the world, yet at the same time, he is suffering from taxes and bad services. Our country has become a colony of America. The Saudis now know their real enemy is America". Cited in *Ibid.*
83. *Ibid.*, p. 29.
84. For details, see, Najm Jarrah, "Saudi Arabia: Jihadis Strike", *MEI,* No. 700, 16 May, 2003, p. 10; Roger Hardy, "Saudi Arabia: Black Saturday", *MEI,* No. 727, 11 June, 2004, p. 19; and Saleh, "Jihad on the Wane?", p. 31.
85. Saleh, "Jihad on the Wane?", p. 32; Francis Daly, "Life after Fahd", *MEI,* No. 756, 5 August, 2005, p. 14. For the data on al-Qaeda's attacks in the kingdom, see James Gavin, "Saudi Oil comes under threat", *Petroleum Economist,* July 2004, p. 3.
86. See Caroline Montagu, "Uncertainties in Saudi Arabia", *MEI,* No. 663, 23 November, 2001, pp. 24-26.
87. Hanson, "Our Enemies, the Saudis", p. 26 and p. 27.
88. See Caroline Montagu, "Saudi Arabia: Crown Prince in US", *MEI,* No. 674, 3 May, 2002, p. 17.
89. Yamani, "Nightmare?", p. 17.
90. Foreign Minister Prince al-Faisal believed that the perpetrators of 11 September attacks on the US recruited Saudis with the aim of "driving a wedge between the kingdom and the US. It was their intention to make it seem that Saudis were responsible for this act." Cited in Jansen, "Changes afoot", p. 18.
91. Cited in Bahgat, "War on Terrorism", p. 55.
92. Colin Powell stated: "In our desire to protect ourselves, we should not go to the point where we rupture our relationship with a country that has been

a great friend to the United States". Defense Secretary Donald Rumsfeld characterized US-Saudi ties as "good military-to-military relationship". White House spokesman Ariel Fleischer called Saudi Arabia "a good partner in the war against terrorism". Cited in Ghada Khouri, "Saudi Arabia: Caught in the Crossfire", *MEI,* No. 689, 6 December, 2002, p. 10.

93. *Ibid*., p. 10.
94. Rouleau, "Trouble in the Kingdom", p. 85.
95. *Ibid*., p. 89.
96. See Anoushiravan Ehteshami, "Reform from Above: The Politics of Participation in Oil Monarchies", *International Affairs,* Vol. 79, No. 1 (2003), pp. 67-70.

7

Indo-Saudi Relations
Past and Emerging Challenges

A.K. PASHA

India's historical ties with the people of Nile Valley, Mesopotamia and Dilmun civilizations, which flourished in West Asia, are well known. The commercial, cultural and other relations enabled both the peoples to interact quite vigorously and many people from both the regions settled in both the areas. Large number of Indians used to go to Arabia to study medicine. With the rise of Islam in seventh century AD Arab traders spread Islam to coastal towns in Kerala, Gujarat and other interior areas. Many Indians also converted to Christianity and Syrian Christians settled in Kerala and the West Coast of India. Many Jews also settled in Kerala and along the West Coast of India especially those who escaped persecution from the Romans in West Asia. This led to visits by large number of Indians to pilgrimage centers—Mecca, Medina, Bethlehem, Jerusalem , Najaf, Karbala, Mashad, Cairo and other centers. Gradually India's sea trade passed into the hands of the Arabs and Persians who came to dominate the Arabian Sea, Red Sea, Gulf region and the Indian Ocean. Many Indian *Hajj's* stayed to trade in the Holy Land, taking local Arab wives as Arabs married Indian women in Kerala whose offspring's are known as Moppliahs.[1] In Jeddah several hundred Indian families especially Hindus had established themselves in a separate colony retaining their self-identity and distinctiveness in manners, dress and employment. According to one writer they had taken the place of Jews, who had formerly been the brokers but, having offended the Sheriff of Mecca, had been driven out to Yemen. Large number of Indian ships from Calicut, Surat and Bombay and other ports of India arrived at Jeddah with cargoes of cotton, textiles, silk, spices, gems and other materials.

The Jeddah merchants made huge profits out of Indian goods, which were later, transshipped to Suez and Europe especially to Venice and Genoa.[2]

The Mongol destruction of Persia and the Abbasid Caliphate especially Baghdad in 1258 and the subsequent Ottoman domination of the region did not substantially disrupt the links between India and West Asia. But the Portuguese, within a decade since the discovery of the Cape route by Vasco da Gamma in 1498, almost monopolized the highly lucrative spice trade from India to the Red Sea and Gulf area at the expense of the interests of Muslim traders and the important seaports of western India like Camby and Chaul. The Portuguese inflicted a crushing defeat on the allied Muslim fleet near Diu in 1509 and established themselves at Diu, Daman and Goa. The Mughal Ruler Jehangir tired of objectionable practices by the Portuguese, especially their religious intolerance, was delighted when the British in 1612 defeated the Portuguese at Surat under the leadership of English Captain Best. Unable to build any credible sea power and having been defeated by the Portuguese, the Mughal rulers were concerned for the safe passage of their Muslim subjects to Hajj pilgrimage. The religiously indifferent English were preferable to the crusading Portuguese whose religious intolerance provoked the hostility of several Indian rulers as well. In 1613 Jehangir issued a *firman* permitting the English to establish a factory permanently at Surat. Since then English traders were welcomed throughout the Mughal Empire which subsequently led to the colonization of India by the British.

But the English as early as in December 1688 had turned against the Mughals and blockaded Bombay and the Mughal naval vessels and their captains (who went to Red Sea and Gulf area often) mainly "to arrest the pilgrim traffic to Mecca". By the middle of the 18th century Indian ships commanded by English officers were a common sight in Red Sea/Gulf area especially at Jeddah, Aden and Muscat. Before Gujarat passed into the hands of Sultan Allaudin Khilji of Delhi in 1297, the King of Gujarat Arjuna had the broad-mindedness to endow a mosque erected by a Muslim ship owner of Hormouz and provided for the expenses of certain Shia festivals. He further laid down that under the management of the Muslim Community of Somnath any surplus was to be made over to the Holy Places of Mecca and Medina.[3] It is interesting to note that the last great Mughal ruler Aurangzeb, between 1661 and 1667, received "complimentary embassies" from several foreign Muslim powers such as the Sheriff of Mecca and others to neutralize harsh treatment of his father and brothers. It was also customary for rich Indian princes to lavish gifts on the Sheriff of Mecca and the Holy Places as the Hashimi family which had ruled Mecca since the 11th century A.D. The Anglo-French rivalry for domination in India sent ripples to the Hijaz. By their conquest of Surat, the English stopped the flow of treasure amounting to Rs. 5000/- a year granted by the Mughal Ruler to the Sheriff of Mecca. The Sheriff complained to the Ottoman Ruler at Istanbul and for a time the port of Jeddah was closed to English ships.[4] More recently when Abdul Aziz (known as Ibn Saud) captured Mecca, Medina and the entire Hejaz and later proclaimed himself King of the Hejaz on 8 January 1926, he encountered opposition both internal and external. Moreover, despite quick recognition of King Saud as the King of Hejaz by the European powers, still he had to "legitimize his position in the eyes of the Islamic world, which had started with a prejudice against Wahabism and had been scandalized by the violence with which the puritans had suppressed the cult of saints in the conquered holy land". The agitated people of Hejaz, especially the followers of Sheriff of Mecca, also had to be won over and their economic grievances redressed. Thus, to legitimize his position as the ruler of Hejaz, guardian of holy places and also to reassure the Muslim world he called an international conference.[5]

Ibn Saud made a proclamation to the Muslim world asking for representatives to come to the Hejaz to discuss the future of the Holy Places. The Islamic Congress opened on 7 June, 1926 at Mecca during the Hajj, which was attended by sixty delegates from all over the world, including the Indian Muslim Community, which was led by the Ali Brothers—the Khilafat Committee members. The Indian members sent to Mecca achieved little as they became embroiled in mediatory efforts to reconcile the Saudis and the Hashemites.[6] The Saudi King apparently disliked the Indian delegation's intervention as the king had declared Sheriff Hussein of Mecca as a traitor for claiming the title of Caliph on 5 March, 1924 made vacant by the deposition of the Ottoman Sultan by Kemal Attaturk. Due to the objections on a number of issues (related to Hajj, Wahhabi control of Holy Places) from the Indian delegation, the Saudi King according to one writer ordered them to leave Hejaz—clearly an undiplomatic move.[7] It was only after the deportation of Indian delegation that Ibn Saud felt secure. The Saudi King went on to merge Najd and Hejaz and established the Kingdom of Saudi Arabia on 23 September, 1932. Some delegates (including Indians) at the Islamic conference had indeed objected to Ibn Saud's assumption of the unIslamic title of King.[8] It must be added that pilgrims for Hajj from the Indian sub-continent formed one of the largest group and the Sheriffs of Mecca and

King Ibn Saud, following the traditional practice, purchased large quantities of tents from India to be used to house the Hajj pilgrims.[9]

After Independence: Soon after India's independence Prime Minister Jawaharlal Nehru had to tackle, amongst other things, Pakistan's relentless propaganda against India over Kashmir and other issues. Pakistan, by convening and hosting a number of Pan-Islamic conferences since 1949 together with its refusal to recognize Israel and the support it had given to Arab causes had managed to establish close ties with certain Arab/ Muslim states especially with Iran, Saudi Arabia, Turkey, Jordan and others. It must be emphasized that more than Islam, it was the cold war politics which enabled Pakistan to mobilize West Asian countries support but could not make much headway. In fact, by the end of 1952, Pakistan's attempt to forge a Pan-Islamic alliance was in shambles and had to be subsequently abandoned. Among all its allies in the West Asian and North African (WANA) region, Pakistan's relations with Saudi Arabia were to prove most rewarding. King Abdul Aziz Ibn Saud, after consolidating his territorial gains and having obtained financial security in terms of oil revenues, charted to follow a more autonomous foreign policy. When King Saud visited Pakistan in 1953, he extended Riyadh's political support to Pakistan on the Kashmir issue.[10] India's recognition of Israel on 17 September, 1950 came as a surprise to many in the Arab/Islamic world in view of India's support to the Palestinians since the Balfour (1917) declaration and persistent opposition to the partition of Palestine by the UN in 1947. Pakistan tried to paint India in the darkest colours in the eyes of the Arabs on this issue. But New Delhi's unequivocal support to the Palestine cause and subsequently her diplomatic and moral support to Arab National Liberation Movements in Algeria, Morocco, Sudan, Tunisia, South Yemen and elsewhere in the Arab world brought it closer even to many conservative Arab states in the area.[11]

The coming to power in 1952 of Gamal Abdel Nasser in Egypt and the emergence of secular nationalist Arab regimes in Syria, Iraq and later in Libya, Yemen's and Algeria to a large extent neutralized the Pakistani offensive against India in the region, especially over the Kashmir issue. Pakistan's open identification with the policies of the US/West in the region made it a suspect in the eyes of most Arabs. Pakistan's attempt to seek support on the ground of common religion did not work among the Arabs.[12] In fact, many WANA countries resented Pakistan's attempt to raise the Kashmir issue in Islamic gatherings and elsewhere. Pakistan's membership in the Western sponsored Baghdad Pact led to its isolation in the WANA region (except Iran and Turkey) because with the exception of Iraq none of the Arab countries joined the military Pact. Even Iraq withdrew after the July 1958 revolution (led by Gen. Abdul Karim Qassem) from the Pact, which was subsequently re-christened as CENTO.[13] Even Saudi Arabia not only appreciated India's non-aligned foreign policy first refused to join the Baghdad Pact and denounced the Pakistani decision to join the Baghdad Pact. In fact, Riyadh was astonished to find that the "Islamic State of Pakistan should accede to those who have joined hands with the Zionist Jews" and spoke of the Pact as a "stab in the heart of the Arab and Muslim states" and urged it "to return to the right path", by withdrawing from the widely unpopular western military pact.[14]

Pakistan, which had launched a campaign against India on the issue of treatment of Indian Muslims, also received a set back when Saudi Arabia publicly sided with India on the issue. King Saud Bin Abdul Aziz paid tribute to the Government of India for its policy of equality and equity towards the Muslims in India. Giving impressions of his 17-day long tour of India, in a now famous public statement, the Saudi King on 10 December, 1955 told the Indo-Arab Society in Bombay, "*I desire to say to my Muslim brethren all over the world with satisfaction that the fate of the Indian Muslims is in safe hands. In my capacity as the guardian of Muslim holy places, I desire to express my gratitude to the great Indian leader, Mr. Nehru, and all those lieutenants of his, through whom he executes this policy of equality and equity.*" A joint statement issued in New Delhi on 12 December, 1955, said that both India and Saudi Arabia are resolved to strengthen the existing friendly ties between the two countries through further cooperation to their mutual advantage in the cultural, political and economic spheres. The statement said the two countries fully subscribe to the five principles of peaceful co-existence. When India's Prime Minister Jawaharlal Nehru returned the visit in September 1956, he was given a rousing welcome with slogans of "Welcome Prophet of Peace" which obviously angered Pakistan. India's support to the Palestine cause, Egyptian stand during the 1956 Suez crisis and opposition to western attempts to pressurize Arab countries which followed non-aligned policies further improved India's credibility among the Arabs. Pakistan on the other hand by siding with the British alienated itself in the region. Egypt went to the extent of declaring that Kashmir was an integral part of India and that "Suez was as dear to Egypt as Kashmir was to India".[15] Taking the cue from Nasser, the Egyptian media blasted Pakistan and its close alliance with the US-UK with an unprecedented anti-Pakistan campaign and branded the latter as "the number one enemy of Cairo and Arabs" who must be cowed before Egypt could handle the West effectively.[16] The Pakistani Prime Minister Hussein Shaheed Shurawardy, whom Nasser refused to receive in Cairo, made the well known statement denigrating the Arabs that "the Arab world is divided among themselves and even if they were united, zero plus zero is after all equal to zero". No wonder Egypt refused Pakistan's offer to contribute a contingent to the United Nations Emergency Force (UNEF) in the Sinai.[17]

U-turn in Saudi Foreign Policy: King Ibn Saud after his visit to the US (after the Suez crisis) became close to the US and endorsed the Eisenhower Doctrine. The US wanted Arab support in the cold war which it failed to get through the Baghdad Pact. No wonder Egypt's Nasser denounced the US Doctrine as imperialist attempt to dominate the WANA region. The secession of Syria from the UAR in 1961, Egypt's military intervention in North Yemen after the 1962 revolution, US decision to supply offensive weapons to Israel under President Johnson, emergence of Faisal as Saudi King and his emphasis on Pan-Islamism rather than Pan-Arabism which Nasser advocated, all this brought about radical changes in the region with implications on India's policy towards the region which had come to be identified as Cairo-centric.[18] In the US-Israeli scheme to contain Nasser and Arab nationalist forces, Saudi Arabia and Pakistan, together with Turkey and Iran (CENTO partners) became prominent players in the game. Moreover, Pakistan's rabid hostility towards Arab nationalism and communism was well appreciated by the House of Saud. No wonder a Saudi-Pakistan alliance virtually came to be established in mid-1960 with Riyadh terming India as an aggressor in the 1965 Indo-Pak war and warned New Delhi not to take undue advantage of its close ties with the Arab/Islamic states.[19] Saudi Arabia at the Arab Heads of States meeting in September 1965 joined with Jordan in demanding a collective Arab disapproval of the Indian stand on the War. Of course the final communiqué did not support India or Pakistan, but Saudi criticism of India was due to close Indo-Egyptian friendship and Nasser's support to Indian position at several forums.[20]

Egypt's humiliating defeat in the 1967 Arab-Israel war, Nasser's death in September 1970 led to a decline in Egypt's influence in the region. Saudi Arabia gradually became the leading Arab state influencing the policies of several Arab states partly due to its huge financial resources. The Saudi's under King Faisal, quickly seized the opportunity by asserting their leadership in the area by reacting strongly to the damage done by the attempted burning to the Al Aqsa mosque in Jerusalem (under Israeli occupation)—the third holiest shrine of Islam on 29 August, 1969 and calling for a conference of Islamic heads of state or government. An Islamic Conference to discuss the Al Aqsa issue was held in Rabat (Morocco) on September 22-25, 1969. The summit was attended by 23 Arab/Islamic heads of states and the PLO as an observer. India was officially invited to participate in the conference at the Saudi request but Pakistan staged a walk out from the conference against the presence of Indian delegation, led by the Indian Ambassador at Rabat and later officially by the Indian Industries Minister Mr. Fakhruddin Ali Ahmed. The Rabat Summit paved the way for the establishment of the Organization of Islamic Conference (OIC) in May 1971. Thirty-eight states became founding members of OIC. Saudi Arabia wields considerable influence in the OIC not only due to the location of head quarters in Jeddah but also due to its major contribution towards the OIC budget. In the OIC Secretariat large number of Pakistani nationals work with some holding key positions. Pakistan which had been taking keen interest in organizing Islamic conferences where it had denounced India and raised the Kashmir issue along with its declaration of world Islamic solidarity found in Saudi Arabia a very useful partner. Pakistan with Saudi Arabia's support always attempted to get the Islamic world use its pressure in favour of its stand on Kashmir especially since the eruption of militancy in the Kashmir valley in 1989.[21]

The Bangladesh crisis and the Indo-Pak war in December 1971 had a major impact on India's relations with WANA states and especially with Saudi Arabia as Pakistan sought to get closer to Riyadh. Riyadh's position on the crisis at the United Nations was that the development in East Pakistan was Islamabad's internal affair and that no other country had any right to interfere in the same. The Saudi representative speaking at the UN on 16 December, 1971 acknowledged that the showdown between East and West Pakistan was "probably for economic as well as for political reasons". He urged a bilateral solution asserting "only India and Pakistan can solve the problem without interference from outside". But during the war and soon after the fall of Dacca, Saudi Arabia adopted an even less friendly attitude towards India by extending support to Pakistan and refusing to recognize Bangladesh. In fact, the Saudi Minister of state for Foreign Affairs Mr. Omar Saqqaf, asserted that India's refusal to hand over the POW's to Pakistan and its move to refer some of them to Dacca for trial as war criminals constituted a "flagrant violation of the Geneva Convention". He warned that India's attitude could result in "further deterioration in the situation". In the UN Security Council debates, the Saudi representative referred to the problem in East Pakistan as a conflict between brothers. Even if one considered India a "cousin" New Delhi had no right to become involved, opined the Saudis. It was reported that Saudi Arabia gave sanctuary to Pakistani fighter planes in the face of heavy Indian bombing of Pakistani airfields in addition to giving nearly $200 million during and after the war. Saudi Arabia, unlike Egypt, named India as the aggressor in the 1971 Indo-Pak war.[22] However, India soon managed to convince the Saudi rulers of New Delhi's sincere desire to live in peace with Pakistan and respect its territorial integrity. The 1972 Simla Agreement and the release of Pakistani POWs by India helped the atmosphere, as Saudi concern for Pakistan's territorial integrity had become an issue in India's bilateral ties. The Saudis who consider themselves as leader of the Arab/Islamic world with their huge financial power and also due to the location of Islamic holy places—Mecca and Medina—also wished to play a more active role in the Non-Aligned Movement and other foras. Many Asian and African states became members of the OIC under Saudi influence especially due to its generous financial assistance. Thus, Saudi aid, loans, and grants has won them many supporters. Moreover the numerous external challenges emanating from Nasser's Egypt, Yemen, Iraq and from Iran since the 1979 Islamic revolution and again Iraq from 1990 onwards and domestic instability (1979 Mecca Mosque takeover) have compelled the House of Saud to use OIC as also for their foreign policy goals.[23]

In the wake of the 1973 Arab-Israeli war, Riyadh (mainly due to the oil embargo and financial resources) emerged as the leader of the Arab/Islamic states as also due to mounting isolation of Egypt under President Sadat due to his separate peace policy with Israel under US auspices. In view of limited military capability (which made them conscious of their vulnerability to external and internal challenges), the Saudis developed close security relations with Pakistan with the blessings of the US. Several hundred Pakistani military advisors had been stationed in the Kingdom during the early period of Iran-Iraq war to bolster the security of the House of Saud. The US-Saudi-Pakistani triangular relationship—which worked effectively to evict the Soviets from Afghanistan to give one instance—has to be kept in mind while discussing the Kashmir issue and the OIC.[24] Since Pakistan's defeat and division in 1971 the United States came to rely increasingly on Iran and Saudi Arabia for its oil and commercial interests in the Gulf area. The twin pillar policy gave Pakistan some room to maneuver in the region's politics. The downfall of the Shah of Iran in 1979 and the Soviet military intervention in Afghanistan aggravated Saudi concern for their national security. Notwithstanding the Carter Doctrine, Rapid Deployment Force and later Central Command and US assertion that it will not allow the repetition of Iranian revolution in Saudi Arabia, in order to enhance Saudi security, the United States was well disposed to Pakistan's decision to volunteer military training and trained men to Riyadh.[25] In return Pakistan received Saudi funding for its arms purchases especially from Washington. Saudi Arabia's military aid to Pakistan became a major irritant in relations between New Delhi and Riyadh. Pakistan also exploited the issue of communal riots in India by propagating that Muslims were not safe in India.[26] The growing challenge from Khomeini's Iran and the Iran-Iraq War among other issues posed serious challenges to the House of Saud. These events coupled with the ongoing Arab-Israeli conflict especially Israeli invasions of Lebanon in 1978 and 1982 and with Soviets fully entrenched in Afghanistan; the Saudis gradually realized that their close ties with Pakistan need not come in the way of establishing good ties with India. Around this time in early April 1981 Mr. Eric Gonsalves, Secretary in the Indian Ministry of External Affairs in an interview published in ***The Washington Post*** said among other things that the sale of US arms to Saudi Arabia and other Gulf States could provide these states with a false sense of security that could lead to their royal families being toppled as the Shah of Iran. He gave the interview on the eve of Saudi Foreign Minister Saud Al Faisal's visit to India for three days in 1981. This created a ripple in India's ties with Arab Gulf monarchies. As seen above the 1979 Iranian revolution, Soviet intervention in Afghanistan and the Iran-Iraq War (1980-88) brought about closer Saudi-Pak ties, which the US supported. This made General Zia ul Haq, the Pakistani military ruler say: "If Saudi Arabia's security was threatened and help was sought from Pakistan he would personally lead Pakistani forces in the defence of Saudi Arabia". It is in this backdrop one should see Prime Minister Mrs. Indira Gandhi's visit to Riyadh in April 1982 which ended the 26 years long communication gap between the two states. Her visit paved the way for better relations and heralded a new era or so, claimed India' Ministry of External Affairs (MEA).[27]

End of Communication Gap: No Indian Prime Minister or top leader had been to Saudi Arabia since Jawaharlal Nehru visited the Kingdom in 1956, until Mrs. Indira Gandhi paid an official visit to Riyadh in April 1982. The only exception was the visit by Fakhruddin Ali Ahmed, President of India, who attended King Faisal's funeral in March 1975. This was the first time an Indian President personally represented India at the funeral of another Head of State, since the practice had been to depute the Vice President or senior Cabinet minister. It indicated the importance India attached to relations with Saudi Arabia. During the period 1956 to 1982, India's relations with Saudi Arabia had never been unfriendly but at the same time they were not close either. A variety of factors worked such as close Indo-Egyptian ties, treaty relationship between India and USSR, close Indo-Iraqi ties, Indian support to the Iranian revolution, and on top of it the Indo-Pak 1965 and 1971 wars. But what materially affected Indo-Saudi ties was the close Saudi-Pakistan relationship.[28] However, despite the lack of political understanding, Indo-Saudi economic ties flourished. It is in this backdrop one should see Mrs. Gandhi's visit to Saudi Arabia in April 1982, which ended the 26 years long "communication gap" between India and the Saudi Kingdom. Her visit, it was claimed by MEA, had paved the way for better relations and "heralded a new era" in Indo-Saudi ties. She herself praised the Kingdom's "constructive role" in the global arena and its contribution in solving many international problems. She supported the Fahd Peace Plan on the Arab-Israeli issue saying, "We have welcomed it. It is in line with our basic principles to which we must adhere to resolve the crisis in West Asia". She also went on to describe the Fahd Plan as "new hope, and conforming to India's stand". More significantly, she sought Riyadh's cooperation to strengthen peace and stability in the South Asian region in the background of Pakistan's support to militancy in Punjab.[29]

Indo-Saudi Economic Ties: While political relations have been far from bonhomie as a result of cold war alignments and Saudi-Pakistani affinity, Indo-Saudi economic cooperation took a more realistic form and flourished. Mrs. Indira Gandhi's visit to the Kingdom paved the way for a new chapter in economic cooperation. The most tangible gain was the setting up of an Indo-Saudi Joint Commission to promote economic and technical collaboration. It was inspired by the assumption that a combination of Indian technology, skilled manpower and Saudi money could work to strengthen South-South cooperation which had yielded tremendous economic gains during the last 25 years forcing rethink on the political front.[30] India's trade relations with Saudi Arabia go back many years and the quantum has increased since Nehru's visit and risen steadily since 1973. The two-way trade in 1963-64 was a mere Rs. 24.3 crores, which increased to Rs. 548 crores in 1979-80. During 1961-62 India's exports to Riyadh were a lowly Rs. 3.33 lakh as compared to Rs. 18.9 lakh worth of imports. In 1973-74 Indian imports from Saudi Arabia (mostly oil) amounted to Rs. 131.35 crores, while it exported goods worth Rs. 25.84 crores. India's exports to Saudi Arabia have always been less than its imports. In 1990-91, imports were valued at Rs. 2,897.73 crores and exports at Rs. 418.42 crores. In 1992-93, India purchased over $1.3 billion of crude oil while it exported goods to Riyadh worth $375 million.

The trade turnover during 1999-2000 was $3.75 billion. India's exports were $741 million and imports $3 billion. Saudi-Indian bilateral trade in 2002-03 was estimated at $5 billion with Saudi exports being $3.65 and India's exports were at one billion US $. Saudi-Indian trade during 2001-02 stood at 1290.42 million US $and in 2002-03 at 1445.47 million US $excluding crude oil and petroleum products. These figures are among the highest between India and an Islamic country. However, much of this adverse balance is made up by the flow of remittances by over 1.5 million Indian workers in the Kingdom. Moreover, Indian companies, both public and private, have taken and completed numerous lucrative projects in the Kingdom and earned huge profits.

The Saudis have given loans to India through the *Saudi Development Fund* as follows: 1977-78 Rs. 75 crore; 1981-82 Rs. 17.70 crore; 1983-84 Rs. 17.23 crore; 1985-86, Rs. 28.72, crore; 1987-88 Rs. 50 crore, 1988-89 Rs. 6 crore; 1989-90 Rs. 43 crore; 1990-91 Rs. 30cr; 1991-92 Rs. 27 crore; 1992-93 Rs. 2 crore and in 1996 Rs. 152 crore. These loans given at low interest rates were for some of the following projects: Sirsailam and Nagarjunasagar power projects, in Andhra Pradesh (1977 Rs. 75 crore); to the Rajasthan Canal Project; Koel Karo power project in Bihar (1981 Rs. 17.70, crore); Koraput Rayagad Railway project (1983 Rs. 17.23 crore); Ramagundan Thermal Power Project II (1985 Rs. 50 crore); Nhawa Shiva Project (T&C, 1987 Rs. 50 crore).[31]

Despite growing economic relations, Indo-Saudi relations became strained in the wake of the militancy in Kashmir (since 1989) and the 1990-91 Iraq-Kuwait conflict. Saudi Arabia called for a solution to the Jammu and Kashmir issue on the basis of the UN resolutions saying that the long-standing problem had cast a shadow over Indo-Pakistani ties. Riyadh helped Pakistan build up support at the UNHRC meeting in March 1994. Its financial muscle gives a great deal of influence to the lending of its name as a sponsor because it would not have to vote on the resolution, not being a member of UNHRC. Moreover, as seen before Saudi Arabia wields considerable influence in the OIC. The Saudis, who co-sponsored the Pakistani resolution at the UNHRC in March 1994 on human rights violations in Jammu and Kashmir by India, compelled India's Minister of State for External Affairs Mr. Salman Khurshid at Geneva to say that India was not asking for special rapporteurs to be sent to investigate the condition of women in the kingdom who were denied basic human rights.

Moreover, Mr. Dinesh Singh India's External Affairs Minister called the Saudi step at UNHRC "quite wrong", and said that the issue should not be given a "communal colour." It would only create "difficulties for the Muslims in India", he added.[32] Many observers felt that in view of India's lack of sensitivity to Saudi national security concerns, whether siding with Nasser's Egypt, Yemen, supporting Iraq or Iran, the Saudis have always looked upon India's close ties with the Kingdom's enemies especially in the WANA region with deep suspicion which, in fact, may have partly driven them to support Pakistan on Kashmir and other issues, affecting India indirectly. The over-reaction to the Surat (Gujarat) plague scare in 1994 by the GCC was perhaps due to the initiative of Saudi Arabia. Earlier, the GCC leaders at Abu Dhabi (UAE) summit meeting at Saudi initiative had described in December 1992 the Babri Masjid demolition as, "sacrilege and an unpardonable act". The severest condemnation from among the Islamic States of India, of course, came from Saudi Arabia on the Babri Masjid issue. The Saudi financed Jeddah based *Rabita-e-Alam-al-Islami*, or the League of the Islamic World, also accused the Indian government of being "fully responsible" for the destruction of the Babri Mosque.[33]

All this clearly indicated that the time had come for India to take the initiative on a summit meeting to prevent stagnation in Indo-Saudi ties. No exchange at the highest governmental level had taken place since Mrs. Gandhi's visit to the Kingdom in 1982 until King Abdullah was invited to visit in 2006. India strived hard to ensure that Saudis took a more balanced view of its relations with India and Pakistan. A directive for opening out towards the Saudis came from the top leadership. There was growing perception that India under the BJP led NDA government due to the Kashmir issue, Indo-Pak tensions, US support to Pakistan and US economic sanctions after the May 1998 nuclear explosions looked at closer cooperation with Israel in a number of fields as additionally useful to reach out to the US. (After having opposed the partition of Palestine by the UN in 1947, India recognised the Jewish State of Israel in September 1950 but established diplomatic ties only in January 1992). One need not underestimate the importance of Indo-Israeli relations, but one has to assess its impact on India's traditional ties with the Islamic countries. In the wake of the end of the Cold War, disintegration of USSR, and the Gulf War over Kuwait, it became obvious that the US was openly welcomed by the Gulf monarchies for regime security and stability in the region. The US has shown (as in the case of Kuwait and Iraq) its determination as to the extent it can go to safeguard its interest in the

Gulf especially concerning oil and the stability of GCC family rule. Undoubtedly in the coming years the US would be preoccupied with the security of the GCC monarchies, which is vital for its status as the sole superpower. It is in this context we have to see the significance of Indo-Saudi ties. If New Delhi can engage the US in a dialogue over security measures in the Gulf area, and achieve a breakthrough particularly in assuring the Saudis and other GCC monarchical States of India's willingness to help them in concert with the US, then in that case Saudi Arabia could hold the key, not only for better Indo-US relations but more significantly for stability in South Asia as well including the resolution of the thorny Kashmir issue and normalization of Indo-Pakistan relations.[34]

Major developments took place after the end of Cold War, collapse of USSR, Madrid Peace Conference, and establishment of Indo-Israeli ties, Oslo Peace Process and improvement in Saudi-Russian ties. More significantly India's nuclear tests in 1998 made Saudi Arabia apprehensive and acknowledge India's growing power. The Pakistani nuclear tests somewhat balanced their apprehensions. The kingdom continued to support the Taliban government in Kabul and could have done much more to restrain Pakistan over military and foreign fighters in Kashmir. However, the emergence in the US of neo-conservatives, election of George W. Bush as US President and the 9/11 events came as rude shock to the Saudis. Strident US criticism of the Kingdom especially over the involvement of Saudis in the 9/11 bombings virtually neutralized what all the Kingdom had done to the US especially keeping oil prices low and supporting the US against USSR among many other things. The Saudis were now accused of giving financial assistance to terrorist groups globally especially to Hezbollah, Hamas, Islamic Gehad as also some groups in the US. Wahabbi Islam was identified as promoting religious extremism worldwide. The Saudis were urged to carry out political reforms and loosen the tight political/security control they exercised over the kingdom. The treatment of Shia minority within the Kingdom, as also human rights situation, came under scrutiny as well. The US didn't appreciate Saudi call for rise in oil prices, King Abdullah's Arab-Israeli peace plan presented at Beirut's Arab League Summit and Abdullah's personal mediation between Iraq and Kuwait.

As seen before, since the emergence of militancy in Kashmir in 1989 and the demolition of Babri Masjid in 1992, India worked hard to improve ties with the Kingdom. The opportunity to cement that effort came following 11 September, 2001 developments when Saudi Arabia responded to Indian overtures, realizing that both countries face the common scourge of terrorism. Since then, Riyadh has condemned all forms of extremism and terrorism, including the attack on Indian Parliament in 2001, while making its fervent appeal for peace in the Indian subcontinent. The healing process was demonstrated by the quick aid dispatched to the victims of the Gujarat earthquake, the same year. Further, much of the political rapprochement comes amid the Saudi shift in position on Kashmir over the last five years. Saudi Arabia's position on Kashmir now emphasizes the bilateral process with a dialogue with Pakistan based on existing Shimla and Lahore agreements, which confirms with New Delhi's stand. Since then the Kingdom has condemned all forms of extremism and on several occasions made a fervent appeal for peace, between India and Pakistan. The appeal was again made during Crown Prince Abdullah's meeting with Najma Heptullah, Deputy Chairperson of Rajya Sabha in Jeddah in 2002. Moreover having seen the limits to their support to Pakistani efforts to use OIC on Kashmir and other issues, India's nuclear tests in 1998, growing Indo-Israeli ties, India's emergence in areas of IT, high economic growth rate and rapidly improving Indo-US relations, Saudi Arabia has apparently concluded that its pro-Pakistani tilt will be a burden in its quest for better ties with India.[35]

Despite growing Indo-Saudi economic ties, the political ties had not progressed and bilateral visits were few. Mr. Jaswant Singh, India's Foreign Minister visited the Kingdom in January 2001. The then Finance Minister Manmohan Singh visited Saudi Arabia for the meeting of the Indo-Saudi Joint Commission in 1994, which was followed by the visit to India of Prince Khalid bin Sultan bin Abdulaziz in October 1996. However in 2005 there were many bilateral visits at the ministerial level with Finance Minister P. Chidambaram visiting Riyadh in April; and India's Petroleum and Natural Gas Minister Mani Shankar Aiyer visiting the Kingdom three times during 2004-05. He was also the first Indian oil minister to visit the Kingdom. Saudi petroleum minister Ali Al-Niami visited New Delhi in January 2005 to attend the first round table of Asian ministers on regional cooperation in the oil and gas economy.

Saudi Arabia is not only a major economic partner of India, it is also a major power in the Gulf region, with substantial influence on other GCC states, major producer of oil, Saudi financial power which gives them enormous ability to influence many groups, parties and states worldwide, location of Islamic holy places (Mecca and Medina) in the Kingdom as also Riyadh wields considerable influence in the 57-member Organization of Islamic Conference (OIC). It is also a major player in the Organization of Petroleum Exporting Countries (OPEC) by virtue of being the largest oil producer in the world at over 10 million barrels a day. Besides the above visits other important visits have also taken place. Mr. Omar Abdullah, India's Minister of State for External Affairs led a delegation to the Kingdom to sign the hajj agreement in Jeddah on 22 August, 2001. A five-member delegation led by the Chairman of Indian Oil Corporation visited Saudi Arabia from 6-8 April, 2001 to renew a term contract with Saudi Arabia for the supply of crude oil and other petroleum products to India for 2001-02. A 12-member team from the National Defence College (NDC) paid a 5-day visit to the Kingdom from 21 May, 2001. This was the first visit of an NDC team after a gap of ten years. The team visited major defence and economic institutes and held discussions with Saudi officials in Riyadh, Dammam and Jeddah. While the campaign undertaken by the Saudi ministry of Labour to achieve full Saudiization in the sectors of gold and tourism (travel agency) have continued to test Saudi-Indian relations during the last two years, India has to look beyond; given that Riyadh is bound to further intensify its unemployment—alleviation drive. The Saudi Arabian General Investment Authority has given licenses to Indian companies to setup joint ventures in different areas. Many Indian companies have also taken advantage of 100 percent foreign ownership of companies in the Kingdom and are establishing themselves in designing, financial services, software, so on. At present, 49 Indo-Saudi joint ventures are operational in India and 82 Indian companies-either fully owned or joint ventures-in the Kingdom. India's information technology software exports to the kingdom are rapidly increasing, amounting to over $170 million and poised to grow further. By April 2005, 42 investments projects from India with an investment of $411 million had been licensed by Riyadh. Further, there were 40 non-industrial projects with an investment of $56.2 million, which took Indian investments in the Kingdom to $467.2 million. Expanding on that relationship, State Bank of India has started functioning in Saudi Arabia and a Saudi group is building a five star, 500-room hotel in Hyderabad in Andhra Pradesh. In addition, the Saudi embassy will soon open a Saudi school in New Delhi and plans are afoot to construct a new Saudi embassy in the capital.[36]

Saudi Arabia has emerged as the 13th largest market for Indian exports and a source for 5.5 percent of India's total imports. India is the fourth largest market for Saudi goods and ranks 10th in the Saudi imports market list. Riyadh is the largest source of crude oil to India supplying half a million barrels of crude oil per day and a total of about 25 million tones annually, which is nearly a quarter of India's total crude requirements. Saudi-Indian bilateral trade in 2002-03 was $5 billion and Saudi exports were of $3.65 billion while India exported one billion dollars worth goods to the Saudi Kingdom.

Emerging Relationship: In a major breakthrough India announced, in November 2005, the visit of Saudi King Abdullah to India in early 2006. The Saudi King was the chief guest at the Republic Day celebrations in New Delhi on 26 January 2006. He became the first Saudi king to get that honour. The tradition of inviting a head of state as chief guest at the Republic Day parade every year is now considered a measure of the importance India attaches to that country, apart from serving as an opportunity to showcase the country's military might as well as secular and democratic traditions. For the last half century no Saudi ruler had visited India as the Kingdom enjoyed close ties with Pakistan. As seen earlier, since the Babri Masjid Issue (1992) and the Kashmir issue (militancy) India had been working hard to improve ties with the Kingdom. Since 9/11, there has been a realization among Saudi circles of the need to improve ties with India. Both the countries have been facing the challenge from terrorism. Saudi Arabia condemned the 2001 attack on Indian Parliament in New Delhi. The Kingdom is also appreciative of Indian stand on the Kashmir issue and signaled that its ties with Pakistan need not come in the way of better ties with India. Setting the stage for economic agreements during King Abdullah's visit to India, the first India-Saudi Arabia Joint Business Council meeting was held on the 21 November, 2005. The meeting acted as a "catalyst" in furthering economic ties between the two countries. Saudi Ambassador in New Delhi Mr. Saleh Mohammad Al-Ghamdi announced that India and Saudi Arabia have concluded 15 agreements: to promote bilateral investments, avoidance of double taxation; youth and sports and on security matters an anti-terror pact during the King's visit to India. Meanwhile a high-level Saudi business delegation to India urged the Indian companies and the investors to take advantage of the tremendous opportunities in the Kingdom and put in their expertise and resources to develop strategic partnerships with Saudi companies. Further, Saudi Arabia is playing a key role in the talks for a Free Trade Agreement between GCC and India that began in January 2006. Based on its new diplomacy of promoting cooperation between importers and exporters of crude oil, India and Saudi Arabia are encouraging cross investments in the industry, mining and energy sectors.

The two countries also signed a memorandum of understanding on meeting challenges such as crime and terrorism. There are over 1.5 million Indian workers gainfully employed in the Kingdom who send valuable remittances in foreign exchange, which form a good part of the trade bill for India. More than one and half lakh Indian Muslims go on hajj pilgrimage annually to the Kingdom besides several hundred thousands making the Umra pilgrimage every year. The visit of King Abdullah to India has given a big boost to the tourist traffic between the two countries with Saudi visitor arrivals in India already up by 16 percent in 2004 to about 15,000 and likely to go up further by six percent in the first half of 2006. Those figures are bound to rise further as Saudis discover India as a viable destination for medical treatment, education and sightseeing. The official international carrier, Air-India, now generates about 19 percent of its revenue from the Gulf, with the Saudi sector accounting for 30 percent of the figure. Clearly relations are likely to see upswing in the coming years. In the broader context of rapidly improving Indo-US ties, closer Indo-Saudi ties are likely to be upgraded which could include security cooperation to meet common challenges. King Abdullah's visit should kick-start a process that will look beyond religion, oil and employment, as well as remain independent of the Pakistani factor.[37]

Indo-Saudi ties began to improve in the aftermath of 9/11 mainly due to Saudi realization that their decision to put all eggs in US basket is risky and that they should build bridges in the neighbourhood. The new "Look East" policy started with Saudi support to India on the terrorist attack on Indian Parliament in 2001, support to Shimla agreement on Kashmir, condemnation of terrorism in India and delinking of their ties with Pakistan and India. Although they had received BJP's Jaswant Singh as Foreign Minister (of the NDA) but it was only with the assumption of UPA-Congress led government that Saudi-Indian ties really matured. Also Ambassadors Ishrat Aziz, M. Hamid Ansari and Talmiz Ahmed had played a crucial role and so was the dynamic and innovative role of Saudi Ambassador in Delhi Mohammad Saleh al Ghamdi. It was said that Crown Prince Abdullah had accepted India's invitation to visit Delhi but the death of King Fahd appears to have finally paved the way for the visit. Breaking protocol India's PM Mammohan Singh personally received the Saudi King at the Delhi Airport. King Abdullah set the tone for his four-day visit to India by describing India as a "second home" and hoped his visit would take bilateral ties to new heights. Manmohan Singh described Saudi Arabia as "an important partner in combating global terror". King Abdullah told India's Prime Minister that his country had "declared a war on terror. It might be a long-term struggle, the battle will continue unless this scourge is eliminated".

Both signed 15 new agreements, including a landmark anti-terror pact, which focuses on strengthening cooperation in tackling transnational crime, terrorism and the smuggling of narcotics. The two sides signed an agreement to eliminate double taxation, a pact on investment promotion and cooperation and an agreement relating to youth and sports. The two sides also signed 11 commercial agreements at a joint business council meeting. The MoU's between Saudi and Indian firms were in the energy, financial and health care sectors. The India Prime Minister thanked the king for increasing the quota of Indian Muslim pilgrims going for Hajj by 10,000 to 1, 47,000. Later both the leaders witnessed the signing of eleven of 20 joint ventures between Saudi and Indian businessmen. The Saudi King underscored the "tremendous developments in economic and commercial ties" between the two countries and invited Indian businessmen to invest in the Kingdom especially in the area of IT, telecommunications, power, pharmaceuticals, minerals and the services sector. He said the new bilateral agreements would play a big role in boosting joint investments and further widening and deepening of bilateral ties. India's Prime Minister said: "We have reinvented and rediscovered our relations after a lapse of time and new winds of change are blowing across the world". He underlined the importance India attaches to the visit and to its ties with the Kingdom, "which have deep-rooted civilization links and have tremendous potential of great economic possibilities". He invited Saudi businessman to come to India and set up Joint projects. The joint business deals cover sectors like pre-engineered buildings, the health sector-opening India's Apollo Hospitals in the Kingdom, water services, pipe manufacturing, finance and oil and gas equipment. Saudi finance minister Al-Assaf said, "There is good scope for widening bilateral cooperation." At the moment there are 106 Indian joint ventures with a global investment of $445 million, in Saudi Arabia and over 50 Saudi Joint ventures in India. India has emerged as the Kingdom's fourth largest export destination with $10 billion worth of exports. Oil accounts for 94 per cent of the exports with the kingdom emerging as the largest exporter of oil to India supplying 26 percent of India's needs. Saudi imports from India are however much lower at $1.6 billion.

The sixth Joint Commission (est. in 1981) was held in Riyadh on 12 April, 2005. India has invited Saudi Aramco to invest in three refineries at Bhatinda, Bina and Paradeep. Reliance, it was reported, has decided to invest $8 billion in refinery and petrochemicals projects in Saudi Arabia. Two other Indian refineries, which will have Saudi investment, are Kakinada and Barmer. Saudi Arabia's Bushnak Group has tied up with Hyderabad based Pallava water Services to invest $80 million to set up desalination plants in Tamil Nadu, AP and Karnataka besides the first project coming up at Karaikal in Pondicherry in early 2007. The Saudis are concerned at Iraqi developments especially the issue of sectarianism, Iran's nuclear programme, as also the future stability of the House of Saud in the face of fast pace development in the region. The King's visit took place in the background of tragedy at Mina during the Hajj in which the largest victims were from India. Year after year, some disaster or the other has been claiming the lives of hajjis especially from India either by fire or stampede. Although this should be a matter of grave concern as it reflects the administrative competence of the Saudi authorities, this issue appears to have not affected bilateral ties. The "Delhi Declaration" signed at the end of the visit spoke of a broad strategic vision between India and Saudi Arabia.[38]

For sometime the Saudis have been taking unusual interest as far as conflict resolution in South Asia is concerned. This initiative may perhaps be on their own, or US inspired but certainly in the knowledge of India. Although in the past Indian leaders have discouraged outside mediation between India and Pakistan, and officially it still does reject it, but New Delhi has been welcoming friendly pressure on Pakistan to reciprocate Indian peace overtures over Kashmir. It is in this spirit one should view the statement of Saudi Crown Prince Sultan, who is also the Deputy PM and Minister of Defence, when he said in April 2006 that it was time for India and Pakistan to reach a just and peaceful solution to the Kashmir issue: "I hope the two countries would have the true vision and ability to continue their peace overtures".[39] The Saudi Press Agency quoting Crown Prince Sultan said, Saudi Arabia is striving to reinforce security and stability in the subcontinent by brokering peace between India and Pakistan.There is no doubt India needs Saudi assistance to convince Pakistan to work seriously in South Asia for peace and stability. In this connection the Saudi Ambassador to India said starting next year (2007) the Kingdom will be sending hundreds of Saudi students on scholarships to study in India. Most of these students would have normally gone to the west as before, but after 9/11 there has been a change in Saudi policy, which is increasingly looking towards India, China and the east in general.[40] India's Lok Sabha (Lower House of Parliament) Speaker Somnath Chatterjee led a high powered Indian delegation to Saudi Arabia in mid February 2007 to 'Keep up the momentum' of high level exchanges between the two countries. Mr. Chatterjee recalled Saudi Foreign Minister Saud-al Faisal telling the delegation that "India should be prepared to educate around 10,000 students from the Kingdom soon". Infact, Saudi Arabia is looking at India as a major destination for education as well as a partner in trade and investments. Asked about the prospect of a high level visit to Riyadh from India, Mr. Chatterjee said, "it was likely" that Prime Minister Manmohan Singh would visit Saudi Arabia in May 2007. During his stay, the Speaker called on the Crown Prince, Prince Sultan Bin Abdulaziz and held talks with the Saudi Shura Council delegation. Other members of the parliamentary group included Deputy Chairman of Rajya Sabha K. Rehman Khan, C. Ramachandraiah, E. Ponnuswamy, Syed Shahnawaz Hussain, Vanlalzawma Furkan Ansari.[41]

In a bid to further strengthen Indo-Saudi cultural ties, India's Minister for Youth Affairs and Sports Mr. Mani Shankar Aiyar led an Indian delegation to Saudi Arabia in mid February 2007. Both countries decided to hold bilateral exchange programmes involving students, youths and sportsperson. It was agreed that a ten member Indian delegation will visit the Kingdom soon. The two countries also agreed on establishing institutional contacts between the Rajiv Gandhi Institute of Youth Development and corresponding institutions of Saudi Arabia. Mr. Aiyar, a former oil minister of India familiar with the kingdom had talks with Saudi officials led by Prince Sultan bin Fahd. The Indian minister visited the Governorate of Muzahmia and met the Governor, members of the Local Council and the Municipality of Muzahmia. In sports, the two sides decided to cooperate in training and group exchange programmes. The disciplines that were taken on priority were football, volleyball, basketball, handball, athletics and equestrian. The two sides discussed ways of activating a Mou signed during king Abdullah's historic visit to India in January 2006.[42]

References

1. See A.K. Pasha, "India and West Asia", *World Focus,* Vol. 25, No. 10-12, Oct-Dec. 2004. pp. 41-46.
2. The Muslim ruler of Gujarat, commonly known as, Mahmud Begarha, who came to power towards the middle of 15th century in alliance with Qwansauhal-Ghauri, Sultan of Egypt, tried to check the rising power of the Portuguese in the Indian seas. The Egyptian fleet, under the command of Amir Husain, the Kurd, Governor of Jeddah, and the Indian Contingent, under the command of Malil Ayaz, a Turk, who had found employment in the court of Gujarat, defeated a Portuguese squadron commanded by Dom

Lourenco, son of the Portuguese Viceroy, Francesco de Alameda, near Chaul, South of Bombay, in 1508. Subsequently after his defeat at the hands of the Portuguese, in 1509, Mahmud granted them a site for a factory at Diu. Begarsha died on 23 November, 1511. For details see R.C. Majumdar *et al. An Advanced History of India* (Delhi: Macmillian, 1978), p. 346. After they took over Constantinople in 1453, and renamed it Istanbul, the Ottomans lost naval supremacy in the Mediterranean in 1571, when they were defeated at the Battle of Lepanto. The Europeans began to dominate trade in the Indian Ocean and Arab *mudarabah* or speculative trade declined, as the former came to dominate territories as well. Historian Bernard Lewis quotes from Umar Talib, one of the Turkish elite, who complained in 1625, AD that: "The Europeans have become acquainted with the whole world sending their ships everywhere and seizing the harbours. The goods from India, Sind and China previously came to Suez and were distributed by the Muslims to the whole world. Now, however these goods are transported by the Portuguese, the Dutch and the English to the Frankish countries, from where they distribute them to the world. The goods they don't need, they bring to Istanbul and the Islamic countries selling them at five times their value, thus, reaping great profit. For this reason, both gold and silver have become scarce in Islamic countries." Quoted from Bernard Lewis, "Some Reflections on the Decline of the Ottoman Empire", *Studies Islamica*, 9,1959 p.118; see also K.N. Chaudhari, *Trade and Civilization in the Indian Ocean; An Economic History from the Rise of Islam to 1950* (Cambridge: 1985); see also Wrike Freitag and William G. Clarence Smith, Ed; *Hadhrami Traders, Scholars and Statesman in the Indian Ocean, 1750's-1960's* (Leiden: EJ Brill,1997); and A.K. Pasha, *"Tipu and the Ottoman Empire"*, in B. Shiek Ali, Ed, *Tipu Sultan: A Great Martyr* (Bangalore: Prasaranga, 1993), pp. 219-32; and A.K. Pasha, Ed.; *Perspectives on Indian and the Gulf States* (New Delhi: Détente Publication, 1999) pp. 1-23; see also Khaldoun Hasan al Naqeeb: *Society and State in the Gulf and Arab Peninsula: A Different Perspective.* (London: Routledge, 1990) pp. 31-42.

3. R.C. Majumadar, *Ibid.*, p. 175; see also M.A. Salem *Khan, Early Muslin Perception of India and Hinduism* (New Delhi: South Asian Publishers, 1997) see also K.N. Chaudhuri, *The Trading World of Asia and the English East India Company 1660-1760 (Cambridge, 1987) and Shafaat Ahmad Khan, The East India Trade in the 17th Century, in its Political and Economic Aspects* (New Delhi: S. Chand and Co.); see also Edward Simpson, *Muslim Society and the Western Indian Ocean* (London: Routledge, 2006); and Asghar Ali Engineer, ed., *Islam in India: The Impact of Civilizations* (New Delhi: ICCR, Shipra, 2002).
4. Michael N. Pearson, *Pilgrimage to Mecca: The Indian Experience*, 1500-1800 (Princeton; Markur Wiener, 1996); see also Document: "Relations between India and Arabia before the Birth of Islam-Early Contacts", *Indian Journal of Secularism* (Mumbai) Vol. 2, July-September 1998, pp.73-89.

5. Soon after the abolition of caliphate in 1924, by the new leader of Turkey, Mustafa Kamal Ataturk an international Muslim Congress was held in Cairo in May 1926 at the initiative of Al Azhar Ulema to discuss the Caliphate issue. Muslim leaders from nearly thirteen countries participated; including representatives from British India-Maulana Shaukat Ali and Mohammed Iqbal were two of the four Indian delegates who attended. All of them took part in their private capacities with non-governmental representation. Other delegates were from Egypt, Libya, Tunisia, Morocco, South Africa, the Dutch East Indies (Indonesia), the Yemen, the Hejaz, Palestine, Iraq and Poland. Interestingly, Turkey, Iran, Afghanistan, the Nejd, and Russia were not represented. The conference decided to meet soon as the feasibility of appointing a Caliph at the moment was found incapable of realization, in view of the situation in which the Muslims found themselves. For details see SAM Pasha, *Islam in Pakistan's Foreign Policy* (New Delhi: Global Media Publications, 2006).
6. See Uri M. Kupferschmidt, *"The General Muslim Congress of 1931 in Jerusalem"*, *Asian and African Studies* (Haifa) Vol. 12, No. 1, March 1978, p. 126; see also, A.K. Pasha, *Indian and Turkey; Past and Emerging Relations* (Delhi: Academic Publishers, 2006)
7. S.M. Burke, *Mainsprings of Indian and Pakistani Foreign Policies* (Minneapolis, University of Minnesota Press, 1974), p. 134; Adbullah Ahsan, *The Organization of Islamic Conference: An Introduction to the Islamic Political Institution* (Herndon, Virginia: The International Institute of Islamic Thought, 1988), p. 11-12 and p. 109; see also Arnold J. Toynbee, *Survey of International Affairs,* vol. 1: The Islamic World since the Peace Settlement, 1925 (London: OUP, 1927) p. 89; H.A.R. Gibb, "*The Islamic Congress at Jerusalem in 1931*", Survey of International Affairs (Oxford: RIIA,1934), p. 99 and p. 105-06; see also Sisir Gupta, *"Islam as a factor in Pakistan's Foreign Policy"*, *India Quarterly*, vol. 18, No. 1, July-September 1956, pp. 230-58.
8. For details see Jacob M. Landau, *The Politics of Pan-Islam: Ideology and Organization* (Oxford: Clarendon Press, 1990), pp. 240-41.
9. John Sabini, *Armies in the Sand: The Struggle for Mecca and Medina* (London: Thames and Hudson,1981), p. 134-35; see also Arnold J. Toynbee, *"The Proclamation of Sultan Abdul Aziz B. Saud as King of Hejaz and the Islamic Congress at Mecca (1926)"*, in *Survey of International Affairs,* Vol. 1, (London: RIIA), 1927.
10. Harpal Singh Bedi, *"India and the Pan-Islamic Conferences: A Case Study of Rabat Conference",* M. Phil disst. SIS/JNU, New Delhi 1987; see also Noor Ahmed Baba, *OIC: Theory and Practice of Pan-Islamic Cooperation* (New Delhi: Sterling Publishers, 1994).
11. Ranjit Kaur, *Islam, Cooperation and Unity* (New Delhi: Deep and Deep Publishers, 1993); see also A.K. Pasha, "Nehru and Crisis in West Asia", *Détente,* Vol. 9, No.1, May-June 1990, pp. 4-9.

12. See A.K. Pasha, *India and OIC: Strategy and Diplomacy* (New Delhi: Center for Peace Studies, 1955); see also A.K. Pasha, *"Security and Stability in the Gulf and West Asian Region*", in A.K. Pasha, Ed; *Contemporary Gulf: State Society, Economy and Foreign Policy* (New Delhi: Detente Publishers 1999).
13. Mujtaba Rizvi, "*Pakistan-Saudi Arabian Relations: An Example of Entente*", *Pakistan Horizon,* First Quarter, 1981, p. 83; S.M. Burke, *Pakistan's Foreign Policy* (London: OUP, 1975), p. 204; see also A.K. Pasha, "Indo-OIC Relations: Perspective and Trends", *Journal of Peace Studies,* Vol. 1, No. 3-4, March-June 1994, pp. 22-50; and M.S. Agwani, *"Pakistan and Pan-Islamism"*, in Surendra Chopra, ed. *Perspectives on Pakistan's Foreign Policy* (Amritsar: 1983), p. 292; Cuyler Young, *"Pan-Islamism in Modern World"* in Harris Proctor, ed., *Islam and International Relations* (London: Full Hebb Press,1965).
14. Pasha, n. 12, p. 3; see also M.S. Agwani, *"India, Pakistan and West Asia*", *International Studies,* vol. 8, July, 1966 April 1967, p. 159; and Shaukat Ali, *Pan Movements in the Third World: Pan Arabism, Pan Africanism and Pan Islamism* (Lahore: United Publishers Ltd. 1976); see also Pasha, n.5, p. 140-53.
15. *Round Table* (London) March 1957, p. 172.
16. *Dawn* (Karachi) 1 December, 1956, cited in Pasha, n.12, p. 3-4.
17. National Assembly of Pakistan Debates (Islamabad) 25 February, 1959, p. 1088; Zulfikar A. Khalid, *"Evolution of Saudi-Pakistan Strategic Relations, 1947-1990;* Military, Security and Economic Factors", *Strategic Studies,* Vol. XII, No. 1 Autumn 1989, p. 58: Naved Ahmed, *"Pak-Saudi Relations*", *Pakistan Horizon,* no. 4, 1982, p. 51: Ajay N. Jha, "Pakistan as factor in Indo-Saudi Relations", *Journal of Political Studies,* (Jallandhar) September 1984, p. 38-51; and Verinder Grover, ed., *International Relations and Foreign Policy of India,* Vol. 4, *West Asia and India's Foreign Policy* (New Delhi: Deep and Deep Publications, 1993), pp. 309-25.
18. Noor Ahmed Baba, "Nasser'a Pan-Arab Radicalism and the Saudi Drive for Islamic Solidarity: A Response for Security", *India Quarterly*, Vol. XLVII, No. 1-2 January-June, p. 1-22; and "Saudi Drive for Islamic Solidarity: A Quest for Security", *Political Science Review,* Vol. 24, Nos. 1 and 2, January-June, 1985, p. 35-34; Abdullah M. Sindhi, *"King Faisal and Pan-Islamism",* in Willard A. Beling, ed., *Modernization of Saudi Arabia* (London: Croom Helm, 1980); see also Nizar Madani, *The Islamic Content of the Foreign Policy of Saudi Arabia, King Feisal's Call for Islamic Solidarity,* Thesis submitted to the America University, Washington DC, 1977; see also James P. Piscatori, "Islamic values and national interest: The case of Saudi Arabia" in Adeed Dawisha, ed. *Islam in Foreign Policy*, (Cambridge: CUP, 1983).
19. *Dawn*, 11, 18, 24 September, 1965; and UN General Assembly official Records, session 20, Plenary meetings, Vol. 2, p. 16, as cited in Pasha, n. 5, p. 16-7.

20. Dawn, 20 September, 1965, *Ibid*, p. 165.
21. Pasha, n. 12, p. 98-100; see also Ishrat Aziz, "India and West Asia/North Africa", and Rajendra M. Abhyankar, "India's West Asia Policy: Search for a Middle Ground", in Atish Sinha and Madhup Mohta, eds.; *Indian Foreign Policy: Challenges and Opportunities* (New Delhi: Academic Foundation, 2007), pp. 293-350
22. Baba, no. 10, p. 78; *Asian Recorder*, (New Delhi) 1971, p. 10473.
23. Z.A. Bhutto called Pak-Saudi ties as "indestructible solidarity", King Khalid called for a settlement of the Kashmir problem in accordance with relevant UN resolutions. The Saudi King was on visit to Pakistan in October 1976. See also Anwar Syed, "Pakistan in 1976: Business as usual", *Asian Survey* (Berkeley) vol. 17, no. 2, February 1977, pp. 187-88; and Rashid Jamal, "Pakistan as the Central Command", *Middle East Report* (Washington; DC) July-August 1986, p. 31 and 43.
24. Anthony Hymen, "Pakistan: Towards a Modern Muslims state" *Conflict Studies* (London) No. 227, January 1990, p. 19; Pasha, n. 5, p. 296-97.
25. *POT* (New Delhi) Vol. VII, Part 265, 15 December, 1980, p. 2241-42; Part 16, January 21, 1981, p. 131; Vol., No. 143; 20 July, 1984, p. 2255 as cited in Pasha, n.5, p. 294-96, See also Howard W. Wriggins, *"Pakistan's Search for a Foreign Policy after the invasion of Afghanistan", Pacific Affairs*, (Vancouver), Vol. 57, No. 2, Summer 1984 see also A.K. Pasha "India and Israel: Growing Cooperation", *World Focus*, Vol 14, No. 8, No. 164, August, 1993, pp. 19-22.
26. Riyaz Punjabi and A.K. Pasha, ed. *India and the Islamic World* (New Delhi: Radiant Publishers, 1998) and Pasha, n. 12, p. 149-64.
27. See A.K. Pasha, *India and West Asia: Continuity and Change* (Delhi: Gyan Sagar, 1999); *Dawn* (Karachi) 16 April, 1981; *The Washington Post,* 13 April, 1981.
28. A.K. Pasha *"Communal Revivalism in India: Its Impact on ties with West Asia and North Africa"*, in Muchkund Dubey, Ed, *Communal Revivalism in India: A Study of External Implications* (New Delhi: Har Anand, 1994), p. 54-88; and A.K Pasha, "India's West Asia Policy: Continuity and Change", *Strategic Analysis,* Vol. XVI, No. 6, 1993, September, pp. 783-804.
29. A.K. Pasha, "Perspective on Indo-Saudi Relations", *Asian Affairs* (London) Vol. I, No. 11, September 1997, p. 24-26; see also A.K. Pasha "Security and Safety aspects of Haj", *The Pioneer*, 24 May, 1997; Mohan Guruswamy, "Dealing with Saudi Arabia: Beware of Unholy Bias", *Indian Express*, 9 May, 1997; *Times of India*, April 24, 1997; *The Pioneer*, 24-25, 28 April, 1997; and 7 May, 1997.
30. A.K. Pasha, *"India and the Gulf States: Challenges and Opportunities"*, in Rajan Harshe and K.M. Seethi, ed.: *Engaging with the World: Critical Reflections on India's Foreign Policy* (New Delhi: Orient Longman, 2005), pp. 389-424.
31. See also Muhammad Azhar, "GCC Aid to India" in A.K. Pasha, ed: *Perspectives on India and the Gulf States* (New Delhi: Détente Publications,

1999); see also Bansidhar Pradhan, "Changing dynamics of India's West Asia Policy", *International Studies,* Vol. 41, No. 1, 2004, pp. 73-84; and A.K. Pasha, "India and West Asia: Past and Future", in N.S. Sisodia and Ashok K. Behuria, ed., *West Asia in Turmoil: Implications for Global Security* (New Delhi: Academic Foundation, 2007), pp. 441-470.

32. A.K. Pasha, n. 12, p. 54-118.
33. A.K. Pasha, "Indian and the GCC", in n. 26, p. 34-48.
34. A.K. Pasha, *"Indo-Saudi Arabian Summit is Long Overdue", The Pioneer,* 3 August, 1992; and A.K. Pasha *"India's Policy towards the Arab World in 21st Century"* in V.D. Chopra, ed., *Indian Foreign Policy in 21st Century* (Delhi: Kalpaz, 2006). pp. 215-50.
35. *Saudi Gazette*, March 29 and 31, 2006; *Arab News*, 28 March, 2006.
36. A.K. Pasha "India-Saudi ties ready for a new Dawn", *GCC-India Research Bulletin*, (Dubai) No. 1, January 2006, p. 6-7.
37. *Ibid.*, See also *Deccan Chronicle*, 24 January 2006; *The Asian Age*, 25 January, 2006.
38. *Deccan Herald,* 25 January, 2006; for major highlights of the Delhi Declaration see *GCC-India Research Bulletin,* Issue No. 2, June 2006, pp. 3-4.
39. *National Herald*, 25, 26 January 2006, p. 8 and 14.
40. *Arab News*, April 17 and 19, 2006; *Saudi Gazette*, 16 April, 2006.
41. *The Hindu*, 13 February, 2007.
42. *The Hindu*, 17 February, 2007.

8

New Trends in Indo-Saudi Economic Relations

JAVED AHMAD KHAN

Introduction

In January 2006, when the King Abdullah bin Abdulaziz Al Saud of Saudi Arabia was about to come as a chief guest on Republics Day celebrations in New Delhi, the major discussion in the media and academic circles centered on whether India would be able to materialize with the Arab world's new "Look East" policy. Its significance was also because the massive oil revenues have refueled the developmental activities in the region as the GCC states along with the public and private sectors are experiencing a broad-based economic boom, thus changing the region's political and economic landscape. The most positive of this development is that the current GCC economic boom is based on sizeable balance of payments and fiscal surpluses, substantial government assets, sound banking systems and strong corporate profits. The economists distinguish this from earlier booms in the region or the Asian experience of the mid-1990s. Further, there are many sound investment opportunities in the GCC countries especially in sectors such as oil, gas and petrochemicals, utilities, infrastructure, leisure and tourism, and also finance and asset management.[1] Another geo-strategic factor now much visible is Arab Gulf's new 'Look East' policy, which can be easily attributed to the 11 September, 2001 terrorist attacks and its repercussion on the Muslim countries. In fact, King Abdullah's recent visit to India and other Asian countries are mainly seen in this context.

In the era of Kingdom's accession to World Trade Organization (WTO) in November 2005, the current Indo-Saudi relations are rightly seen as passing through an exciting phase. Because, it is the first time that Saudi Arabian businessmen are increasingly becoming aware of the rich opportunities for investment in India.

In Saudi Arabia, the post-WTO scenario shows that rules, regulations and procedures are being continually simplified and streamlined to facilitate business. The phenomenon of this emerging trends can be seen in Indian companies current penetrations in Saudi market. However, before the liberalization process started, Saudi regulations for registration of foreign companies were very stringent and Indian companies found uneasiness to comply with them. In fact no competitive biddings were in practice, as the Kingdom would offer its projects and joint ventures to the high profile western and US companies. Now, in a rather open and market driven economic activities in the entire Gulf region Indian companies have responded very positively. Especially the Kingdom's efforts to attract foreign investment has provided new opportunities for the Indian companies to compete with their Western rivals. This is clearly evident from the fact that since the promulgation of new investment laws by the Saudi government in mid-2000, more than 58 licenses have been granted to Indian companies by the Saudi Arabian General Investment Authority (SAGIA) for establishing joint ventures or 100 per cent Indian owned companies.

Similarly, gaining the trust from the Indian investors in the Kingdom, the growing number of Saudi businessmen have also started visiting India to source their business needs and look for business partners. In May 2003, a high-level Saudi Ministerial delegation visited India and another high-level business delegation organized by the Council of Saudi Chambers of Commerce and Industry visited during October 2003. The growing number of investment ventures, including in the Small and Medium Enterprises (SMEs) sector, clearly indicate that businessmen on both sides now do not feel much constraints.[2]

Today both Saudi Arabia and India are each other's major partners in trade, investment and joint ventures. The total volume of annual bilateral trade exceeds US $5.1 billion. Saudi Arabia's exports to India are worth more than US $4.1 billion with substantial oil exports and a steadily growing portion of non-oil exports. But all this became possible with the process of economic reforms both in India and Saudi Arabia, facilitating for more and more participations of private sectors. On the other hand, India is in the second phase of economic reforms launched in early 90s. In fact, this new Indo-Saudi economic relations can be traced only since the 1990s, the period of reforms in both the countries. In December 1994, then India's finance minister, Dr. Manmohan Singh (now the Prime Minister of the country) visited Saudi Arabia and the meeting of the Indo-Saudi Joint Commission revived the interest in strengthening economic ties and resumption of dialogue and frank exchanges on difficult issues.

In the late 1990s, India and Saudi Arabia were drawn to each other and the Kingdom saw India as a source of stability and moderation in the region, and as an important economic partner both as a market for crude oil and energy products and as a source of technology. In February 2000, the Saudi Assistant Foreign Minister, Dr. Nizar Obeid Madani, visited India and stressed the Kingdom's desire to strengthen bilateral relations, and establish a framework for co-operation with India in different fields. But the Indo-Saudi bilateral relations got a further boost with the first ever visit of India's Minister of External Affairs, Jaswant Singh, to Saudi Arabia in January 2001 focusing on issues of bilateral interest.[3]

At a time when surplus oil revenues in the region started the developmental projects, the importance of Indo-Saudi economic relations can be seen in that perspective also. Saudi oil exports in the world market in 1998 was merely $35 billion, and it soared a record of $160 billion in 2005. The Kingdom's daily oil income, according to the Middle East Association, has increased from $196 million in August 2004 to $630 million in August 2005. This has led to an unprecedented budget surplus and levels of liquidity in the country.[4] Saudi Arabia is one of the 25 major economies in the world and its gross national product (GNP) accounts for one fifth of the total Middle East GNP. The Saudi economy makes an annual growth rate of more than seven percent, which is the largest in the region. The booming Saudi stock market, where about two million Saudis invest in the bourse, which is the 11the largest in the world as shares valued at about $1.7 billion are exchanged there daily. Since the increased income and wealth also provides the economy with the savings needed to finance the new investments, this is seen as a golden opportunity for domestic business to set up new factories and businesses in the country to produce related goods and services. The rising oil revenues have also stepped up the developmental activities in the Gulf region. In Saudi Arabia too, this started at the accelerating pace.

Saudi Access to WTO and the New Investment Climate

In early November 2005, when the World Trade Organization (WTO) gave its approval for Saudi Arabia to join the global body after more than a decade of talks, the Kingdom has adopted 42 new regulations and measures as part of its efforts to join the international trade body and its accession to the WTO is expected to open new markets for Saudi products and services. After joining the WTO, oil giant Saudi Arabia aims to become one of the world's top 10 countries for attracting business by the end of the decade, and has taken steps to lure investors, including easing visa rules and preparing to set up special courts to arbitrate commercial disputes. But the most important thing about the WTO is that it gives comfort to foreign investors that Saudi Arabia's laws and regulations are in line with international standards.[5]

Saudi Arabia announced a series of measures to improve the country's investment climate, removing obstacles facing private investors, allowing foreign manpower recruitment and speeding up licensing procedures. The Supreme Economic Council in charge of economic reforms approved the implementation of various agreements between the Saudi Arabian General Investment Authority (SAGIA) and the relevant government departments to make Saudi Arabia more investment-friendly. They also feature streamlining judicial procedures to resolve trade disputes, strengthening guarantees for investors, and speeding up the process of collecting imports from entry ports.

In fact, The Kingdom is seeking foreign investment to carry out a large number of projects worth SR2.34 trillion ($624 billion) in the core areas such as petrochemicals, natural gas, electricity generation, water desalination, railways, telecommunications and other vital sectors. According to Omar Bahlaiwa, secretary general of the foreign trade development committee at the Council of Saudi Chambers of Commerce and Industry, infrastructure projects offer the largest investment opportunity of $140 billion. The petrochemicals sector comes second with $92 billion projects followed by electricity and water $88.9 billion, telecommunications $60 billion, tourism $53.3 billion, natural gas $50 billion, agriculture $28.3 billion and information technology $10.7 billion.[6]

With the joining of WTO there started the flow of foreign investments and till the November 2005 alone the Kingdom received record 17.3 billion dollars in Foreign Direct Investment (FDI). Saudi Arabian General Investment Authority (SAGIA) has already started an aggressive policy to attract foreign funds, providing incentives and tax breaks for investors and removing hurdles facing them. In its efforts to improve the Kingdom's investment climate and attract more foreign direct investment, Saudi Arabian General Investment Authority (SAGIA) has started surveying the Kingdom's 13 regions in order to establish new investment projects. SAGIA has recently started an aggressive policy to attract foreign funds, providing incentives and tax breaks for investors and removing hurdles facing them. The authority concluded 17 agreements with various government departments aimed at knocking down hurdles to local and foreign investment.[7]

With the flow of massive oil resources due to high oil prices, Saudi Arabia seeks to raise a staggering $624 billion in foreign direct investment (FDI) over the next 14 years, of which some 37 percent is earmarked for the oil and gas industries; 30 percent for water and electricity projects; 26 percent for refining and petrochemicals; and 7 percent for transport. The sectors identified as the most potential ones like Housing, Infrastructure, Electricity, Railways, to draw FDI are the sectors where India could emerge as a major player. The oil and gas sectors are also planning massive expansion with Saudi Aramco planning to spend $46 billion over the next five years. At least six mega oil and gas projects are planned to push production capacity to 12 million barrels per day. Saudi Basic Industries Corp. (SABIC), now a major global petrochemicals player is also planning a major expansion with much greater private sector involvement.[8]

Prospects for India

In April 1981, both India and Saudi Arabia established a Joint Commission for Economic, Trade, Scientific, Technical and Cultural Cooperation and now they are trying to stimulate relations not only in area of trade but in the scientific development also. A Technical Cooperation Agreement in 1993, which provides for cooperation in the areas of metrology, scientific and industrial research, standardization and quality control in different fields. A team of Indian agricultural experts is working with the Saudi Ministry of Agriculture and Water in the Red Palm Weevil Pest Control Project. A Joint Business Council (JBC) was also established during the last JCM (Joint Cooperation Mission) between the Council of Saudi Chambers of Commerce and Industry and FICCI. ISRO has signed a MOU with ARABSAT for imparting training to the ARABSAT personnel. KACST is also negotiating with ISRO for cooperation in designing and launch of micro satellites, launching of joint remote sensing satellites and training of KACST personnel.

The Kingdom is also embarking on an ambitious privatization programme in the wake of its accession to the World Trade Organization which will see a further estimated $800 billion worth of state assets sold off over the next 14 years.

The process of economic liberalization is creating an environment that is more attractive to private investment thereby marking strong growth in the private sector. Privatization, which has resulted in more inflow of foreign direct investment, has already started showing a positive impact on the industrial sector, with many Saudis venturing into light industries either for self-employment or as a matter of diversification.[9] In case of India for example, Saudi investors have shown much interest. Similarly, the financial reforms are going in the Kingdom and the financial sector is being opened for foreign investment, flexible laws for foreign institutions, reviewing its copyright laws and pushing for privatization and thus paving the way for its accession to the organization. In this context, the entry of Indian financial institutions, banks and investment companies points towards the opening of vast opportunities to tap the region's excessive finance for productive investment. In recent years, Indian finance houses, such as Unit Trust of India (UTI), ICICI Bank, State Bank of India have already penetrated in the Gulf market.

In April 2005, India's Finance Minister P. Chidambaram showed keen interest in Indo-Saudi cooperation in financial sectors. He explored the prospects of Indian banking sector gaining a foothold in Saudi Arabia. State Bank of India has now opened a branch in Jeddah. There also are prospects of a Saudi-Indian insurance company being set up.[10] Chidambaram reminded them that India had an independent judicial system that held guarantees for investment. He formally announced there on the setting up of a SR100 million Saudi-Indian insurance venture. Life Insurance Corporation of India, its foreign arm LIC International and the New India Assurance Co. have combined to set up the joint company Saudi Indian Insurance Company—with Saudi investors to offer life and non-life insurance products to the Indian expatriates (NRIs) there and other residents.[11]

But the most attractive area for Indian financial institutions in the Gulf is equity fund market, because with the massive oil revenue the private equity business has grown significantly in the recent years with a number of foreign players investing in the region. Currently there are more than 29 private equity firms operating in the region which deals worth over $6 billion. The success of private equity has been largely attributed to the relatively high returns it offers investors with an average internal rate of return (IRR) of more than 15 per cent. As of now, there are a number of significant private equity players with sizable funds (by regional standards) that are actively making investments in the region. In the recent years the regional governments, especially in Saudi Arabia and UAE have liberalized the process of acquisition and transfer of companies and this provide more attraction to foreign investment companies.[12]

With the joining of World Trade Organization (WTO) Saudi Arabia is now bound to remove certain forms of protection especially the subsidies and tariffs and the sectors being forced to compete internationally. Kingdom has made major commitments to reduce tariffs, open services sectors of the economy to greater foreign participation, and to implement WTO rules upon membership without recourse to transition periods.

But with the accession of WTO, one genuine fear among the Saudis and also other Gulf states is that many domestic companies will have to either enter into partnerships with foreign companies or merge with other companies to avoid bankruptcy. For example, the insurance and the agriculture sector are expected to suffer the most due to high competition. Consequently, the Saudi companies will either have to enter into partnerships with foreign companies, merge with other companies or face bankruptcy. Because, before joining the WTO, Saudi private sector was not competitive internationally and that its efficiency was not comparable to that of the international private sectors.[13]

There are in fact much concern in the country that the local businessmen and entrepreneurs would not prepare themselves for the competitive advantage in the presence of multinational companies as the small and medium businesses in the Kingdom still work in a traditional way. In order to achieve this distinction the Saudi government did much to restructure administrative procedures and educate the workers in each sector to improve the quality of service to add to their competitive strength and negotiation leverage.

India and Saudi Arabia signed a "few agreements" to promote bilateral investments when the King Abdullah visited in January 2006. Some 100 Saudi businessmen came to India along with King Abdullah to take Saudi-Indian relations to a new pitch. Earlier, the Council of Saudi Chambers of Commerce and Industry (CSCCI) and the Federation of Indian Chambers of Commerce and Industry (FICCI) signed a Memorandum of Understanding (MoU) for setting up the Saudi Indian Business Council for promoting greater interaction between the two business communities as part of their strategic alliance. In order to boost bilateral trade from the current level of $6.63 billion Saudi Arabia and India are now eager to diversify their relations in oil and gas, infrastructure, telecommunications, IT and health care sectors as and promote investments in both directions.

India is Saudi Arabia's fourth largest trading partner and sources about 26 per cent of its total crude oil requirement from the kingdom.

Both the countries are exploring opportunities for collaboration in the oil and petrochemical sector. There are currently 49 Indo-Saudi joint ventures in India, while there are 82 Indian companies either fully owned or joint ventures. Up to April 2005, some 42 investments projects from India with an investment of $411 million were licensed. In addition, there are 40 non-industrial projects with an investment of $56.2 million taking the tally of Indian investments in the kingdom to $467.2 million.[14]

With its rapidly increasing population and their changing lifestyle, Saudi Arabia's market for consumer goods and fashion accessories is running into billions of dollars In recent years, the rising oil revenues means the increasing cash flow especially among the Saudis who constitute more than three quarters of the estimated over 23 million population or its large expatriate population belonging to various nationalities. With women increasingly attending schools and colleges and even aspiring for jobs, the market for fashions and fashion accessories is also maintaining a fast pace. Readymade dress market in Saudi Arabia, which is now estimated at SR8 billion, is poised to grow by 20 percent in the next three years. According to one report (*Arab News* 21 April, 2005), sales of women's dresses represented 65 percent and dresses of men and children 35 per cent.

Sensing this growing garment market in Saudi Arabia, the delegations of businessmen sponsored by the Power Loom Development and Export Promotion Council (PDEXCIL), Synthetic & Rayon Textiles Export Promotion Council, and Gem & Jewellery Export Promotion Council, all based in Mumbai, and Tea Board, Dubai, visited the Kingdom and received good and positive response from Saudi businessmen.

Promotion of India as a tourist destination among Saudis is also a major focus area, and efforts are under way to device a new approach and plan effective strategy. Thus we can see that Indian public and private sector companies are already carrying out operations in the kingdom and have established trading relations with their Saudi counterparts for marketing and distributing Indian products.

For India, Saudi Arabia is also emerging as a prime market for medical equipment and healthcare companies around the world, with recent research suggesting that the Kingdom accounts for almost 60 per cent of total sales in the Gulf. Market analysts have predicted that this decision will help to grow the private healthcare market, and stimulate growth in spending across the Kingdom. Healthcare companies and hospital equipment designers are signing up to exhibit with specific objectives for reaching Saudi decision-makers in the medical sector. India's Apollo

Hospital is already in the race for establishing its branches in the Kingdom.[15]

Keeping in view the lucrative market, Indian businessmen have started investing in the Kingdom, as the Mena report 2005 indicates, Indian investments reached some SR1.5 billion ($400 million) with 39 companies and 30 joint ventures in Saudi Arabia. In March 2005, a two-day meeting between the two sides witnessed the launch of Saudi-Indian Business Network (SIBN). The membership of SIBN is restricted to Saudi businessmen having business interests in India and senior Indian executives working in Saudi companies having trade and commercial interests in India. Again, in September 2005, India's vast investment potential and taxation policy favouring Saudi and other overseas investors were in focus at a seminar organized by Saudi Indian Business Network and Jeddah chapter of the Institute of Chartered Accountants of India.[16]

Indo-Saudi Trade in the Liberalized Market

Although Indo-Saudi bilateral economic and trade relations started some half a century back, but the major drive in this area can be seen only since the early 1990s, the era of economic liberalization. While both countries have now opened up their economies to the foreign trade and investment, this provides tremendous opportunities to expand their trade horizon. In 1997-98, Saudi Arabia was the second largest trading partner of India from the GCC countries accounting for 32.12 per cent of India's total trade with the GCC. Saudi Arabia is also considered as the 14th largest target market of India within the country-product export strategy formulated by the Ministry of Commerce. Significantly, exports have been picking up steadily from 16.93 per cent over the 1995-96 period to 18.08 per cent in 1997-98 period. Indian exports to the Kingdom stood at US$681.586 million in 1997-98, up from US$577.183 million in 1996-97. The export growth rate with Saudi Arabia (9 %) is nearly double the growth rate of India's total exports to the GCC countries (4.59%). India's global exports growth rate is 1 per cent. Indian imports from Saudi Arabia constitute 4 per cent (6.2% in 1997-98) of India's total imports. However, Indian imports from Saudi Arabia have fallen from US$2554 mn during 1997-98 to US$1857mn in 1998-99, a decline by 27 per cent. Crude oil and petroleum products continue to top the list of India's imports from the Kingdom. Saudi Arabia is the largest supplier of crude to India. During 2002-03, India's imports of crude oil and petroleum products from Saudi Arabia amounted to 18.816

million tons worth $3.6 billion. Saudi Arabia meets 26 percent of India's crude requirements annually. For Saudi Arabia, India is the fourth largest market for its exports, accounting for 4.84 percent of its total exports. Other items heading the list are Organic Chemicals (Rs. 21 billion), Artificial Resins, Plastic materials (Rs. 1.7 billion) and Inorganic Chemicals (Rs. 1.7 billion). Basmati Rice continues to head the list of exports to the kingdom with a total value of Rs. 9.6 billion. Cotton garments and accessories, non-basmati rice and man-made Yarns Fabrics/Made-Ups are next. Saudi Arabia is the third top source of Indian imports, behind the USA (Rs. 135.097 billion) and Switzerland (Rs. 95.278 billion). Indian imports from Saudi Arabia constitute 6.2 per cent of India's total imports. The following table shows the increasing trade between India and Saudi Arabia and it also points that under the WTO regimes the prospects of the trade growth would be higher than ever before.

Trends in India's Imports and Exports to Saudi Arabia

($million)

\Year	2000-2001	2001-2002	2002-2003	2003-2004	2004-2005
EXPORT	822.94	826.43	940.74	1,123.31	1,379.18
%Growth		0.42	13.83	19.41	22.78
IMPORT	621.12	463.99	504.72	737.77	1,264.20
%Growth		–25.3	8.78	46.17	71.35

Source: Ministry of Commerce, Govt. of India, 2006.

Since the provisions of the World Trade Agreement (WTO), enables WTO member states to gain market access for industrial and agricultural products besides boosting inward and outward remittances, the Indo-Saudi trade is expected to boost in the coming years. Agricultural items constitute nearly 57 per cent of India's total exports to the Kingdom followed by cotton/silk textiles and ready-made garments, metals, ores and minerals, machinery and instruments, manufactures of metals, plastic and linoleum products, glassware, ceramics and refractoriness', inorganic, organic and agro-chemicals, handicrafts, etc. With their all-time record of exports worldwide, Indian spices such as cardamom, pepper, chilli, ginger, turmeric and curry powders have maintained an increased lead in Saudi Arabia as well as the Gulf and Middle East markets. Export of spices during 2004-05 exceeded 3,00,000 tons in volume for the first time in the history of spice export. Export of spices during the 2004-05 was estimated to total 3,35,488 tons valued at $490.60 million, marking a growth of 32 percent in terms of quantity.[17]

It became possible only in post-reform period that India has gained success in establishing substantial trade relations with Saudi Arabia in the non-crude oil sector also, and sees the Kingdom as an important economic partner in respect of investments, joint ventures, transfer of technology projects and joint projects in third countries. The Kingdom is trying to woo Indian investors in a big way. Similarly, Saudi interests in the bilateral relationship are related to India's emerging economic profile as one of the largest and most diversified economies in the world and as a stable market for Saudi crude and petro-chemical exports.

Energy Relations

Although India's energy hungry economy's dependence on the oil-rich Saudi Arabia has shown increasing trends in recent years, there are also debates whether India should feel threatened with this phenomenon in the new globalized energy market?. For, in order to achieve its energy security India is pursuing acquisition of equity in oil and gas abroad, besides exploration acreages and producing properties. The government is willing to invest up to $25 billion for acquiring oil fields overseas.[18]

In March 2005, Indian minister of petroleum and natural gas, Mani Shankar Aiyar, delivered a lecture on "Asian Energy Vision" and addressed the energy challenges that India is facing and outlined New Delhi's new energy diplomacy and looked for long-term oil contracts with Saudi Arabia. "We now want to secure long-term contracts with an assured delivery every year", said the minister. For, India plans to build strategic oil reserves of five million tons by 2008 to cover 15 days' domestic demand for oil products. The country imports nearly 70 percent of its crude oil requirements. Currently, India imports about 4,30,000 barrels per day from the Kingdom. In January 2006, finally both the countries agreed to develop further energy strategy as the Kingdom has now realized the long-term secured supply of its oil reserves for the huge energy market in India.[19]

Saudi Arabia's proved reserves were estimated at about 88bn barrels in 1970. Today, these are estimated at more than 264bn barrels despite having produced some 91bn barrels over the intervening 35 years. At the 18th meeting of the World Petroleum Congress in Johannesburg on 27 September, 2005, Saudi Petroleum and Mineral Resources Minister Ali Naimi in his speech had observed that behind this impressive growth are the technological advances which have enabled us to economically recover a great portion of the resource base, thus adding to recoverable reserve estimates. The upstream expansion projects now underway in Saudi Arabia represent a combined production capacity addition of around 3mn b/d, part of which will be utilized to offset natural decline and the rest to expand capacity. By 2009, Saudi Arabia's maximum sustainable capacity will reach 12.5mn b/d.[20] This also shows that foreign participation opens various investment opportunities for technologically advanced yet competitive Indian companies in Saudi oil fields

The Saudi oil minister, Ali Naimi has recently expressed his views that for the Saudi Arabia, there is not a challenge of resources, or of availability, but what the global oil industry confronts today is a challenge of "deliverability". By that he meant that the petroleum industry faces infrastructure constraints and bottlenecks that are causing market volatility and restricting its ability to bring oil from the ground to the consumer. The oil exporting nation now realize, that the current deliverability difficulties emerged because of the inadequate return on investment caused by a prolonged period of low oil prices and low product refining margins from the mid-1980s to the late-1990s. The argument that alternative energy such as coal, nuclear, solar, wind power, natural gas, will replace the oil is still not valid. For, in the transportation sector, where oil accounts for 95 per cent of the energy consumed globally, there are currently no competitive alternatives to petroleum-derived fuels.

However, with the Arab Gulf's shrinking oil market in US and Western Europe, it appears that Saudi Arabia's main concern is the maintenance of the stability in the oil market so that the future supply could be assured to the giant Asian energy consumer countries such as China and India. In this context, we can imagine the significance of Asian Oil market conference in January 2005 in New Delhi where both Asian consumers and producers discussed the benefits from stable and reliable oil markets. This also explains why Saudi Arabia has vowed to boost supplies, to secure stability in the market. In March 2005, Saudi Oil Minister expressed his readiness to increase oil supplies to India from the current level of 4,30,000 barrels per day. Pursuing an aggressive exploration programme for oil and gas, Kingdom is expanding its production capacity from the current 11.0mn b/d to 12.5mn b/d bid by 2009.[21]

Saudi Arabia is willing to extend long-term crude oil supply contracts to India. In January 2006, Saudi Minister of Petroleum and Mineral Resources discussed with Indian counterparts the security of oil supplies and stability of market. They also proposed on mutual investment opportunities in the two countries. Saudi oil minister in fact welcomed investment by Indian companies in Saudi Arabian oil fields, and was keen on setting up an export refinery with Indian companies. One notable development in this context is that India has invited Saudi ARAMCO to set up a refinery in India that would refine crude oil produced by Gulf producers and the Indo-Saudi joint venture could retail petroleum and petrochemicals produced by the unit in India and neighboring countries. On its part, Saudi Arabia has invited Indian companies to set up an oil refinery there, mainly for export of petroleum products to third countries, and has cleared Oil and Natural Gas Corp.'s (ONGC) bidding for gas field development projects. Another public sector oil company HPCL is looking at partnering Saudi ARAMCO for setting up refineries in both Saudi Arabia and India. Moreover, Saudi ARAMCO and Indian Oil Corporation Ltd. (IOC) have already signed a Memorandum of Collaboration to evaluate future cooperation in petroleum research and development and the commercial exploitation of any resulting technologies. The new joint venture will import crude oil from the Kingdom and supply refined products to India's burgeoning market in the oil and gas sector. India's prestigious joint ventures with the Kingdom, the Saudi-Indian Petrochemicals located in Yanbu, has an installed production capacity of 1,00,000 tons of regular paraffin and 8,00,000 tons of alkyl benzene, annually.[22]

India's decontrolled oil sector has already engaged both the public and private oil companies in upstream as well as in downstream activities. The ONGC invest in overseas oil and gas projects to secure energy supplies for the country. The company is operating in 12 countries including Russia, Sudan, Vietnam and Myanmar and is scouting for opportunities in several countries including Venezuela, Yemen, Kazakhistan, Kuwait, Nigeria, Angola and Ecuador. Its overseas output rose from 31 percent to 5 million tons in the year 2005. The public sector oil firms in India have a long term contract with Saudi ARAMCO to purchase 7.5 million tones of crude per annum, which is about 16 per cent of their total annual crude imports. In addition, certain private Indian companies have also term contracts with Saudi ARAMCO, which accounts for another 6.5 million metric tons per annum. Under such a scenario both the oil producers and consumers are heavily interdependent on each other's and the concept of 'energy threat' especially for India is no more relevant in the contemporary oil and gas market.

Indo-Saudi Joint Ventures

In this vast investment and joint venture opportunities, a number of Indian firms have since 2000, taken advantage of the new Saudi laws and established joint venture projects or wholly owned subsidiaries in the Kingdom. Major Indian public sector and private sector companies like

TCIL, IRCON, BHEL, ACC, LIC and New India Assurance Company are already carrying out operations in the Kingdom. In the private sector too, companies like TATA, Oberoi, Godrej, Voltas, Videocon, Raymonds, etc. have established relations with their Saudi counterparts. At the invitation of the Council of Saudi Chambers of Commerce and Industry, in April 2001, a delegation of the Confederation of Indian Industry visited Saudi Arabia. Soon after new investment regulations came into force in the Kingdom two Indian firms obtained licenses involving a total of $287.2 million for the manufacture of linear alkyl benzene and natural paraffin. A few other Indian companies also took advantage of the new regulations providing for 100 percent foreign ownership of projects in the Kingdom. For example, Indian pharmaceutical firm Ajanta Pharma has set up a joint venture in Jeddah to produce a variety of prescription and over-the-counter medicines for Saudi and Gulf markets.[23]

In the recent years there is an increased tendency among the Indian companies to take, joint ventures in the Kingdom. For instance, Wockhardt Ltd. has invested $5 million in a pharmaceuticals JV with two Saudi firms with a 50 per cent equity stake while KEC International, a company specialized in erecting electrical towers, plans to invest $4.22 million in its JV in the Kingdom. In October 2003, a high-level Saudi business delegation sought the Indian entrepreneurs to look at the Kingdom as a preferred trade and investment destination because of the massive development activity being undertaken in the country. In power projects alone, Saudi Arabia is expected to invest $100 billion over the next few years and is in the process of strengthening its industrial base particularly in the non-oil sector.

With the Kingdom having taken steps to initiate privatization, investment law has been liberalized. Saudi Arabia is now open for foreign investments and in certain areas 100 percent foreign ownership is being allowed. What Saudi Arabia needs is technology and expertise more than money. India with its experience of industrialization is very well placed to share it with Saudi Arabia.

Since the 1990s, Saudi Arabia has also felt the need to give greater importance to developing economic cooperation with India especially in non-petroleum sector. Bilateral Investment Protection and Promotion Agreement (BIPPA) are prime agendas between the two countries. Currently, there are 82 Saudi-Indian joint ventures valued at $467 million in the Kingdom. Indian companies have established 21 joint ventures in Saudi Arabia in different sectors such as management and consultancy services, construction projects, telecommunications, information technology, pharmaceuticals, etc. There are also collaborations between Indian and Saudi companies in the areas of designing, consultancy, financial services and software development.

Keeping in view the open business climate in the Kingdom, India's software giant Infosys Technologies is enhancing its presence in the region, in the Saudi Kingdom where the Nasdaq-listed company plans to set up a Technical Support Centre. Infosys has signed a contract with Arab National Bank (ANB) in Saudi Arabia to provide IT solutions and services. The Indian National Fertilizer Company is currently conducting negotiations with Saudi ARAMCO to establish a fertilizer company in Saudi Arabia. Tata Motors, a Bombay-based automobile manufacturer, also targeted the Tata passenger cars to hit roads across Saudi Arabia following the successful acceptance of Tata trucks across the Kingdom. Tata Motors is setting up a bus-building facility in Turkey, and had similar plans for the Kingdom.[24]

In November 2005, Indian participation in joint ventures was asked by a high-level business delegation from Saudi Arabia to take advantage of the tremendous opportunities in the Kingdom and put in their expertise and resources to develop strategic partnerships with the Saudi companies. The delegation headed by Abdulrahman Abdulaziz Arabiah, the co-chairman, Saudi-Indian Business Council, held an interactive session with several Indian businessmen and companies under the aegis of the Confederation of Indian Industry. Under the new business climate, Saudi-Indian Business Network (SIBN) now foresee "wonderful land of opportunities" in Saudi Arabia and India. The newly established Saudi-Indian Business Network (SIBN) has decided to institute a "Distinguished Friend of India Award" to the Saudi entrepreneur, annually. The award will be presented to the Saudi businessman who excels in promoting business with India and mutual investments. SIBN has also decided to develop a data bank on various Indian investment projects, Indian business houses active across the Kingdom, and liberalization of rules and regulations to promote and facilitate investment.[25]

Saudi Arabia is now experiencing a second boom after the first boom of 1970, which was based solely on the increase in the price of oil. Saudi Arabia is heading toward becoming a $300 billion economy by 2010, and has introduced a new industrial policy to drive speedy growth and improved infrastructure, and created a special economic zone to attract overseas investors.[26] The present oil boom, however, still plays an important factor but it is not the only factor. The reforms, the openings of new sectors, opening of market in Saudi Arabia are all playing an important role.

Summary

Two important developments have coincided with Saudi Arabia's emergence in the global market. First, the economic reform initiated some one and half decades back has in fact resulted into the massive diversification both in the oil and non-oil sectors in the country. This has greatly paved the ways for the entry of private sectors in Saudi economy. Another notable feature is the Kingdom's joining of WTO in November 2005 and this along with the rising oil revenues due to high oil prices, has further boosted the developmental process. Inevitably, all these have pushed up the foreign direct investment in the Kingdom that was never seen before.

Under the new investment climate, and keeping in view the new geo-strategic position after the 9/11 incident, Saudi Arabia is as much eager to seek its market in the Asian region where India now figure prominently, both because of its huge oil demand in the coming years and also because of the abilities of its companies to compete the western rivals.

An Indo-Saudi economic relations should be seen in this framework because India, once considered being in a high vulnerable position due to its energy dependency on the Kingdom, though still importing higher volume of oil than before, but under the globalized market both India and Saudi Arabia are tending towards more interdependency rather than causing imbalances to each other's economies. As we have also seen the Asian oil conference in New Delhi has already brought these Gulf oil producers for the first time to discuss the oil market security in Asia.

In the new era of business and investment climate both countries are projected to benefit from their complementary strengths. For example, the Kingdom has substantial sources and expertise in petroleum and petrochemicals industry and Saudi companies can reap considerable benefits by making investments in India. On its part, India has many strengths that have attracted foreign investors to its shores, its stable polity and democratic framework; well-developed legal system and independent judiciary to safeguard the 'rule of law'; a free press; a rapidly growing economy with a huge market; and a strong tradition of entrepreneurship. India's vast reservoir of knowledge resource and skilled personnel—are among the best in the world. Hence, there are promising new horizons for Indian companies in almost all sectors of the Saudi economy, major among them being petroleum and petrochemicals power, water, railways, roads, telecommunications, information technology (IT) banking, and financial services. As we have seen, this has enabled India's public and private companies to penetrate in Saudi Arabia and other Gulf countries.

This is a new trend in the Indo-Saudi economic relations but the onus would be more on India as how it competes with its other Asian competitors in one of the highly rich region on the earth. This would be the real challenge.

References

1. *Daily Gulf News*, 16 March, 2006.
2. http://www.indiaonestop.com/face2face/kamaluddin.htm.
3. http://www.meadev.nic.in/foreign/saudiarabia.htm.
4. In the 2005 budget for instance, some SR75.5 billion was earmarked for capital expenditure mainly in education and health sectors. The value of actual construction contracts awarded in the Kingdom in the first six months of 2005 totaled SR61.5 billion. *The Economist*, 7 January, 2006, p. 11.
5. Negotiating its membership since July 1993, Saudi Arabia formally became the WTO's 149th member on Dec. 11, 2005. It has leapt 29 places to 38 in a World Bank ranking of countries based on competitiveness in attracting investment, becoming ahead of its freewheeling neighbour, the UAE. *Arab News*, 21 December, 2005
6. *Arab News* 7 July, 2005.
7. According to the decision issued recently by Saudi authorities, foreign businessmen will be granted visas within 24 hours to facilitate their entry into the kingdom. There is no restriction for foreigners to buy 100 percent of Saudi companies or totally own their projects," Foreign investors can now establish projects totally owned by them. But 75 percent of the staff in most foreign projects must be Saudi nationals. *Arab News*, 30 November, 2005
8. *Arab News,* 21 November, 2005.
9. In May 2005, a dozen countries including India took part in the fair dubbed as Saudi Arabia's multi-sectoral trade expo. *Arab News,* 15 May, 2005
10. *Arab News,* 11 April, 2005.
11. The initial share capital is SR100 million. LIC, (Bahrain) and New India Assurance will together have a 31 percent equity stake in the new venture. *Arab News,* 13 April, 2005.
12. *Khaleej Times,* 20 March, 2006.
13. Monica Malik, 'The Role of Private Sector", In: Rodney Wilson, *Economic Development in Saudi Arabia*, London: Routledge-Curzon, 2004, p. 128-29.
14. *Khaleej Times*, 22 November, 2005.
15. *Khaleej Times*, 20 June, 2004.
16. *Arab News*, 14 September, 2005.
17. *Arab News* 22 May 2005.
18. See online; www.petroleum.nic.in
19. The lecture, hosted by International Energy Forum (IEF), was attended by

a number of Saudi officials, diplomats and newsmen. *Arab News* 29 March. 2005.

20. Ali Naimi, 'Shaping The Energy Future: The Role of Saudi Arabia', *Middle East Economic Survey*, Vol. XLVIII, No. 40, 3 October, 2005.
21. *Gulf Daily News* 30 March, 2005.
22. *Arab News*, 6 January, 2005.
23. http://www.saudia-online.com/business326.htm
24. Tata Motors trade having increased in Saudi Arabia from $2.5 million in 2002 to $6 million in 2003. *Arab News*, 21 November, 2005.
25. *Arab News* 8 April, 2005.
26. *Arab News* 10 July, 2005.

Appendices

I

Saudi Arabia: Basic Law of Government

CHAPTER 1
GENERAL PRINCIPLES

Article 1: The Kingdom of Saudi Arabia is a sovereign Arab Islamic state with Islam as its religion; God's Book and the Sunnah of His Prophet, God's prayers and peace be upon him, are its constitution, Arabic is its language and Riyadh is its capital.

Article 2: The state's public holidays are Eid al-Fitr and Eid al-Adha. Its calendar is the Hegira calendar.

Article 3: The state's flag shall be as follows:

(a) It shall be green.

(b) Its width shall be equal to two-thirds of its length.

(c) The words *"There is but one God and Mohammed is His Prophet"* shall be inscribed in the center with a drawn sword under it. The statute shall define the rules pertaining to it.

Article 4: The state's emblem shall consist of two crossed swords with a palm tree in the upper space between them. The statute shall define the state's anthem and its medals.

CHAPTER 2
[MONARCHY]

Article 5: (a) The system of government in the Kingdom of Saudi Arabia is that of a monarchy.

(b) Rule passes to the sons of the founding King, Abd al-Aziz Bin Abd al-Rahman al-Faysal Al Sa'ud, and to their children's children. The most upright among them is to receive allegiance in accordance with the principles of the Holy Koran and the Tradition of the Venerable Prophet.

(c) The King chooses the Heir Apparent and relieves him of his duties by Royal order.

(d) The Heir Apparent is to devote his time to his duties as an Heir Apparent and to whatever missions the King entrusts him with.

(e) The Heir Apparent takes over the powers of the King on the latter's death until the act of allegiance has been carried out.

Article 6: Citizens are to pay allegiance to the King in accordance with the holy Koran and the tradition of the Prophet, in submission and obedience, in times of ease and difficulty, fortune and adversity.

Article 7: Government in Saudi Arabia derives power from the Holy Koran and the Prophet's tradition.

Article 8 [Government Principles]: Government in the Kingdom of Saudi Arabia is based on the premise of justice, consultation, and equality in accordance with the Islamic Shari'ah.

CHAPTER 3
FEATURES OF THE SAUDI FAMILY

Article 9: The family is the kernel of Saudi society, and its members shall be brought up on the basis of the Islamic faith, and loyalty and obedience to God, His Messenger, and to guardians; respect for and implementation of the law, and love of and pride in the homeland and its glorious history as the Islamic faith stipulates.

Article 10: The state will aspire to strengthen family ties, maintain its Arab and Islamic values and care for all its members, and to provide the right conditions for the growth of their resources and capabilities.

Article 11: Saudi society will be based on the principle of adherence to God's command, on mutual cooperation in good deeds and piety and mutual support and inseparability.

Article 12: The consolidation of national unity is a duty, and the state will prevent anything that may lead to disunity, sedition and separation.

Article 13: education will aim at instilling the Islamic faith in the younger generation, providing its members with knowledge and skills and preparing them to become useful members in the building of their society, members who love their homeland and are proud of its history.

CHAPTER 4
ECONOMIC PRINCIPLES

Article 14: All God's bestowed wealth, be it under the ground, on the surface or in national territorial waters, in the land or maritime domains under the state's control, are the property of the state as defined by law.

The law defines means of exploiting, protecting, and developing such wealth in the interests of the state, its security and economy.

Article 15: No privilege is to be granted and no public resource is to be exploited without a law.

Article 16: Public money is sacrosanct. The state has an obligation to protect it and both citizens and residents are to safeguard it.

Article 17: Property, capital, and labor are essential elements in the Kingdom's economic and social being. They are personal rights which perform a social function in accordance with Islamic Shari'ah.

Article 18: The state protects freedom of private property and its sanctity. No one is to be stripped of his property except when it serves the public interest, in which case fair compensation is due.

Article 19: Public confiscation of money is prohibited and the penalty of private confiscation is to be imposed only by a legal order.

Article 20: Taxes and fees are to be imposed on a basis of justice and only when the need for them arises. Imposition, amendment, revocation and exemption are only permitted by law.

Article 21: Alms tax is to be levied and paid to legitimate recipients.

Article 22: Economic and social development is to be achieved according to a just and scientific plan.

CHAPTER 5
RIGHTS AND DUTIES

Article 23 [Islam]: The state protects Islam; it implements its Shari'ah; it orders people to do right and shun evil; it fulfills the duty regarding God's call.

Article 24 [Holy Places]: The state works to construct and serve the Holy Places; it provides security and care for those who come to perform the pilgrimage and minor pilgrimage in them through the provision of facilities and peace.

Article 25 [World Peace]: The state strives for the achievement of the hopes of the Arab and Islamic nation for solidarity and unity of word, and to consolidate its relations with friendly states.

Article 26 [Human Rights]: The state protects human rights in accordance with the Islamic Shari'ah.

Article 27 [Welfare Rights]: The state guarantees the rights of the citizen and his family in cases of emergency, illness and disability, and in old age; it supports the system of social security and encourages institutions and individuals to contribute in acts of charity.

Article 28 [Work]: The state provides job opportunities for whoever is capable of working; it enacts laws that protect the employee and employer.

Article 29 [Science, Culture]: The state safeguards science, literature and culture; it encourages scientific research; it protects the Islamic and Arab heritage and contributes toward the Arab, Islamic and human civilization.

Article 30 [Education]: The state provides public education and pledges to combat illiteracy.

Article 31 [Health Care]: The state takes care of health issues and provides health care for each citizen.

Article 32 [Environment, Nature]: The state works for the preservation, protection, and improvement of the environment, and for the prevention of pollution.

Article 33 [Armed Forces]: The state establishes and equips the Armed Forces for the defense of the Islamic religion, the Two Holy Places, society, and the citizen.

Article 34 [Military Service]: The defense of the Islamic religion, society, and country is a duty for each citizen. The regime establishes the provisions of military service.

Article 35 [Citizenship]: The statutes define the Regulations governing Saudi Arabian nationality.

Article 36 [Arrest]: The state provides security for all its citizens and all residents within its territory and no one shall be arrested, imprisoned, or have their actions restricted except in cases specified by statutes.

Article 37 [Home]: The home is sacrosanct and shall not be entered without the permission of the owner or be searched except in cases specified by statutes.

Article 38 [Punishment, *nulla poena*]: Penalties shall be personal and there shall be no crime or penalty except in accordance with the Shari'ah or organizational law. There shall be no punishment except for acts committed subsequent to the coming into force of the organizational law.

Article 39 [Expression]: Information, publication, and all other media shall employ courteous language and the state's regulations, and they shall contribute to the education of the nation and the bolstering of its unity. All acts that foster sedition or division or harm the state's security and its public relations or detract from man's dignity and rights shall be prohibited. The statutes shall define all that.

Article 40 [Communication]: Telegraphic, postal, telephone, and other means of communications shall be safeguarded. They cannot be confiscated, delayed, read or listened to except in cases defined by statutes.

Article 41 [Residents' Duties]: Residents of the Kingdom of Saudi Arabia shall abide by its laws and shall observe the values of Saudi society and respect its traditions and feelings.

Article 42 [Asylum, Extradition]: The state shall grant the right to political asylum when the public interest demands this. Statutes and international agreements shall define the rules and procedures governing the extradition of common criminals.

Article 43 [Royal Courts]: The King's Court and that of the Crown Prince shall be open to all citizens and to anyone who has a complaint or a plea against an injustice. Every individual shall have a right to address the public authorities in all matters affecting him.

CHAPTER 6
THE AUTHORITIES OF THE STATE

Article 44: The authorities of the state consist of the following: the judicial authority;

the executive authority;: the regulatory authority.

These authorities cooperate with each other in the performance of their duties, in accordance with this and other laws. The King shall be the point of reference for all these authorities.

Article 45: The source of the deliverance of fatwa in the Kingdom of Saudi Arabia are God's Book and the Sunnah of His Messenger. The law will define the composition of the senior Ulema body, the administration of scientific research, deliverance of fatwa and it's (the body of senior Ulema's) functions.

Article 46: The judiciary is an independent authority. There is no control over judges in the dispensation of their judgments except in the case of the Islamic Shari'ah.

Article 47: The right to litigation is guaranteed to citizens and residents of the Kingdom on an equal basis. The law defines the required procedures for this.

Article 48: The courts will apply the rules of the Islamic Shari'ah in the cases that are brought before them, in accordance with what is indicated in the Book and the Sunnah, and statutes decreed by the Ruler which do not contradict the Book or the Sunnah.

Article 49: Observing what is stated in Article 53, the courts shall arbitrate in all disputes and crimes.

Article 50: The King, or whoever deputizes for him, is responsible for the implementation of judicial rulings.

Article 51: The authorities establish the formation of the Higher Council of Justice and its prerogatives; they also establish the seniority of the courts and their prerogatives.

Article 52: The appointment of judges and the termination of their duties is carried out by Royal decree by a proposal from the Higher Council of Justice in accordance with the provisions of the law.

Article 53: The law establishes the seniority of the tribunal of complaints and its prerogatives.

Article 54: The law establishes the relationship between the investigative body and the Prosecutor-general, and their organization and prerogatives.

Article 55: The King carries out the policy of the nation, a legitimate policy in accordance with the provisions of Islam; the King oversees the implementation of the Islamic Shari'ah, the system of government, the state's general policies; and the protection and defense of the country.

Article 56: The King is the head of the Council of Ministers; he is assisted in carrying out his duties by members of the Council of Ministers, in accordance with the provisions of this and other laws. The Council of Ministers establishes the prerogatives of the Council regarding internal and external affairs, the organization of and co-ordination between government bodies. It also establishes requirements to be fulfilled by ministers, their prerogatives, the manner of their questioning and all issues concerning them. The law on the Council of Ministers and its prerogatives is to be amended in accordance with this law.

Article 57: (a) The King appoints and relieves deputies of the prime minister and ministers and members of the Council of Ministers by Royal decree.

(b) The deputies of the prime minister and ministers of the Council of Ministers are responsible, by expressing solidarity before the King, for implementing the Islamic Shari'ah and the state's general policy.:

(c) The King has the right to dissolve and reorganize the Council of Ministers.

Article 58: The King appoints those who enjoy the rank of ministers, deputy ministers and those of higher rank, and relieves them of their posts by Royal decree in accordance with the explanations included in the law. Ministers and heads of independent departments are responsible before the prime minister for the ministries and departments which they supervise.

Article 59: The law defines the rules of the civil service, including salaries, awards, compensations, favors and pensions.

Article 60: The King is the commander-in-chief of all the armed forces. He appoints officers and puts an end to their duties in accordance with the law.

Article 61: The King declares a state of emergency, general mobilization and war, and the law defines the rules for this.

Article 62: If there is a danger threatening the safety of the Kingdom or its territorial integrity, or the security of its people and its interests, or which impedes the functioning of the state institutions, the King may take urgent measures in order to deal with this danger And if the King considers that these measures should continue, he may then implement the necessary regulations to this end.

Article 63: The King receives Kings and Heads of State. He appoints his representatives to states, and he receives the credentials of state representatives accredited to him.

Article 64: The King awards medals, as defined by regulations.

Article 65: The King may delegate prerogatives to the Crown Prince by Royal decree.

Article 66: In the event of his traveling abroad, the King issues a Royal decree delegating to the Crown Prince the management of the affairs of state and looking after the interests of the people, as defined by the Royal decree.

Article 67: The regulatory authority lays down regulations and motions to meet the interests of the state or remove what is bad in its affairs, in accordance with the Islamic Shari'ah. This authority exercises its functions in accordance with this law and the laws pertaining to the Council of Ministers and the Consultative Council.

Article 68 [Consultative Council]: A Consultative Council is to be created. Its statute will specify how it is formed, how it exercises its powers and how its members are selected.

Article 69: The King has the right to convene the Consultative Council and the Council of Ministers for a joint meeting and to invite whoever he wishes to attend that meeting to discuss whatever matters he wishes.

Article 70: International treaties, agreements, regulations and concessions are approved and amended by Royal decree.

Article 71: Statutes are to be published in the Official Gazette and take effect from the date of publication unless another date is specified.

CHAPTER 7
FINANCIAL AFFAIRS

Article 72: (a) The statute explains the provisions concerning the state's revenue and its entry in the state's general budget.

(b) Revenue is entered and spent in accordance with the rules specified in the statute.

Article 73: Any undertaking to pay a sum of money from the general budget must be made in accordance with the provisions of the budget. If it is not possible to do so in accordance with the provisions of the budget, then it must be done in accordance with Royal decree.

Article 74: The sale, renting or use of state assets is not permitted except in accordance with the statute.

Article 75: The statutes will define the monetary and banking provisions, the standards, weights and measures.

Article 76: The law will fix the state's financial year and will announce the budget by way of a Royal decree. It will also assess the revenues and expenditure of that year at least one month before the start of the financial year. If, for essential reasons, the budget is not announced and the new financial year starts, the budget of the previous year will remain in force until the new budget is announced.

Article 77: The competent body will prepare the state's final statement of account for the passing year and will submit it to the head of the council of ministers.

Article 78: The same provisions will apply both to the budgets of the corporate bodies and their final statements of account and to the state's budget and its final statement of account.

CHAPTER 8
CONTROL BODIES

Article 79: All the state's revenues and expenditures will come under subsequent control and all the state's movable and immovable funds will be controlled in order to confirm the good use of these funds and their preservation. An annual report will be submitted on this matter to the head of the Council of Ministers. The law will define the competent control body and its obligations and prerogatives.

Article 80: government bodies will come under control in order to confirm the good performance of the administration and the implementation of the statutes. Financial and administrative offenses will be investigated and an annual report will be submitted on this matter to the head of the Council of Ministers. The law will define the competent body in charge of this and it's obligations and prerogatives.

CHAPTER 9
GENERAL PROVISIONS

Article 81: The implementation of this law will not prejudice the treaties and agreements signed by the Kingdom of Saudi Arabia with international bodies and organizations.

Article 82: Without violating the content of Article 7, no provision of this law whatsoever may be suspended unless it is temporary such as in a time of war or during the declaration of a state of emergency. This temporary suspension will be in accordance with the terms of the law.

Article 83: This law may only be amended in the same way as it was promulgated.

II

Delhi Declaration, Signed by King Abdullah bin Abdulaziz Al Saud of the Kingdom of Saudi Arabia and Prime Minister Dr. Manmohan Singh of India

27/01/2006

The Custodian of the Two Holy Mosques King Abdullah bin Abdulaziz Al Saud of the Kingdom of Saudi Arabia held historic meetings with the President of the Republic of India, His Excellency Dr. A.P.J.Abdul Kalam and the Prime Minister of the Republic of India, His Excellency Dr. Manmohan Singh during his State visit to the Republic of India from 24 – 27 January, 2006. The two sides exchanged views and had in-depth discussions that touched upon the mutual interests of both countries as well as the security, stability, peace and prosperity in the whole region.

Realizing that this visit heralds a new era in India-Saudi Arabia relations and constitutes a landmark in the development of increased understanding and cooperation between the two countries and creation of a mutually beneficial partnership,

Reflecting the view that both countries are developing a broad strategic vision, and are determined to work together closely for the welfare and benefit of their peoples and for peace and stability in the region and the world,

Desirous of building upon and expanding the close ties and friendship and the many commonalties between the two countries and peoples,

Affirming their commitment to the ideals of tolerance, harmony and diversity between societies and the importance of dialogue and peaceful resolution of disputes,

Conscious of their responsibility for promoting peace, stability and security in the region and the world,

Recognizing the close inter-linkage of the stability and security of the Gulf region and the Indian sub-continent and the need for maintaining a secure and peaceful environment for the development of the countries in the region,

Desirous of further strengthening people - to - people ties,

The two sides have agreed as follows:

Exchanges of high-level bilateral visits and consultations should be intensified in order to give an impetus to and expand the scope of bilateral cooperation and understanding.

Terrorism is a scourge for all mankind and there is a need to intensify and coordinate bilateral, regional and global cooperation to combat and eradicate the menace of terrorism.

The two Governments would closely and actively cooperate to fight the menace of terrorism and other transnational crimes like money laundering, drugs and arms smuggling in a sustained and comprehensive manner. The signing of the Memorandum of Understanding between Saudi Arabia and India on Combating Crime will help in the fight against terrorism, extremism and criminal elements. The two countries shall make concerted efforts for an early realization of the proposals to conclude a Comprehensive Convention on International Terrorism which is before the UN General Assembly, and the setting up of an InternationalCounter-Terrorism Centre as called for by the International Conference on Counter-Terrorism held in Riyadh in February 2005, in response to the idea proposed by King Abdullah bin Abdulaziz Al Saud.

To expand and diversify mutual trade and investments and, noting with satisfaction the signing of agreements regarding Promotion and Protection of Investments and Avoidance of Double Taxation, called for the exploration of investment opportunities in all sectors, including infrastructure, in both countries.

Both sides affirmed the importance of stability in the oil market for the world economy. The Indian side expressed understanding and appreciation of the balanced petroleum policy of Saudi Arabia which is considered a trusted and reliable source of oil supplies to international markets in general and the Indian market in particular. In this context, the Saudi side appreciated the Indian initiative to initiate a regional forum for dialogue among Asian oil and gas producers and consumers.

Both countries will develop a strategic energy partnership based on complementarity and interdependence. The elements of this partnership would include, inter alia:

— Reliable, stable and increased volume of crude oil supplies, through "evergreen" long-term contracts.
— Cooperative and joint ventures, both in the public and private sectors, in the upstream and downstream oil and gas sectors in India and Saudi Arabia as well as in third countries.

— Saudi investments in oil refining, marketing and storage in India, subject to commercial viability.
— Setting up of India-Saudi ventures for gas-based fertilizer plants in Saudi Arabia.

The two governments would encourage and support entrepreneurs in both countries to harness each other's strengths for mutual benefit and promote economic cooperation actively.

The two countries would work for closer cooperation in the field of technology, in particular in the field of information and communication technology, agriculture, bio-technology, and non-conventional energy technologies. India will assist in setting up an ICT Centre of Excellence as well as institutes of higher learning, involving both education and research, in the field of technology in Saudi Arabia. India would offer opportunities for Saudi students to pursue Post-Graduate and Doctorate level studies in technical institutions in India, and enhance cooperation in human resource development related to telecommunications. It was agreed that an Educational Exchange Programme between the two countries should be finalized and concluded at an early date.

The two countries would explore the prospect of cooperation in the health sector to realize the promising possibilities for enhancing cooperation in this sector, including health services, exchange of health personnel, health education and pharmaceuticals.

It was agreed that cooperation in the field of science and technology, tourism, youth affairs and sport, agriculture research and education, technical education and vocational training and other fields of mutual benefit should be intensified through signing of agreements and memorandum of understanding as necessary.

The two sides agreed to cultivate and encourage cultural exchanges between the two countries, both at official and popular levels.

The meetings of the bilateral Joint Commission will be held frequently and regularly, and the next meeting of the Joint Commission to be held later in 2006 has been tasked to ensure follow-up and implementation of the decisions taken by the two leaders during King Abdullah's visit to India.

In the field of political cooperation, both sides exchanged views about international developments, especially those related to the Middle East, and affirmed their commitment to the principles of international legality and the importance of maintaining international peace and stability. The two sides agreed to work together towards resolving outstanding conflicts in the world through peaceful means.

Both countries emphasized the importance of the Beirut Arab Peace Initiative and the Road Map. They realized that the complementarity between the two plans would invigorate the peace process in the Middle East, and lead to the establishment of a viable and independent State of Palestine living in peace and prosperity within secure borders side by side with Israel.

With regard to the Iraqi situation, both sides expressed their hope that Iraq would turn a new page in history that would assure its security, unity, territorial integrity and prosperity, and respect for its sovereignty and independence.

The two sides welcomed the ongoing dialogue between India and Pakistan and their continued efforts aimed at settling the outstanding issues between the two countries.

Done in New Delhi on the 27th of January, 2006 corresponding to 27th of 12, 1426 H.

Dr. Manmohan Singh
Prime Minister of the Republic of India

Abdullah bin Abdulaziz Al Saud
King of the Kingdom of Saudi Arabia

Joint Declarations
Ministry of External Affairs, New Delhi

Contributors

Alam, Anwar is an associate professor at the Centre for West Asian and African Studies, School of International Studies, JNU.

Dietl, Gulshan, is a professor and the Director, the Gulf Studies Programme at Jawaharlal Nehru University. Her publications include The Dulles Era: America Enters West Asia, Through Two Wars and Beyond: A Study of the Gulf Cooperation Council, Saudi Arabia: People, Politics, Policies; and nearly a hundred book-chapters, research papers and articles.

Jain, P.C., is on the faculty of the School of International Studies, Jawaharlal Nehru University, New Delhi. The author of *Racial Discrimination against Overseas Indians: A Class Analysis* (1990), *Indians in South Africa: Political Economy of Race Relations* (1999) and *Population and Society in West Asia: Essays in Comparative Demography* (2001), Dr. Jain has to his credit a number of articles published in Indian and foreign journals. He has also co-edited a book on *Contemporary Iran and Emerging Indo-Iranian Relations* (1996). Dr. Jain has done field works on Overseas Indians in Canada, Guyana, South Africa and some of the Persian Gulf countries.

Khan, Javed Ahmad is a Reader at the Academy of Third World Studies, Jamia Millia Islamia, New Delhi. He received his Ph.D in West Asian Studies (Economics) from Aligarh Muslim University. Among his publications include; India's Energy Security and the Arabian Gulf : Oil and Gas Market in Decontrolled Regime (2005), Islamic Banking in India - Scopes & Challenges (Edited volume, 2003), India and West Asia : Emerging Markets in the Liberalization Era (1999) and Islamic Economics and Finance: A Bibliography (1995). His areas of interest include Arab Economies, Indo-Arab Economic Relations and Islamic Business and Finance. He may be contacted at: javedadkhan@rediffmail.com

Pant, Girijesh is Professor and Chairperson in Centre of West Asian and African Studies at Jawaharlal Nehru University. Has authored and edited eight books. Published more than fifty articles in various journals. His specializations include Political economy of Development, West Asian Economies and International Energy Security. He has also been Vice Chancellor, GGD University, Bilaspur and Vice President Indian Academy of Social Sciences and Senior Fulbright Fellow. India:The Emerging Energy Player is his forthcoming book.

Pasha, A.K., Professor, Gulf Studies, CWAAS, SIS, JNU where he has served as Chairman and Director. Also served as Director, Indian Cultural Centre, Cairo and Visiting Fellow at the Faculty of Economics and Political Science, Cairo University, Egypt and at Gulf research Centre, Dubai, UAE.He has published twelve books on West Asia and North Africa and edited ten books besides contributing chapters to over twenty edited books and numerous research articles to international journals and in Indian and Gulf newspapers.He is a frequent commentator on West Asian affairs in Indian and foreign media.

Pradhan, Bansidhar is Associate Professor at the Centre for West Asian and African Studies, Jawaharlal Nehru University. He is the author of three books, the most recent being Dynamics of Conflict and Peace in West Asia (2003). He has also contributed articles to edited volumes and refereed journals like International Studies.

Talmiz Ahmad, joined the Indian Foreign Service in 1974. He was Indian Ambassador to Saudi Arabia (2000-03) and Oman (2003-04), after which he was Additional Secretary (International Cooperation) in the Ministry of Petroleum and Natural Gas (2005-06). Since April 2006, he has been the Director-General of the Indian Council of World Affairs (ICWA), New Delhi.

Index